D0464333

c

Paul N. Schaeffer

DELINQUENTS AND CRIMINALS

THEIR MAKING AND UNMAKING

By the Same Authors

W. H.

THE INDIVIDUAL DELINQUENT
PATHOLOGICAL LYING, ACCUSATION AND SWINDLING
HONESTY
MENTAL CONFLICTS AND MISCONDUCT

A. F. B.

A COMPARATIVE STUDY OF THE INTELLIGENCE OF
DELINQUENT GIRLS
THE PSYCHOLOGY OF SPECIAL ABILITIES AND DIS-
ABILITIES

In Collaboration

JUDGE BAKER FOUNDATION CASE STUDIES, SERIES I

DELINQUENTS AND CRIMINALS
Their Making and Unmaking
Studies in Two American Cities

BY

WILLIAM HEALY, M.D.

AND

AUGUSTA F. BRONNER, Ph.D.

DIRECTORS, JUDGE BAKER FOUNDATION, BOSTON, FORMERLY DIRECTORS, JUVENILE PSYCHOPATHIC INSTITUTE, CHICAGO

(JUDGE BAKER FOUNDATION PUBLICATION No. 3)

New York
THE MACMILLAN COMPANY
1926

All rights reserved

Criminology
Collection
H434d

COPYRIGHT, 1926,
BY THE MACMILLAN COMPANY.

Set up and printed.
Published September, 1926.

Printed in the United States of America by
J. J. LITTLE AND IVES COMPANY, NEW YORK

PREFACE

Convinced that the first step toward improvement in the treatment of delinquency is measurement of the effectiveness of methods of treatment, we began several years ago a special research concerning outcomes. Our case studies of a large series of juvenile offenders, the first extensive group studied by scientific methods, we have reviewed in the light of what was done with and for the individual. The work has grown and we have entered into other inquiries concerning the results of treatment in other series and in another city, all for the sake of what might be learned by comparative studies. Such evaluations offer the only possible basis for the shaping of wiser policies for the prevention and treatment of delinquency and crime.

We gratefully acknowledge once more the inspiration received from Mrs. W. F. Dummer and the material aid from her which made possible for this study the field work in Chicago. The facts were gathered through the fine coöperation of a number of Chicago workers under the intelligent supervision of Miss Marion Schaffner, and particularly with the aid of Mr. Joseph L. Moss, Chief Probation Officer of the Juvenile Court. Part of a grant from the Commonwealth Fund of New York financed some preparation of data. The work in Boston for the most part has been done by the staff of the Judge

Baker Foundation; we are indebted to Miss Stella Abrams and to Mr. Truman Heminway for obtaining the facts of a series of after-careers.

For the future we see yet deeper understandings of delinquents and criminals, of why they do what they do, and of what changes are wrought, for social weal or woe, by any and every step of treatment accorded them by their fellow-men. Offering high adventure, difficult and challenging, incomparably more beneficial to our time and civilization than polar exploration or unearthing ancient cities is the discovery of the springs and sources and later conditionings of human conduct.

WILLIAM HEALY
AUGUSTA F. BRONNER

April, 1926.

CONTENTS

vii

DELINQUENTS AND CRIMINALS

THEIR MAKING AND UNMAKING

PART I
GENERAL STATEMENT

DELINQUENTS AND CRIMINALS

CHAPTER I

INTRODUCTION

ANY sound rebuilding of social and legal treatment of delinquency and crime must have as its foundation established facts, such as are presented in this volume.

It is amazing that modern civilization, with all its frank devotion to conceptions of efficiency, has not yet undertaken thoroughly critical studies of what really are the results of its dealings with delinquency and crime. Despite the tremendous equipment and expenditure for protection, detection, apprehending, for courts, jails and prisons, reformatory education, probation, little or nothing is spent to ascertain with care what is or is not accomplished. In industry, business or active science such an inquiry into results is regarded as absolutely fundamental.

Our huge system of attempt to meet the social problem of delinquency and crime has gradually grown up during the centuries, so unquestioningly granted funds through public largess that its existence and extension have not depended upon any measurement of its success. The body of the tradition of the law has been steadily accompanied in its development by the general idea that the law unaided is competent to decide what is adequate

3

treatment of delinquency and crime. Though sharp criticisms of the whole situation by judges and others now and again appear, no shrewd, long-continued, commonsense self-inquiry has ever been initiated.[1] A scientific study of outcomes of treatment in this great business has never been set about, nor has scientific method been introduced into it.

Now it may easily be known that through and under the law, a very poor business indeed is done in the handling of delinquents and criminals, for social offenses seem certainly not to be diminishing and offenders who have once been in the hands of the law all too frequently do not cease their offending.

One may readily argue either that the difficulty is with the law itself, its machinery and procedure, in that it fails primarily to aim at maintaining itself as an effective social agent, or that the main trouble lies in the limitations of legal education, study of the criminal law affording nothing of a scientific or business-like attitude toward the problems which the law attempts to solve according to its traditions and theories.

Then one may insist that the political selection of

---

[1] This curious fact is emphasized by a "unique crime statistics survey: the first of its kind in the United States," *Crime and the Georgia Courts* (Journal of Criminal Law and Criminology, Aug. 1925). This study made under the guidance of the legal profession quite ignores commonsense inquiry into success and failure in handling offenders; it is no research into causations and cures. But if how to cure delinquent tendencies should not be our chief quest in such studies, what should?

The various studies of procedure under the law, or of groups of reformatory inmates, appearing from time to time, and some of which certainly do embody scientific method, bear but seldom on the practical points we have so strongly in mind, namely, the handling of offenders as successfully as possible from the different levels of police, court and institutional treatment.

officials, almost entirely those who lack special education and training for the tasks they assume, is what
is to blame all along the line, which very curiously extends from the judges, who without particular interests
or special knowledge in scientific criminology, have,
nevertheless, to prescribe treatment, to the probation
officers or prison officials who, equally without specific
training, deal directly with the offenders.

And, finally, one may say that perhaps of primary
importance is the fact that, as yet, because of lack of
application of scientific method in the field, there has
been built up no large body of solid knowledge to be used
as a guide to treatment. This accounts for the prevalence of the idea that justice is achieved, above everything, by the treatment of each and all alike, certainly
a very pernicious principle, since it takes no account of
the multitude of differences in human beings and situations, and brings about indiscriminate herding of
individuals in institutions, with consequent tremendous
moral contaminations and formation of anti-social
grudges of which those who are students of offenders
could give many examples. And, second, the judge very
humanly influenced by his moods, notions, prejudices,
has to make without aid from science many decisions
which involve errors, if outcomes are the criteria.

At any rate, science, which has such commanding
victories to its credit elsewhere, has never, either as research or as practical guide, had its inning in this field.

This state of affairs is not due to lack of interest. The
public discussion of delinquency and crime continues
endlessly, even though without apparent result either in
prevention or cure. But practically all the discussion
represents mere unvalidated opinion, based on little or

no appraisal of the results of different forms of treatment. Of theory, belief, preconception, it is to be seen there is aplenty, but of patient willingness to gather hard facts over long years and of genuine desire to discover new truths as they may be slowly revealed there are discernible only the smallest traces. And yet where so much is at stake, the great need is for *proof* rather than for mere *belief*, for *knowledge* rather than for *guess-work*.

The great requirement of the present is more information, such as may only be gained through careful survey of facts which represent long experiences, first, with different types of offenders, offenses, and causations. Then we must impartially ask what actually develops when an offender of known abilities and personality characteristics, guilty of certain offenses, with such and such a background situation, has prescribed for him some socio-legal punishment or treatment. Do facts obtained from scientific observation indicate that the chance for reformation of the individual and for protection of society are greater if some special form of dealing with a given offender is used?

Whether expressed in the main theories of criminology or in the diagnostic work of the modern conduct clinic, explanations and interpretations are not ends in themselves. Principally, they should be means to the planning of efficacious treatment. And the correctness of the interpretations or explanations can often only be determined in the light of outcome of treatment. Hence the point of critical attack on the problems of delinquency and crime must be analytic study of the later careers of offenders who have earlier been subjects of scientific investigation, their personality and experiences and life situations being known as each bears on the offense committed.

Only from accumulated data showing the significance of original situations and later careers can there be built up the knowledge that is fundamental to intelligent effort in any field where there is attempt to control or modify material and situations. For the establishment of sound legal and social measures, and for the development of an effective technic of handling the individual offender, we need above all to know the extent to which we are succeeding or failing. The profit gained from being on the right track not only concerns the immediate, personal reformative work in hand, but also is imperative for the larger plannings of the ever-necessary combat by society against delinquency and crime.

To these ends the careful ascertainment of details about individuals and groups, and about their life-adjustment, is necessary—and equally important is the formulating of generalizations soundly based on the specific facts. If for no other reason than the considerable potentiality of success and the immense cost of failure, the endeavor to modify human beings and their situations should constantly be accompanied by clear-sighted investigations into what really happened during the process of attempted modification and also into later history of the individuals dealt with.

This country long ago committed itself extensively and in costly ways to the idea of reformation rather than the mere punishment of offenders, and later to the scheme of dealing separately with juvenile offenders in juvenile court, through special procedure. It was tacitly assumed that the establishment of reformatories and juvenile courts would accomplish the desired end of diminishing deliquency and crime. Has this aim been realized?

We can find very few attempts at evaluation of success and failure under these procedures, certainly none whatever according to critical scientific method. There are, to be sure, the New York, Chicago and Philadelphia Juvenile Court publications, mines of statistical information; the Chicago reports are exceptional in that they honestly give juvenile recidivism for the year. And one institution, the New York House of Refuge, tells frankly what is superficially known of the after-careers of its inmates. But we look in vain for any study by any judge or court or institutional official of outcomes of considerable numbers over sufficient years and as classified according to conditions of the individual and of his life situation. Such studies would offer the only valid means of estimating the efficacy (a) of the definite prescriptions of the law or those uttered under authority of law and (b) of special forms of treatment developed under legal sanction—either of these as punitive, deterrent, or reformative.

The truth is that bare opinion, or opinion and theory most meagerly supported by facts, whether as represented by statutory law or by judicial pronouncement, has been dictating official policies in the treatment of delinquency, deciding the specific treatment that each offender shall receive. It is the experience of ourselves and many other observers that different judges and other officials have entirely different and even opposed scales of values according to which they decide upon treatment. There is no compendium from which to teach, for example, whether young shoplifters, or forgers, or sex offenders, of certain types and having had certain experiences, tend or not to reform under constructive probation or other treatment.

Clearly, then, it still remains for sufficient scientific knowledge to be gathered and disseminated before methods of treatment can evolve to the point of bringing a larger measure of success in the prevention and diminution of delinquency. It is following the paths of science and, in fact, of commonsense procedure to insist that the gathering of data for study and analysis is a practical prerequisite for advance to formulation of conclusions upon which sound methods may be based.

It is because of our realization of the lack of scientific method in this field and the necessity for it, if progress is to be made, that we have felt impelled to assemble in this volume some data that have been accumulated during the seventeen years of our actual studies of delinquents and to marshal them for comparison and interpretation.

In this present work we are making a first attempt to estimate just what has actually been accomplished through society's handling of some groups of offenders, an attempt that at least shows the great absurdity of going on, year after year, ordering the same methods of treatment without stopping to inventory the effectiveness of the treatment.

The data presented may disturb some complacencies of those who feel content to rest with formulations of theories, or of those who would trust in the law as it now stands and in the present types of treatment operating under the law. That the results now achieved are distressingly poor surely almost all will acknowledge, and that only through reliable gathering of facts and analysis of them is the way of betterment to be found.

Knowing the treatment prescribed for the juvenile offenders we studied and having the opportunity offered to follow many of these same individuals the raw material has been developed for studies of correlations of outcomes with types of offenders and types of treatment. Specifically, the data have been utilized for (1) critical analysis of outcomes of a large number of careers, (2) comparison of outcomes in two very different, typical American cities, (3) statements concerning treatment as it differs in the two communities. From original case-studies are gathered (4) statistics concerning several extensive series of delinquents, adequate in number for some generalizations relative to causes of delinquency and possible conditionings of results of treatment.

Although our daily work ever shows more strongly that the prime interest of all who actually deal with offenders should be with the particular individual, his peculiarities, his background and his needs, yet accumulation of studies and analyses of statistics based thereon are necessary to point the way for the adoption of effective policies and procedures. It is only by finding features common to whole groups of individuals or conditions that safe generalizations are to be made for criminological science. The newer criminology does not object to the science of the earlier criminology, but has its point of departure in utilization of a vastly better technic for deriving the facts underlying behavior in individual instances.

Two years ago we issued a series of case studies [1] for teaching purposes to show in detail methods of studying

[1] Judge Baker Foundation Case Studies, Series I. 1923.

delinquents and some of the many factors involved in delinquency and in the treatment of the individual. The present study of large groups is in antithesis to the case-study method, but it is based on just such actual studies as the published series of cases illustrate.

We have made wide use of the comparative method in the present volume, offering comparisons of the human material, comparison of methods of treatment, and of results. We have attempted also to compare Chicago and Boston in social attitudes toward delinquency and its prevention and treatment, but attitudes, not being reducible to statistics, we have found somewhat difficult to set forth—there is so much in the difference of the spirit of communities that is elusive.

Realizing the temptation that some of our data may offer for upholding one theory or another concerning delinquency or crime, we urge readers to refrain from selecting and overweighting for interpretation any single factor without taking other findings into consideration. Conclusions cannot be drawn fairly from the figures on any one topic; the forces which make for human misconduct are complex.

It may seem that in some of the pages which follow we tell a sorry tale of society's failure to make much headway in the prevention of delinquency, even when a criminalistic career is seen impending, and in spite of great public expenditure directed toward prevention. But as our own experience grows we are becoming more and more convinced that there are many untapped possibilities for doing finer work and realizing more profitable returns.

CHAPTER II

MATERIAL AND METHOD

OUR present research is based on material gathered by us in the form of case studies of juvenile repeated offenders in Chicago and in Boston,[1] and on follow-up work, a study of after-careers, all done as a part of our regular routine or under our direction.

We have deemed it quite unnecessary to review in this book the well known facts which show the utter weakness of handling adult offenders by prevailing methods: placing them under conditions which so tend to weaken personality; that often lead the incarcerated to become further imbued with ideas of crime; releasing the offender without the thorough supervision and aid that alone can prevent recidivism. Society has not yet learned to protect itself by what it prescribes by way of punishment. More efficient methods must be forthcoming in the treatment of adult offenders—we see that plainly—but nowhere shall we learn better what to do than by studying the careers of younger delinquents.

By juvenile repeated offenders we mean young people who have continued in delinquency after very definite

[1] Studies in two cities were undertaken because of the value of comparison as scientific method. We began with no preconceptions; we had no idea of what would be revealed in outcomes. The comparisons have been made solely to determine facts and principles, not in the spirit of praise or blame. Through daily companionship we know full well and respect greatly the fine work of many who have steadily given of their best in both cities.

12

efforts on the part of some one in authority to check their misconduct. By far the most of our cases had been in the juvenile court at least twice. (There is little practical value in taking first offenders for scientific comparisons, because their delinquencies sometimes are accidental or so slight that the offender in essence or by intent is non-delinquent, and the treatment given may properly have been merely nominal or little more than that.)

Utilized for this study are: (1) three groups of juvenile repeated offenders with later careers traced: (a) a series of 920 studied by us in Chicago between 1909 and 1914 and followed up as a special research in 1921-1923, (b) a series of 400 young male offenders who appeared in the Boston Juvenile Court in 1909-1914, whose careers were studied in 1923 in relation to further delinquency, (c) a series of 400 boys, also repeated offenders, originally studied by us in Boston, 1918-1919, and very well known to us in their after-careers through our regular following of cases.

(2) For statistical analysis we used 4000 cases consisting of 2000 offenders studied by us in Chicago between 1909 and 1915, and 2000 studied in Boston from 1917 to 1923.

These larger series, used in groups of 1000 each, represent no selection whatever except as they were repeated offenders of juvenile age. The methods of study of the cases comprising these series are entirely comparable for the points given, although we hope that we have steadily bettered our procedure in detail, and it is a fact that in the Boston group the data of social background are fuller and more accurate. The later years have seen much better development of psychological and personality studies, but this hardly bears upon the general classifications as given in the statistics. Nobody who has read our published case studies can doubt that our statistical findings are based on very careful investigations made with the aim of giving advice about treatment for the individual.

This study of 4000 cases may be regarded as an expansion of our report before the Second Pan-American Scientific Congress in 1916, "A Comparative Study of Two Groups, Each of 1000 Young Recidivists." (*Amer. Jour. of Sociology,* July, 1916). In the present study there is the greatly added value not only of increased numbers, which makes by far the largest series of carefully studied cases reported on in the literature of criminalistics, but also of comparison of findings in two cities, both large centers, each representing a distinct type of development in our American civilization.

Outcomes in the Chicago series were investigated only in cases that had originally been studied sufficiently well to know the individual's physical and mental make-up and the background and probable causations of delinquency.

The main purpose of studying outcomes was an attempt to discover what had become of these young offenders as part of an effort to determine success or failure of the types of treatment given to juveniles. For this purpose it was essential to obtain the facts for entirely unselected cases provided they met the following requirements:

(a) The individual at the time of the initial study was not above juvenile court age, so that treatment, the effects of which we are studying, was administered through the juvenile court itself or through agencies dealing with juveniles.

(b) The individual was old enough at the time of study to be well above the juvenile age at the time when the last follow-up report was made, so that there was a chance to judge of the outcome in the career of the individual. Since most cases were 14 years or over when first seen by us, the average age of the group at the time of our follow-up was approximately 25 years.

(c) All cases had been actually dealt with by the juvenile court. A very few came from Illinois juvenile courts other than Chicago.

(d) No cases were included that were dealt with by the court for only short periods, such as those of runaway boys returned to their own homes in other cities or states.

In the original studies careful records had been made of all findings, of physical examination, of psychological test results, of family and personal history, of sociological facts, and of mental analysis. In each there was also made an interpretive summary, including what were then considered to be probable direct causations. During the years we were in Chicago, that is, up to 1917, many items concerning adjustments made and the results of them were recorded. Thus it was known what court action followed the appearance in court subsequent to our study. And through contact with probation officers and social agency workers it was possible, during the years we were in Chicago, to receive reports informally as to how affairs were going.

The later data were obtained by field workers under the direct supervision of one who knew through first-hand experience our methods and aims, herself earlier a worker in the juvenile court. Visits were made to homes, official sources for obtaining information were utilized, and outcomes were traced, and facts obtained from social agencies other than the court. Frequently all these sources were made use of for corroboration.

It was found that fulfilling requirements for inclusion in the group were 920 cases. When follow-up was sought, a certain number of these could not be found; some were dead, some were custodially held in institutions as mentally abnormal. (See Table 1.) Remaining for study of outcomes were 675 cases whose careers in young adult life could be ascertained reliably enough to permit of evaluation in some measure, and where the general type of treatment that the individual had undergone could be known for correlation with the other facts.

It was recognized when this study was planned and before data were sought that it would not be possible to estimate successful outcome or failure on too fine a scale. Without much more detailed accounts than were available, indeed without personal contacts and restudy of the individuals, it would be impossible to make fine discriminations, to evaluate success or failure in terms of use or development of best potentialities, for example, or in terms of happiness or economic productivity. In the outcomes of girls' cases when marriage had occurred, it was, of course, impossible to ascertain in many instances the subtler facts of marital life. But it could be learned if homes were clean, children cared for, and the mother's attitude toward them good. Nor could the adjustments made and the treatment attempted be known in specific detail, as, for instance, the effect on the individual of any person who had tried to be helpful.

Coarse measurements, however, were possible, and

even these offered opportunity for learning much that is of value and that is badly needed to further the development of better methods of dealing with delinquents.

More specifically, outcome was to be counted as Success when the individual was living in the community, without known detriment to the community and had engaged in no criminality. (Whether he was utilizing his abilities to the fullest, or presented some problem in his personality, or was content with his lot, it was considered not practicable to determine.)

Conversely, Failure denoted actual delinquency. All individuals having adult court records and adjudged guilty, as well as those committed to adult correctional institutions, were regarded as Failures. From the point of view of effectiveness of the juvenile court treatment one who comes in conflict with the law as an adult must be regarded as having failed to be cured by earlier court efforts. A few were regarded as Failures who, though not known to have been arrested, were an actual drag on the community, vagrants, excessive drinkers, extreme loafers, those grossly immoral and thus indirectly costly to society.

Aside from these two groups there were some individuals who, though not actually delinquent or criminalistic and not genuine "sore spots" in the community, yet were found to be irregular workers or non-contributors to their families even in time of great need, or who were themselves victims of bad habits. These latter were designated as being "indifferent" outcomes, but there were only 29 of these.

For comparison we undertook first to obtain male repeated offenders as they appeared in the Boston Juvenile

Court during the same years, 1909-1914, that the above group was studied in Chicago. (Why the study was limited to boys is explained later.) We desired to compare a group equal in number and as similar as possible in the offenses committed. In order to obtain these we ruled out all those who had appeared for very petty offenses, such as selling fruit without a license or playing ball on the street. With such standards in mind we were able to find only 400 repeated offenders appearing in these years. Then, too, in order to make a fair comparison we were limited to those of an age that would at the time of our follow-up research be at least two years above juvenile court age as in the Chicago series of follow-up cases. In addition to these considerations concerning the selection of this group we may state that from the court records we were able to obtain ages, offenses, birthplace, nationality of parents, but since the cases were not studied by us we cannot compare the physical and mental make-up of the offenders and their backgrounds with such known facts of the Chicago group. But from the comparisons of 2000 cases in each city it is easy to determine whether there are significant differences between delinquents and their backgrounds in these two cities, differences that would invalidate clear comparison of treatment and outcome.

The later careers were traced through consulting juvenile and adult court records, institutional and parole records, and the admirable central recording system of the Massachusetts Probation Commission which registers court appearances and dispositions in Boston and vicinity and for certain other more important districts of the state. This registry of information concerning delinquents, while of course not completely accurate, is much more complete than any other source of similar information we have found elsewhere. In Chicago our follow-up had to be done partly through the difficult searching of court records and partly through correspondence with institutions, as well as through field inquiry. In Boston we had official data which makes our knowledge of adult careers, so far as court record is concerned, very much more thorough. For neither of these two groups have we many facts about offenses committed outside the state; lacking a central registry of offenders in our country, such information is very difficult to obtain, unless as in the Boston cases studied by us there is continuing acquaintance and careful following.

Also for comparison a second group of 400 Boston juvenile repeated offenders has been taken consecutively from our own case records of 1918-1919 with the following of careers that has been carried on consistently since that time by our own staff. All of these, too, are at least two years above juvenile court age so that they are very well along in the years when criminalistic behavior predominates. The facts known about this group are much more thorough than any of the earlier series.

Concerning treatment, only gross adjustments have been considered, commitments to institutions, placement in foster homes, probation, rather than the more subjective influences brought to bear, for it was felt that, coarse in measure though these standards are, they offer very much more than is yet at hand concerning the whole matter of the treatment of delinquency.

We recognize clearly that one would like to know specifically "what turned the trick" where outcomes were successful, and why "the trick was not turned" where failure resulted, but such knowledge must await the time when careful, detailed study can be made of individual adult offenders and of the individual adult reformed. Meanwhile there is great practical value in determining, in so far as is possible, the effectiveness of court procedure, of institutional work, the tools of probation and parole employed in the endeavor to check delinquency among the young.

For those unfamiliar with the institutions used by the Chicago Juvenile Court we give here a brief description of them.

The Chicago Parental School is an institution for truants maintained by the Board of Education. It is on the cottage plan, with excellent buildings and equipment. Boys are committed there through the Chicago Juvenile Court at any time during the age that attendance at school is legally required. The length of stay is approximately five months. The curriculum consists of ordinary school subjects with courses in manual arts. There are splendid facilities for outdoor play and exercise.

The John Worthy School, to which boys were committed during the period under discussion, is no longer in existence, having been in some sense replaced by the Chicago and Cook County School for Boys. It was an institution for short commitments on the theory that short "terms" under strict disciplinary control might act as a deterrent for those who were rather in need of being sharply checked than in need of prolonged training. A section of the House of Correction was utilized, but under different supervision, the boys coming in no way in contact with adult offenders. The school was abandoned because it was believed that more injury than benefit ensued from the more repressive type of life and the banding together in one building of quite seriously delinquent youths.

The St. Charles Training School is the state correctional school where boys of all ages up to 17 are sent from all parts of Illinois. It is on the cottage plan, has a thousand acres of farm land and is very well equipped. Commitments are for an indeterminate period, release occurring when in the judgment of the managing officer the boy is ready to return to the community. Boys leaving the school are on parole from the institution, but this parole is nominal and is virtually non-existent, for at the period our study covers there was only one parole officer for the entire state, and as a matter of actual fact the boys included in this study were for the most part sent home from the institution without any later supervision.

Of the institutions for the care and training of girls the Refuge (now called the Chicago Home for Girls) and the House of the Good Shepherd are in the city. The former, non-sectarian, accepted girls sent there by families or committed by the court. Though privately supported, its academic work is conducted by the Chicago Public Schools and its training comprises not only this but also household arts. Much personal help is given to the girls. The House of the Good Shepherd is, of course, a Catholic institution. It maintains one department for non-delinquent or mildly delinquent girls and another for more serious delinquents.

At Geneva is the State Training School for Girls, comparable to the St. Charles for boys. Girls are committed by the court up to the age of 18 though they may be retained there until they are 21.

The Illinois institutions for dependents which are mentioned incidentally in this study vary greatly in size, the larger ones being of the congregate type. Some are on the cottage plan. All are educational in character, giving ordinary school work and often supplementary shop or trade work. They are all either church or private institutions.

The Massachusetts institutions to which boys are committed consist of the Industrial School at Shirley to which juvenile offenders over 15 are sent, and the Lyman School for boy offenders under 15. In general scheme and equipment these are similar to the training school at St. Charles in Illinois. Another school for delinquent boys was formerly on an island in Boston Harbor. This was the Suffolk School, a county institution which went out of existence several years ago. Boston formerly maintained a parental school for truants which was given up many years ago.

Various other facts concerning the treatment of delinquents have been brought out in subsequent chapters, particularly the extent to which placing in foster homes is utilized both through the State Department of Public Welfare and through social agencies. Among the large number placed out by the state there are some cases of younger delinquents, and especially during the last eight years a definite campaign of placing even seriously delinquent juveniles has been undertaken by social agencies, the number limited not by policy but entirely by practical resources. Much of this will be mentioned in our chapter "Analysis of General Social Backgrounds."

The institutions to which adult male offenders are committed are very similar in the two cities. The houses of correction and reformatories, the county jails, penitentiaries or state prisons in general scheme are much alike. In both cities these institutions are of the types common to the more populous centers of this country.

Under adjustments we have included service in the army or navy because this represents a period of time spent by the individual under a very definite type of life and discipline. Figures for such service are, we recognize, quite incomplete. And they do not represent in any way what might occur at some other time, for the years covered in this study include those when our country was taking part in the World War. Of course, those individuals who were at that time serving sentences in correctional institutions were not drafted.

For girl delinquents we have made no attempt at inquiry concerning outcomes in a Boston series because, as our Chicago series shows, very few of the failures reach court in adult life, and field inquiry would have been a most difficult task without the prior studies which form the practical basis of reliable contacts for gathering later information.

Furthermore, had we attempted to select a group of girls for comparison with the Chicago series we would have found it difficult to obtain sufficient numbers to make the comparison worth much. In proof of this point, and incidentally as bearing on the immense difference which may obtain in the practice of a juvenile court, we may refer to the figures for Boston and Chicago, Table 21. In the years covered by our series, the ratio of girls seen in the court in Chicago is sometimes four times as great as the ratio in Boston.

PART II

OUTCOMES IN RELATION TO TREATMENT
OF OFFENDERS

CHAPTER III

STUDYING the extensive problem of crime in America it may perhaps be best to begin by asking how well public authority copes with crime's earlier manifestations. How successful is the treatment of juvenile delinquency, particularly through that notably American institution, the Juvenile Court? Is it possible to follow the careers of the young people who have come before the Juvenile Court, to determine its influence upon them, to estimate the wisdom of its dicta, the effectiveness of its control?

As a matter of fact, one is able not only to follow juvenile offenders step by step, recording observations concerning them, their conduct, and the court's efforts in their behalf; one can also stand aside later and after a lapse of years view, with better perspective, the process as a whole, and endeavor to estimate its accomplishments.

Our inquiry may begin, specifically, by the questions, How many young offenders ceased their delinquency, and how many later became criminals? Who constituted the former group and who the latter? And what differences, if any, existed concerning the treatment of the two groups? These questions can only be satisfactorily answered from actual data and it is such data that we have assembled.

First, and before making comparisons between the two cities, we shall take the young repeated offenders studied

27

by us in Chicago during the years beginning with 1909
who are now all old enough to be well along in and most
of them beyond the great crime period of life, the ages
between 18 and 23, and inquire what have been their
outcomes? What do their careers show concerning the

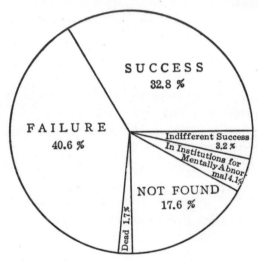

CHART 1.

Findings for 920 Chicago cases studied 1909-1914. (Percentages on
total 1920.)   675 or 73.4% classified as Success or Failure.

efficacy of the legalistic and social treatment accorded
them?

Outcomes on the 675 Chicago cases are as follows:

	Males	Females	Total
SUCCESS	164 (39%)	138 (54%)	302 (45%)
FAILURE	256 (61%)	117 (46%)	373 (55%)
	420 (100%)	255 (100%)	675 (100%)

Quite apart from attempt at analysis of what made
for or against Success or Failure, these first figures must

arouse serious concern. Gauged by outcomes in adult life, what was done to these young offenders in the period when the court or the correctional institutions had the power to attempt modification and control, has failed more often than it has succeeded.

The answer to our first question is thus altogether distressing. But it is necessary to face the facts, and know, as a first prerequisite to betterment that the treatment administered has so frequently failed of its purpose.

In any line of effort should one be content with such a showing? If one considers the net results as business returns, profit and loss, the seriousness of the situation is evident; such losses in the long run inevitably would mean bankruptcy. There is an immediate challenge in this lack of correlation between expenditure and accomplishment.

Another fact apparent from the above general figures is the noteworthy difference in outcomes for the sexes; 39% of the males rate as Successes, 54% of the females. This is in striking contradiction to the tradition that it is extremely difficult for a girl who has been immoral to reform and fill an accepted place in society; for it may be said at once that over half the girls represented in the statistics appeared in court as sex offenders, and 75% of them were to be classified as such sometime during juvenile court age.

Concerning sex differences in outcomes, it is quite certain that special interest and greater effort may have been given to girls' cases, sufficient to account for their relatively greater success. We have some indication that this is the fact, if for no other reason than that the ratio of girls to boys found in the follow-up of our series (1:1.6) was much larger than the ratio (1:2.3) in the series as originally studied during the same years (see Table 20). Other clews to the differences will be revealed in the factors discussed in subsequent chapters.

Since our criteria of Success and Failure are based almost entirely on the keeping or breaking of laws or moral codes there is little that need be said in detail about outcomes of the Success cases. It must suffice to know that these individuals were apparently satisfactorily maintaining themselves in the community, and that, whatever the more intimate facts of their lives might have been, they had not, after juvenile court age, come into contact with the law, nor were they complained of by their families or by agencies as living lives detrimental to the general welfare.

For the Failures details need to be known because their offenses differ so in kind and in amount of repetition. However, the entire picture of the Failures of the males, for example, cannot be sketched with completeness; the nature and extent of later law-breaking it is practically impossible to know accurately; the record even of arrests and criminal charges of such a group will always be far from complete until there is a general Federal system of recording data concerning criminals, and much must be missed in any large city unless there is a central agency for court registration.

What one is able to give concerning Failure is, therefore, an understatement. Through field work some facts can be ascertained about offenses which may have been committed and not registered. But there will always remain a certain amount of delinquency, undetected, known only to the perpetrators themselves. Of crimes committed outside of Chicago or outside Illinois we have some knowledge, but doubtless it is quite incomplete.

Homicide

Without pretense of completeness, but as illustration of the extremity of Failure among the males, and because of the interest in what is generally regarded as the worst of all crimes, we may cite, first, *homicide*. Of the male failures, 5%, 13 individuals, were found guilty of 14 homicides, their offenses being designated as murder or manslaughter. The crimes were perpetrated as follows:

```
4 in connection with burglary
2  "      "        "   street robbery
7  "      "        "   robbery (hold-up) of store or office
1 jealousy murder, love affair
```

One homicide or murder we have not included because it was not part of a career after treatment instituted under the law, which is the subject of our present study; it was the occasion of the offender's first appearance in court. Another case studied and excluded, because not properly in our Chicago series, is that of a 14 year old lad who after release from a correctional institution to which he had been sent from a country district, murdered his foster-mother and her children.

Two of the 14 homicides were committed by a feeble-minded thoroughly criminalistic young man; the second one very shortly after his release from a prison sentence for his first homicide. Then it should be added that records show that 3 others of our total group have been arrested and perhaps justly accused of homicide, but without sufficient evidence for conviction.

The youthful age at which many of the homicides were committed is remarkable:

2 committed homicide at 15 years
2   "   "   " 17   "
4   "   "   " 18   "
2   "   "   " 19   "
1   "   "   " 20   "
1   "   "   " 21   "
1   "   "   " 24   "
1   "   "   " 26   " (a second homicide)

This appalling frequency of homicides among those who had been known earlier as boys with delinquent trends and after treatment of some sort had been undertaken with them need hardly be stressed even for the casual reader. But it must not be forgotten that society earlier very specifically had its hands on these offenders when they were in a formative period and yet accomplished so little with or for them. Whether or not there was reasonable chance of avoiding desperate careers may be inferred from the illustrative cases given in the next chapter.

Of course the question may be raised whether these findings really are representative of the after-careers of Chicago's juvenile repeated offenders. In response we would say that our group was not selected because of peculiar viciousness of behavior, or because they received treatment unusual in any way.

Another query that naturally arises in the light of modern interest in mental disorder concerns the mentality of these offenders. (For these and other facts, see Table 3.) Although in a future chapter mentality of the entire series will be discussed, it may be stated here that of the 13 who committed homicide, 7 had been diagnosed by us as normal mentally, 2 as psychotic, 1 of psychopathic personality, 3 as mentally defective. Recent psychiatric reports concerning several of these young men confirm our early diagnosis of mental normality as well as of abnormality.

Reviewing our first study of these cases we find that for all the mentally abnormal except one clear warnings were given that the future was fraught with very serious possibilities. Their danger to the community was recognized and proper segregation was recommended, but no suitable provisions for the care of such individuals existed—nor do they now.

"Professional" Criminalism

Less spectacular, but immensely burdensome to society are careers continued into "professional" criminalism.[1] Of our group of male Failures, no less than 39 (15%) have been reported as so frequently engaging in crime and so largely earning their living by such means that they may fairly be designated by the police term "professionals." While some of these may engage in more than one variety of crime, the reports are specific that these 39 are "professionally" as follows:

> 16 burglars
> 5 "hold-up" men
> 2 swindlers
> 14 thieves
> 2 sex perverts

The fact that such careers were carried on so steadily is indicative that for the most part these offenders for years escaped serving long sentences. Sometimes arrested and dismissed, sometimes they have served short sen-

[1] Our figures for professional criminalism and prostitution are very conservative. We have included only those definitely and reliably reported as following such careers. Many others we know from our records to be repeatedly, but only intermittently, engaged in crime and immorality. In classifying them we have taken the major offenses but most of them have been engaged in other delinquencies; for example, one burglar also operated a confidence game. It would take a long chapter to tell the story of the delinquencies of this group.

tences, in some cases it is reported by their families or by social agencies who knew them well that they have committed crimes without being apprehended, but all are well known to the police and have had court appearances.

They represent a group that from the standpoint of mentality is largely normal. Among the 39 (see Table 4) there were 30 normal mentally, 5 feeble-minded, 1 psychotic, 3 psychopathic personalities.

Violent Deaths

Violent deaths (Table 6) among our group offer some information about the desperate nature of the misconduct engaged in: 3 were killed in committing crime, 1 each during a burglary, a "hold-up," a brawl, 4 committed suicide, 2 of them after careers of crime.

Other Male Failures

For the other Failures we have made no attempt to enumerate offenses committed after juvenile court age; as we have already stated, it is well nigh impossible to do this in entirety. But from the number of arrests and sentences it is clear that for the most part the careers of the Failures have not been mild. The tables and charts of court appearances and commitments (Tables 7 to 10) partly reveal the story; incomplete as they are, they show that many individuals appeared frequently in court and served several sentences.

Female Failures

Turning to the outcome of the girls' cases we find that even though the percentage of Failure was less than among the boys, it still seems distressingly large.

What we know about the later lives of the females cannot be told in terms of prison sentences or even court offenses. Much more of our knowledge than in the cases of boys was gained directly by field work, through probation officers and social workers who had kept in touch with the girls.

Only 9 of the entire 117 female Failures (Table 7) were committed to adult correctional institutions and there were only 19 other known adult court appearances. Yet of the 117, there were 97 who were definitely known to be adult sex offenders.

That so few of these offenders were brought to court and still fewer sent to adult correctional institutions is possibly due to matters of policy, the wisdom of which one may question. Without arrest and court appearance these women, of course, felt no deterrence in their careers, nor had they whatever help probation might have contributed. Perhaps the small number of the total known offenders who were committed is due to the lack in Illinois of any separate institutions for adult female offenders and a consequent dislike of sending women to an institution so largely utilized for men offenders.

Comparable to the "professionals" among the male offenders, there are (Table 5) among the females one chronic thief and one swindler and forger, and 22 are specifically reported as being prostitutes.

The most common offense among the females, as one might expect, is sex delinquency, and it is of interest to note at once the proportions of Success and Failure among the juvenile sex offending group. Of the entire group of 255 females, 191, or almost 75% (see note following Table 55), had during juvenile court age engaged in sex irregularities. And of these 191, 99, or 52%, were known to be Failures in adult life, as compared with 92 (48%) Successes. Whether or not these proportions accord with expectations, it is at least of great value to know, from actual data, that 92 of these young women were able to reëstablish themselves and to make satisfactory adjustments as adults. This group constitutes 66% of the total female Successes.

Or, differently stated, of all the female juvenile offenders who met our qualifications requisite for classification as Successes, two-thirds had been sex offenders when known to us as juveniles.

Another point of great interest lies in the fact that, combining juvenile and later years, of the 117 female Failures, 111 (94%) were sex offenders, and of these, 99 had been so already at juvenile court age. From these figures it would seem that among our Failures, sex delinquency, in the vast majority of cases, began at an early age.

Of the 64 of the entire group of 255 females who had not been sex offenders during juvenile court age, only 6 were found to have later become so. As we shall show in the next chapter of illustrations, the Successes include some of the girls who, during early years, were flagrantly involved in sex irregularities, the extent of sex affairs seeming much less a factor in the production of Success or Failure than was the quality and extent of care and treatment accorded them.

While the cost of the female Failures is relatively small in terms of court and official expenditures, yet it requires no argument to show that their cost to society is very great indeed. Nor does their problem end with themselves—16 of them have already produced 21 illegitimate children; and there is no knowing the amount of disease which these young women have spread.

It requires very little figuring to demonstrate that all this Failure over years, involving such expenditures for police, court, and institutional work, far exceeds what would have been the expense of more adequate treatment earlier under the law—during the years when something effective might have been done to check criminal careers. The considerable cost of early work with offenders may be what deters from more constructive effort, but whatever in treatment would prove effective, whatever would check careers of delinquency would doubtless in the long run be vastly less costly than are the prolonged careers which many of our cases show.

No thoughtful reader can have accompanied us thus far in our portrayal of careers without wondering whether the large amount of Failure is necessary. Reverting to our earlier queries we may ask for more particulars; wherein lay the differences between the groups of Failures and Successes—in the individuals themselves, in the experiences through which they had passed, in the treatment accorded them? Could more have been accomplished had greater effort been expended, or had the efforts made been more wisely directed toward the individuals' specific needs?

Though the later sections concerning the Successes and Failures present the details upon which our final answers must be based, in this section we may undertake to gain light on the general question.

We shall attempt to determine whether Failure was so inevitable by utilizing comparisons, the very gist of the scientific method. Because of our experience in Chicago and Boston, we are able to compare the later careers of juvenile delinquents in the two cities where the prevailing methods of treatment have been widely different, while from our statistics of four thousand cases of young repeated offenders in the two cities it will be possible to gain information concerning the nature of the human material that comes into their juvenile courts.

CHAPTER IV

ALTHOUGH this present work is planned to deal with the classification of data, comparisons of mass facts, and generalizations from them, yet both statistics and conclusions may perhaps be illuminated by illustrative cases. From our extensive records we have chosen a few fair and typical examples of careers to demonstrate certain clear necessities, if disaster is to be averted, and to show something of the reconstructive possibilities of better methods of dealing with the young offender. Of particular value may be:

(a) Cases which show the fundamental weakness of not segregating or otherwise adequately controlling mentally abnormal individuals of delinquent proclivities. We have many illustrations of the fact that often it was easy enough to discern, by a thorough study of the case, what really should be done, and what very probably would prove availing for the protection of society and for treatment of the individual. And yet, the common-sense adjustment was never made and the young offender went on to develop a career of crime. The expense of non-prevention has been vast.

(b) Instances in which, without alteration of pernicious conditions ascertained through study of the case, the outlook has seemed to be thoroughly bad for reasons other than mental abnormality, instances in which, with nothing fundamental done, the career has been tragically extended. And in every case, such an outcome was preventable.

(c) Cases in which the conditions and outlook were apparently similar to those given above, but where rational and strong measures for reconstruction of the situation were carried out, with results absolutely in contrast to those of the Failure series. These few illustrations quite inadequately represent what our many case studies show by way of humanitarian and economic possibilities.

(d) Cases in which observation of the individual himself seemed to suggest that he was of good promise, but his external situation in life, certainly alterable, or the situation within his own mind, perhaps alterable, was not changed—and he continued in the ways of delinquency and even into severe crime.

(e) Cases, too obvious for extensive presentation, in which the individual appeared of good promise, and with modification of circumstances or of mental attitude or ideational life there was a thoroughly good outcome.

Among such cases as we speak of in (a), (b), (d) are some whose careers have gone on until they committed murder or homicide; we present these first because their failure involves the offense most costly and abhorrent to society. Even a short sketch of what they were as human beings and what were their situations in life, and how they were dealt with as young offenders will serve to show some clear preventabilities.

Some mentally diseased who committed homicide were:

A., one of the most desperate young criminals ever known in Chicago, was seen by us when he was 15 years old. He had been arrested several times by the police for minor offenses, such as staying away from home or gambling, and he had already during two or three years established a reputation with the police by engaging in fights with them. When we first saw him he was accused of being implicated in the death of a peddler who was shot by some one of a crowd of boys who had robbed him. There was no direct evidence that this boy did the shooting, although we found that outside the court room he boastfully maintained that he had. It was perfectly clear that he was mentally abnormal, an over-active, extremely excitable fellow of somewhat poor intelligence. His constitutional excitability was accentuated at times into a frenzied condition, when he was extraordinarily reckless. We learned that already he had engaged in excessively bad habits, smoking, drinking, and sex immorality with girls, by whom he was evidently liked because of his volubility and general liveliness. On account of all this we urged that he receive prolonged segregation and care. Although in Illinois, as elsewhere, there was very little provision for adequate treatment of children and young people with psychoses,[1] and there were and are many objections to putting them among adults in the state hospitals, yet in this case, on account of the boy's sophistication very little harm could have been done.

This boy readily ran away from the correctional school to which he was sent and then was at large, part of the time at home, without supervision of either probation or parole officers, utterly reckless, especially about encounters with the police. He was once shot and slightly wounded by a policeman. He himself shot at a fellow with whom he had a quarrel, and he had by this time become a regular "hold-up man" and burglar. Then after a few months at another correctional school he was released only to become a member of a gang of "auto bandits." At 18 he committed murder for which he was convicted. In the court room he made a serious attempt to injure the judge who sentenced him for a long term of years. In the penitentiary he has desperately attacked guards and made bold attempts to escape.

The reader can readily perceive the weakness of treatment throughout this career. If this fellow's essential condition could not be cured, at least he could have been held away from associations which inflamed his criminalistic ideation or tendencies and thus have been prevented

---

[1] Almost nowhere, even now, are there special wards or hospitals where children showing signs of mental disease may be taken care of. They fit in badly with the older patients who have gone on to the complete development of mental disease. In the meantime disasters impend and the expense to society, represented by these cases, accrues.

from being the social scourge he has been. His trends and traits were to be recognized early in boyhood. *The treatment accorded him served only to add to his tendencies.*

B. was recognized by us as being psychotic and we strongly recommended, three years before he committed murder, that he be taken care of as a mental case. It was not only that he was showing schizophrenic (dementia precox) symptoms, but also he was already showing definite and serious delinquent trends. When first seen, at 15 years, he was an excessive runaway, had been in burglary, and was associating much with bad companions. He came from a very decent family, and his mother's appeals for him always awakened sympathy. He was at the correctional school for boys for a time, but returned to old associations. At the trial for murder the judge decided he was sane, but at the time of our last report, he was about to be transferred from the penitentiary to a state hospital because he was in the catatonic stage of dementia precox.

C., also a boy of 15 when seen by us, was subject to fits of depression. He was in court for stealing and with good insight told us about his delinquent ideation and impulses, which he insisted he had derived from previous confinement in a boys' correctional school. His father had been insane for years. Nothing essential was done in this case either; he was not placed in country life as we recommended. In the city he continued to develop criminal tendencies and finally, entering a store, he demanded two dollars from the storekeeper, a total stranger, and upon refusal shot the man dead. He received an indeterminate sentence to the reformatory.

Because it presents clearly the absurd weaknesses that so frequently obtain in this country in the management of criminalistic abnormal personalities, we add here the case which, incidentally, represents the single instance in which any individual of either of the Boston followed-up series committed homicide.

We studied C 2 when he was a boy of 16, a pleasant appearing lad, with signs of some early developmental defects and of an unstable nervous system. He graded as having distinctly good mental abilities in various ways (intelligence quotient 101) and he had made a very good impression in his school career, which extended to the 8th grade. We found that he was fond of attempting to write both prose and poetry, but showing only moderate talent. He appeared and was reported to be notably companionable and of good address, active, impulsive, for the most part frank and truthful; in no way demonstrating outstanding bad personality traits.

His background was thoroughly unfortunate; the heredity was defective; he had suffered from severe convulsions in young childhood, followed by years of frequent temper fits, he had some sort of an attack with unconsciousness when at 12 years he was picked up on the street and taken to a hospital, at times he had developed peculiar nervous habits. Then home life had been anything but stable, principally on account of desertion of the father.

At 9 years he already began episodes of running away from home, and by the time he was 12 he was taking long trips even to distant parts of the country, sometimes stealing considerable sums for his purposes. Detained by the police in a number of cities he was always returned except once in the west when he was "written up" in the papers and then taken by a wealthy man who obtained a tutor for him and offered him many advantages. However, he soon ran away from this patron. More recently he had stolen in serious fashion from his employer.

We saw in this young fellow a very important case, a thoroughly unstable individual with marked anti-social trends, alleging himself to be the victim of uncontrollable impulse. No chance was found for him to go to sea on a long voyage as we suggested, so he was sent to an industrial school for older boys. There, after once running away and staging on the return trip a serious attempt at a headlong escape from a train window, he was found quite trustworthy. On parole he joined the Navy, but was soon in the Municipal Court for some petty charge. His mother reported to us that within a year he had deserted some three times and that on his home visits he appeared to be in excessively nervous state. She suspected him, evidently correctly, of drinking and of having acquired a venereal disease. He had been held for the Grand Jury once for burglary, but was released as merely being intoxicated at the time of the alleged offense.

Next heard from he had joined the Army in a distant part of the country. Army hospital reports state that a few days after enlistment he made off to another town, held up an automobile party, took the machine and rode around "shooting up" the town. Then he feigned insanity but changed his mind and made a full confession. An examining board, who had at hand full information about his previous career, held that he was "a menace to public safety," and "irresponsible for his actions."

Notwithstanding his mother's urgent request that he be permanently committed because she was certain that he would continue in serious criminality, he was transferred after three or four months to a general hospital from which he readily walked away. During all this period his intelligence was found good by tests and he was reported as clean, neat, and well liked. But he wrote a "terrible letter" about what he would do; later one came from the south stating that he was on his way to the gallows and was going "to have a grand, good time on the way." Next he served in two penitentiaries for short terms and finally, at 22 years of age, became the center of notoriety in a midwestern town because in a hold-up he shot 5 men and killed two of them. Clergymen and others became interested in him and aided his defense on the ground of abnormality. He received a life sentence.

It is obvious that at several stages of his career measures for proper custody should have been taken that would have prevented the hideous disaster that this criminalistically unstable young fellow otherwise was almost bound to be involved in. A competent study of his personality and a knowledge of his history, which easily could have been obtained, was necessary. But proper legal provisions for such cases and institutional colonies in which safely to control them are in most states non-existent.

Cases of mental defectives who committed homicide:

D. came from a family in which there was much feeblemindedness and tendency to criminality. From the time we saw him when he was just 9 years old we repeatedly urged his mother to have him permanently committed as defective, but this was never done although he was sent three times to correctional schools. At 15 he killed a peddler whom he attempted to rob—robbing peddlers in alleys or barns being rather a favorite occupation of young toughs, we found, in Chicago. D. at once left Chicago and at last report had never again come into the hands of the Chicago police, his whereabouts and after-career being quite unknown to us.

E. was a feebleminded boy, the only child of a hard-working mother whom we knew well; her husband and her other two children were killed in a frightful accident when she was pregnant with this boy. At 15 years he was classed by the police as "an expert young burglar" because he had mechanical skill remarkable in comparison with his generally defective intelligence, and he early learned to use his skill in unlawful entering. After our study he was placed in the country; he was contented and did very well for over a year on a farm where he had a chance to exercise his mechanical powers. Then, unfortunately, he returned to the city. He himself preferred staying on the farm, but his mother was sickly and needed his help. Under no supervision, he quickly fell in with old companions and with one of them perpetrated a burglary in which a man was killed. He was sentenced to the reformatory. This is the case mentioned above in which the young man recently accused himself of a second murder committed since his release from the reformatory. He and his criminalistic common-law wife, who played an active part in the affair, have each received a life-sentence.

F. was a mild youth who, at 16, graded mentally at a ten-year level. He was in court for stealing. We felt that in a decent environment he would do well, but he went to live with brothers who had become criminalistic. However, he did not do so badly, except that he began drinking. Then in simple-minded fashion he became infatuated with an immoral woman and spent his earnings on presents for her. When she spurned him he killed her and himself.

Cases of others who committed homicide: The seven who belong in this group were of clearly normal mental ability, none of them having been graded even as low as "poor, but normal ability." One fellow, I., whom we classified as having good ability, has, in the institution where he is serving a long sentence, been graded as having "very superior adult intelligence."

On the physical side, four of them, G., K., L., M., were of normal development and good strength; I. was slight in build but healthy; H. was of very poor development and strength, a pathetic youngster; J. was small, tired-looking and listless. None of them showed stigmata of degeneracy or anything peculiar in their physical make-up.

G. was an Italian boy who immigrated at 9 years of age. When we saw him at 15 he was decidedly bright mentally but poorly educated, having gone very irregularly to school. He had been several times in the juvenile court and once to the Parental School. A few years later he was a member of a gang notorious for their robberies and which, according to the Chicago Crime Commission "commanded some political influence and was said to resort to intimidations to prevent their conviction for various charges for which they had been indicted." After having served a term at the reformatory, he is reported at 24 years to have killed a man in a street hold-up.

H. was a sad, repressed boy, very small for his age, who had a weak, untruthful mother and sickly father. The boy became very dissatisfied with school yet, on account of poor physical condition, he was not permitted to work. The judge's orders for him to live with relatives in the country, following our advice, were never carried out. He was truant, drifted into bad companionship and much delinquency until finally with companions he killed the cashier of a bank they were attempting to rob. He is serving a long term in a reformatory.

I. was a defiant, stubborn boy, suffering for long from a mental conflict concerning his parentage. Although bright and showing no evidence whatever of mental abnormality, he developed a distinct anti-social attitude, shown even towards benefactors. He became a chronic runaway, going off alone. Penniless and hungry, he crept into a shanty with the purpose of robbery and assaulted the old man occupant so that he died. This boy needed understanding treatment which he never received. He was sent to an industrial school.

J. was an orphan, said by the aunt who raised him, to be a masturbator and exhibitionist at 4 years of age. When we saw him he was a sneaky-looking, undertoned boy, the victim of long standing, severe masturbation. He was lewd in speech and objectionable with little girls. He associated with bad companions and developed a tremendously long court record for forgery, stealing, assault with intent to rob. He was early immoral, married, divorced. Finally with companions, while burglarizing a store, he shot and killed a policeman. In the penitentiary he has an average adult mental rating. The intensive care that we urged for this case was never undertaken.

K. was a likeable, frank boy when we saw him, dissatisfied with school because of retardation caused by his family's moving about. His father had deserted and was immoral, and the boy knew it. He was a suggestible lad who was influenced much by bad companions. Murder was committed during robbery of a store and he received an indeterminate reformatory sentence.

L. was a boy with a nice, open face, who demonstrated good loyalties to the father who looked after him; the mother, an immoral woman, having deserted. At one time he was allowed to live with her. Bad companionship was a big factor in his downfall; except for a short time in a correctional school, he was never removed from his thoroughly bad environment. He, too, was implicated in killing a bank official while a member of a gang of "auto bandits." His sentence was 15 years in the penitentiary.

M. seemed to us to be a well-intentioned, adventure-loving, direct-spoken boy, who had been systematically engaged in store robberies, but who, at the time we saw him, wanted, he said, to turn his back on it all. He had a wretched family, known to many social and relief agencies. He was placed on probation, but nothing was done to alter his situation and satisfy his needs. He kept on engaging in burglaries, hold-ups, etc., with companions, until in one escapade a store proprietor was killed. M. received a life sentence to the penitentiary.

It would seem that the tragic outcomes in most of these seven cases could have been avoided. One only, J., was at all vicious when first known to the court; the remainder were likeable lads, but in need of definite constructive adjustments. One, I., presented a very difficult problem, but he probably could have been handled successfully by very patient treatment. In the remaining five instances very specific needs were clearly indicated, needs not impossibly difficult to meet, and it was predicated that without the meeting of these needs further delinquency would ensue.

We may next offer a few examples showing something of the variety of individuals and of backgrounds involved in the production of "professional" criminal careers, not that these instances by any means give a complete picture of the multiplicity of facts and of the intricacies which range through our case histories.

N., American born of Italian parents, we saw three times when he was between the ages of 12 and 16. From the first he was in poor physical condition, with very large tonsils and adenoids, poor color, choreic jerkings, and valvular heart lesions. At 14 after having been nine months at the Parental School, he was only four feet, six inches, and was fifty pounds under the average for boys of his age. We found him normal mentally and of striking personality characteristics. He was a leader, never coming to report to his probation officer without bringing a crowd of boys. We observed him to be forceful, bad-tempered, and reckless. His home was just moderately good, his mother being a grim-visaged, illiterate woman whose treatment of her boy's delinquencies was excessive scolding. In general the family attitude was, "Let him alone; he's sick."

The delinquencies of N. were serious from the beginning. With his crowd there was very repeated petty thieving, burglary, truancy, and staying out late at night.

It was clear that he needed physical up-building and firm disciplinary control over a very long period. After these three court appearances he was tried with a well-to-do farmer uncle, who could not manage him. He was sent twice for short periods to the John Worthy School and on numerous occasions was held in the Detention Home. Each time he was allowed to return home.

We find that at 24 N. has had an exceedingly long court and police record for burglary, robbery, assault, and assisting in an attempt to murder. He has served two terms in the House of Correction, has been in the army and deserted, is a gambler, and has twice had gonorrhea. His people tolerate him when he is at home and regard him as a burden with which they have to put up.

The story of O. covers ten years from the time he was 13 years old. He was short, of sturdy build, healthy. Mentally he was of average general ability; one of his teachers said that he was an unusually bright boy, "but with a mind full of badness." His delinquent tendencies, beginning at 7 years, comprised stealing from home, school, and employers, sometimes with companions, but not always with the same crowd. At home he showed signs of irritation and nervousness in certain "spunky spells" and in biting his finger nails. The family circumstances were good, but his father was a peculiarly "hard" man "who never could be told anything." His mother was religious, affectionate, anxious to be helpful to the boy.

Even so young this boy showed marked reticence, his lips firmly set, though his chin appeared decidedly weak. One of his remarks to us was that he hadn't stolen nearly so often as he had been tempted.

He was frank with nobody, apparently not even with himself; he lied excessively to officials of the juvenile court and to others. He showed a rather defiant attitude, but sometimes tears were in his eyes and he very evidently was suffering from some inner stress. We came to feel strongly that the dominant feature of his case was inner conflict and obstinate repression. Later he grew more and more indifferent and more anti-social.

His record has been a long career of frequent thieving, fraudulent misrepresentation, forging, robbery, cashing of stolen money orders, etc. Earlier he was befriended by many, including the judge, and jobs with good firms were found for him, but in every case he proved dishonest. Of recent years he has not worked, living by dishonest methods. He was tried on probation to several officers. He was sent to St. Charles twice and he was returned on other occasions when he ran away. He was twice sent to the John Worthy School. He was committed to the state reformatory as a young adult and finally to the penitentiary. He is well known to detective agencies because of the type of delinquency in which he mainly engages.

From the time of our earliest study we recognized that we did not know the essential trouble with this boy, and unfortunately no prolonged analysis of the motivation of his career was ever made. We regret greatly that this was never done; it might have proved a difficult professional task, but certainly no rational therapy could be undertaken without such an analysis.[2] This fellow has been a costly member of society; nothing that has been done in the way of punishment has availed. In those earlier days there was little understanding of the nature of such cases; indeed there is still too little recognition of this type of causation.

P. was very poorly developed, weighing only 65 lbs. at 14 years of age but with strength good for his size. Mentally he was a middle-grade moron with special ability for dealing with concrete material.

He came from an Italian family all of whom were much brighter than he. His mother had typhoid fever during his pregnancy. On account of meager income, a very large family, and poor control at home we felt the outlook to be bad, and we advocated the boy's commitment as

[2] See Cases 5, 16, 20, Judge Baker Foundation Case Studies, 1923.

defective. His delinquencies consisted in much staying away from home and stealing in petty ways when thus living out. He had once been to the Parental School.

During the next two years he was several times placed on probation for stealing. In the Detention Home he was reported one of the worst of sex perverts, continually teaching other boys. Later he was in a series of robberies. Despite the renewed objections of the family he was, at 16, sent to the institution for the feebleminded, but he ran away in a few days, returning to his old haunts and engaging in more daring delinquencies, the loot of his gang being found in a room which he had secured for himself. By this time he had developed leadership in delinquency. He was returned to the institution, again escaped, and after some new affair was sentenced to the House of Correction. After release he was in automobile stealing and other affairs, and his gang had a long battle with the police, one companion being shot. Then followed burglary, "hold-ups" with a gun, etc. Some others of his gang we knew to be normal mentally. P. was ordered again to the institution for the feebleminded by the adult court. However, it is reported that this time he did not reach there on account of the long waiting list. In the meantime he was released. Since then he has served at least one sentence for burglary in the reformatory.

That delinquencies may continue on into long careers of crime is well illustrated by the above three cases, in all of which no adequate treatment was early administered. Each case had its own special needs, all perhaps difficult to meet, yet intensive study, prolonged and patient effort, skillful adjustments and personal interest would have been well justified in an attempt to save, both from the humane and economic standpoint, the vast losses likely to be incurred.

In the next six cases of males there was successful outcome after a beginning certainly unpromising, indeed after a criminalistic career had already been begun. Either mental attitudes were changed, environmental conditions altered, bad companions given up, stability increased with advancing maturity—something caused the desisting from further delinquency.   Among the Successes, two cases of mental abnormality are introduced showing that Failure is not a necessary correlate of defect and psychosis.

Q., when seen at 16 years, had been in court several times.   He had been in the Parental School; following release, he had run away from home many times, remaining as long as several months at a time.   He had been in homosexual affairs with one man who had been sentenced for it, and probably with others.   Leaving school, he refused to work, though it was said employers liked him.   He associated with undesirable companions, smoked heavily and gambled.   When 14 he had been sent to the John Worthy School, where his behavior was so bad that he was twice refused parole; this did not improve his conduct.   On release he resumed old habits, left home often, lived in cheap hotels, earning enough to live on by selling papers.

His parents, both by report and from our impressions, were decent, honest people.   Of their six children only this boy had given trouble. The mother claimed she had spoiled him by too great leniency because he had early been sickly.   At 10 months he had typhoid, a little later diphtheria; at 10 years he was very ill with bloodpoisoning, and again at 12 with scarlet fever.   When, however, he became so troublesome she concurred in his being sent to the Parental School and later to the John Worthy School.

We found Q. just fairly well developed, slouchy and rather weak in appearance.   Normal in ability, his mental attitude was most striking. He seemed to take his delinquencies as a joke, claiming he did not know the name of his probation officer, he had had so many he was too mixed up to know.   He freely gave details of his career; but when discussing either his family or his future he showed himself most embittered.   He insisted that he was utterly indifferent about what might be done to him; he would be "railroaded" through court and to another institution; his mother didn't care for him; she had been the one to send him to the Parental School; institutions had made him "a bum." Rather than go home he preferred, he said, to return to the John Worthy School.   He met with sarcastic laughter our suggestion of possible placing in the country.   Perhaps he would like it, but he knew that it was out of the question—no one was really interested in his welfare. He made no effort to earn a good record in the Detention Home; indeed he was reported by the superintendent as one of the most hardened boys she had ever met.   On his way to court, with bravado he attempted to smoke, and urged other boys to follow his example.

When, however, we recommended country placing, since institutions had been such a failure and there seemed every likelihood that the boy, were he sent again, would come out with a more firmly-set anti-social attitude, the judge was willing that this be done. During the month that he was in the Detention Home awaiting placement he was involved in much more trouble, especially through teaching vicious habits. Then an excellent farm home having been found, he was placed there. To the astonishment of every one, from that day he gave absolutely no trouble. He remained on this farm for about four years. He grew strong, liked the work, and stayed for two years after his permanent release from the court. Then he joined the army and was in the service for two years. Since that time he has lived away from home, having even changed his name, and communicating with his family only rarely. Although details of his more recent life are not known, he did not have any court record in the more than six years after his last juvenile court appearance.

R. at 16 years was a tall fellow, of good strength, rather stoop-shouldered, and depressed in expression. We found him of fairly good mental ability, but of rather poor school acquirement. He was in court as a participant in a street robbery, the hold-up of a citizen whom his gang had followed. His only record previously was for a minor offense —picking up coal on the railroad track. But his family reported him earlier truant and lately extremely irregular in work, leaving jobs upon the slightest provocation. He engaged considerably in dice playing, a common amusement in his neighborhood; he smoked excessively, frequented pool rooms, and for years had picked out the worst type of associates.

His father died in delirium tremens; he had been a shiftless man and R's mother who herself worked steadily, felt that he resembled his father.

The boy himself maintained that he wanted to be a brakeman on the railroad or go into the navy, but his mother would not sign papers, and he was too young for railroad work. R. told us how he hated inside work, and in general how he disliked being "hollered at like a slave." He felt himself to be a man and wanted an active life. Though his family wanted him sent there, we strongly advised against St. Charles, particularly because of the boy's attitude and desires, and because he tended to form grudges.

But nothing constructive was done and in two or three months the boy was in court again for stealing with companions from a garage. Now more active measures were undertaken and, following our suggestion, R. was easily found a place on a ranch in the West. He did well there and after some months came back to Chicago and obtained employment as a shipping clerk in a large concern. He was soon found to be worthy of advancement. He served honorably during the war and then was given back his good position. At the time of our study it is eight years that he has done very well indeed.

S., 16 years old, was in court for burglary. He was in good physical condition and had quite average mental ability. His sharp eyes gave him a rather ferrety expression. He was small and in sex development retarded. Twice he had been at the John Worthy School, first for excessive truancy and violent bad school behavior, and the second time for repeatedly running away from home and much petty thieving.

The probation officer reported the hard-working, somewhat alcoholic father as saying, "Do anything to get rid of him; shoot him or kill him. I don't care what you do. He's no good." The boy had been away from his home for two months, sleeping in basements and frequenting parks in the daytime. But once when very hungry, so he told us, he watched a house until he found out how he could get in. Entering, he took a revolver and a considerable sum of money with which he bought clothes and food.

When we proposed that, since institutional treatment had not corrected him something different might be tried, the probation officer objected, saying that if he were placed in the country he would not stay more than a day or two—"You can't expect anything from a boy who is thoroughly without honor."

But the judge did allow him to go with an officer who placed boys, and this man found for him a home in the country with people who not only had high religious impulse but much commonsense. S. settled down from the first. The people had nothing but praise for him. He worked well and enjoyed hunting and the other sports of the farm. He stayed until he was 18 and then found it possible to live at home. He has held one position for a long time and altogether has had a continuously good record for over ten years.

In fairness to the fact that some individuals undoubtedly do profit by institutional commitment which to them is punishment we may cite the following:

T. at 14 years, had been extremely delinquent for a year or so. He had associated with a very bad crowd, sometimes staying from home over night, terrifying his family by his violent behavior when reprimanded. He had become quite practised in shoplifting, once successfully making off with a suit of clothes.

He was a handsome boy with personality characteristics that readily gained him employment; but he soon lost his jobs because of dishonesty. He had average mental ability. He came from a good family in which he was the only delinquent. His father had been away much on business and there had not been sufficient control of this boy.

His story to us was straight-forward indeed. It was "kind of sport" to steal—it was "good fun." He had started with some other boys, and then in the Detention Home earlier he had met one specially bad fellow and recently had associated with him in more desperate delinquencies. But he insisted that he didn't want to keep on with this career; he would "make good" if he were somewhere out in the country. His probation officer was in favor of his going for a long term to St. Charles, and we were against his going to the John Worthy School, which housed so many bad young fellows for shorter terms.

However, he was sent to the latter place for three months. This resulted in bringing about an utter change in him. When released he began at a trade which he learned speedily and by the time he was 19 he had been so successful that he was in business for himself.

It is clear that punishment did deter in this case, though just why it did or why, as was so common, there was not development of worse trends than before, through miserable human contacts in the institution, we confess we do not know.

U., a younger brother of L., one of the above cases of homicide, like his brother was early engaged in excessive stealing though not with the same crowd. Indeed he was in more desperate affairs, burglaries and staying away nights from home and for several days at a time. In contrast to L., he graded as feebleminded and in school never advanced beyond fifth grade. Similarly to his brother he was sent several times to correctional institutions, altogether four times. But at 15 years of age he settled down to work, living with his mother who earlier had deserted her family, and evidently has had a continuously good record for the past eight years. The interest in this case lies in the fact that the mentally bright brother kept on with bad companions while this feebleminded boy, though living under what might be supposed to be bad circumstances, and himself being earlier one of the worst of his delinquent crowd, now stayed out of trouble by keeping away from other delinquents.

V., 15 years old, unenergetic, with weak features and babyish voice, lied excessively in a silly manner to the judge and to us. Now in court for a serious but foolishly undertaken burglary and larceny, he had earlier appeared for petty stealing, and had been in homosexual affairs with a man. His irrationality was shown in his delinquencies as well in his conversation and general behavior, though his school progress had been fair and he did not grade as defective. He was classified by us as psychotic, without definite diagnosis, but perhaps dementia precox. His mother, though the victim of mental disease, lived at home; his father had a court record for abusing his family. This boy was placed on probation and a place found for him away from his miserable home. He had no further police record and worked until he entered the army. Upon release from service he became part owner of a store which he runs successfully and supports a wife and child.

The careers of girl offenders who as adults were Failures present little that is worth illustration. Unlike the boys, there are few instances of criminalistic careers with commitments; and continuance in immorality or desertion of families is obviously what was to be expected unless very good treatment was undertaken, unless there was much more done than commitment as a juvenile to an institution and upon release, return to a bad environment.

But to select cases where there was early extreme misconduct with later Success is justified because of the encouragement these outcomes offer toward better efforts for such offenders. Nothing has impressed us more than the fact that individual effort may and very often does succeed in cases of girls that, according to social tradition, have been considered irrevocable.

A.A. had lived with a man for a week, following a chance acquaintance with him. She was 16 years old and had been on probation for about a year because of immorality with several men, one of whom was tried by the grand jury. At that time she had a miscarriage. Her introduction into delinquency had been through a group of school companions, and her reading of love stories had developed much sex feeling as she voluntarily confessed.

A.A. was in fine physical condition and attractive in appearance. Mentally she had good ability. Her parents bore an excellent reputation, and her home afforded thoroughly good interests and recreations.

During her time on probation, in order to break up her companionships, she had been placed in a foster family where she did well until she became infatuated with this last man whom she met on the way home from work. She was once more placed in a good home and this time much personal help was given her. Again she did well. A year later she married. For eight years all has gone well with her. Her husband has a responsible position. Her later history is well known because she keeps steadily in touch with the people who so befriended her years ago.

A. B., at 11 years, was not only an excessive masturbator but she had been in numerous sex affairs with boys. By her step-mother and neighbors she was declared to be disobedient, immodest, and very obscene in her language. Physically she was in good condition except for somewhat defective vision. Mentally she was diagnosed by us as subnormal, but not definitely feebleminded. The father was reported as alcoholic; the mother, a quick-tempered woman, who died six years earlier. The step-mother was an intelligent woman who, however, seemed, according to others, more devoted to her own child than to this girl.

A. B. was sent to the Refuge for three years until it was felt certain that her old habits had been corrected and new and better interests established. From there she went to her grandmother, where she remained for the next two years, working steadily and having very good supervision. Later she went to live with a friend of the family, of whom she was very fond, worked regularly as a machine operator, earned quite well, was considered industrious and neat. She has visited her relatives frequently and seemed quite content with little else in the way of recreation.

A. C., at 16 years of age, was large and overdeveloped both in general and in sex characteristics. She had normal mental capacities, quite a keen sense of humor, and was pleasure-loving, but perhaps only to a normal extent. She came, however, of a repressively religious family and found her satisfactions in companions who happened to have poor standards.

When we saw her she had been repeatedly immoral and was at the time pregnant. She was committed by the court to the Beulah Home, the superintendent of which kept in touch with her even after her release. She was said to have been very wild up to the time of her marriage at 22 years, but since then she has done very well. It is reported that her husband is a thoroughly good man, and that she has changed very greatly in her habits and interests since her marriage.

A. D. at 16 was exceedingly strong and well developed; in sex characteristics she was considerably overdeveloped, with very mature, strong features and a particularly strong chin. Mentally she was quite fair in ability. She was self-willed and energetic, although at times lazy and fond of her own physical comfort. She had been repeatedly immoral with a young man of bad reputation and had stayed away from home some nights, frequenting the house of a woman of poor reputation. She engaged in much misrepresentation and had been generally incorrigible and bad tempered at home. She made accusations of immorality against her mother which were probably untrue.

The mother was in some respects the prototype of her daughter, a woman of great physical strength and fiery temper. She felt that her daughter should be put in an institution for the purpose of breaking her spirit. Our view was that since she was a girl of so much force possibly with healthy, vigorous activities outside of an institution she would become more stable after adolescence had passed. We believed, too, that with her attractiveness and interest in the other sex she would probably soon be married, and that through this some of her problems would be solved. But within a few days after she had been placed and before anything else could be carried out for her she ran away to meet the man with whom she had been earlier immoral. She said she always liked him because he was a gentleman, dressed well, and "talked nice" to her. She helped herself to a gold ring before going away and was arrested in a park by a detective while walking with this man. She was sent to the House of the Good Shepherd.

In about a year she was released and was then supervised by a probation officer for a few months until she married. This was about seven years prior to our follow-up study. She is reported to be a good housekeeper and mother, and has already several children. Her mother is now her good friend and reports that A. D. has vastly changed in personality.

A. E., living with a thoroughly immoral mother, was herself immoral at 10 years and at 12 years was already supporting a man, a "cadet," by prostitution. Seen by us when 15 years old, she was hardly so much a girl as a beautiful young woman, really magnificently endowed physically—although she had contracted gonorrhea. Mentally A. E. was somewhat better than average in ability; she seemed essentially refined. On the basis of our study we felt that the outlook with proper treatment was distinctly hopeful, in spite of her five years of sordid immorality. She was placed in country life with a vigorous, intelligent woman who became a genuine friend, confidante and source of inspiration. All her old experiences seemed to drop away from her without leaving any defect of character. Two years later A. E. entered a training course for nurses where she did admirably; but before completion of her course she married. Frequent reports have come of her continued success in her family life.

CHAPTER V

Is such a large proportion of Failure inevitable in the treatment of delinquents? Comparisons which seem to make possible an answer to this question are as follows: The careers of 420 males, studied by us in Chicago in the years 1909 to 1914 (the group for which we have reported Success or Failure in the previous chapter) have been set side by side with the careers of 400 males, also juvenile repeated offenders, consecutive cases, who appeared in the Boston Juvenile Court during these same years.[1] Because of the differences, social and industrial, between pre-war and post-war conditions, it seems necessary, for the sake of fairness, to compare the same year periods.

But since there may be criticism of the comparison of a studied with an unstudied group, on the basis that information gained with field inquiry is not comparable to that obtained from public records, we have utilized as a check, a second group of 400 Boston juvenile male repeated offenders, studied by us during the years 1918

[1] In the desire to make comparisons that represent the deepest truths we have been extremely cautious and have omitted from this Boston series all cases brought into court, even repeatedly, for distinctly petty offenses. As it stands, after this culling, the 400 cases constitute practically all the more serious repeated offenders who appeared in the Boston Juvenile Court during the years mentioned.

59

and 1919, the youngest of whom is now two years above the juvenile court age.[2]

As a matter of fact, we are quite certain that for both the Boston groups our information concerning adult offenders is much more complete than for the Chicago series, not only because in the second Boston group our field work has been carried along, year by year, very thoroughly, but also because for even the first series the well-kept records of the parole department of the juvenile correctional institutions and of the state Department of Correction dealing with adults have been available. Furthermore, and most important, the Massachusetts Probation Commission records are a very valuable source of information concerning both juvenile and adult delinquents. No such sources of information were existent in Chicago.

For girl delinquents we made no attempt at inquiries concerning outcomes in any Boston series because, as our Chicago follow-up shows, very few of the Failures reach court in adult life, and field inquiry would have been a most difficult task without the prior studies which formed a practical basis of reliable contacts for gathering later information.

Comparing, then, the careers of male offenders in the two cities we are at once confronted by startling differences in the figures relating to court records, commitments and types of misconduct. From Table 8 it will be seen that in the Chicago cases there were adult court records for 50%; in the Boston cases of the same years,

---

[2] We believe, though, that the comparisons with this second group are hardly sound, for conditions following the world war have been so unusual in regard to delinquency; special problems in the increase of extent and seriousness of crime have been quite general.

only 21%; in the later Boston group there were adult court records for 26%.

But these figures do not tell all the story of the differences. We must go a step further and compare the seriousness of the crimes committed. We find that while 14 homicides are known to have been committed by our Chicago cases, in the first Boston series there were none, and in the second series only one. And, then, compared to the 39 reported professional criminals among our Chicago cases, there was in the first Boston series only one.

Besides this, we note that the offenses for which the young men of our Boston series were in the adult court are by no means comparable to the much more serious offenses for which alone there were the adult court appearances of our Chicago group. The astonishing difference in the number and severity of sentences given, as shown below, indicates this, but here we may say that, listed, the largest single offense in Boston was "larceny" undifferentiated, and next "breaking and entering," a category which includes petty offenses. Next in order of frequency were "gaming," "drunkenness," "violation of automobile laws," "being present at gaming," offenses not charged against our Chicago cases [3] in the court records reported to us.

[3] Study of the records of the Boston courts makes it clear that many arrests and court appearances are for offenses so minor that they do not find representation at all in our Chicago follow-up records. We found in the 400 Boston careers that we should have to subtract 32 cases from the total court appearances, because they were brought in for such offenses as violating minor city ordinances, automobile laws, park rules, etc. It would be ridiculous to offset against our Chicago records such complaints as violating the spit law, or cruelty to animals, or gaming on the Lord's day, nor can we fairly include the "repeater" whose two appearances were for nude bathing and gaming, or the fellow who was in court once for throwing missiles and again for "refusing to

Quite apart from its statistical import this is a point for earnest consideration, for while some may think that the Boston procedure sometimes represents much ado over very little, we ourselves could suggest that perhaps it is this very attention to minor offenses that leads to respect for law and may deter from the commission of more serious misdeeds. It is from the collection of just such data as these, comparing practice and results in different communities, that principles should be evolved in order that law-makers and administrators of the law may shape effective policies of treatment.

We may next logically review in some detail the records of adult commitments of our groups as throwing light upon the seriousness of their offenses.

Of the 420 Chicago males, 209 (50%), as we have already stated, actually appeared in the adult courts as offenders. And of these 209 (Tables 7 and 9) 157 received 272 sentences to adult correctional institutions.

While our figures, particularly for court appearances, are undoubtedly incomplete for the Chicago group, we know that, aside from the offenses for which some of them were sentenced as adults to an institution, 90 individuals appeared 160 times in court for offenses [4] and

obey officer." If arrests for such offenses are made in Chicago at all they are not handled by the courts so as ever to appear among the offenses, always of much graver nature, which we have found recorded against the young men who were the boys of our Chicago series.

(But even if we did include the above 32 cases, the total court appearances become only 29 per cent in Boston as compared with the Chicago 50 per cent.)

[4] In connection with our statements in this chapter it should be reiterated that the totals we set forth represent a considerable understatement of the facts. Through the strange and unbusinesslike absence of any scheme or system of recording facts concerning criminals and crime, whereby court appearances, dispositions and institutional records

were fined, put on probation, or other disposition of the case was made. Of these 90, 38 served sentences for other offenses and consequently figure among the committed. We do not pretend to know the exact extent of the court records of these 90 individuals, but we do note (Table 7) that 19 had three or more appearances, and one already as a young adult had been tried in court 9 times. Most of these young men, at the time of our follow-up study, were not more than twenty-five years old—their careers are not yet ended. Six of the 52 who according to our information had not served sentences as adults are to be classed as professional criminals.

Concerning the 157 sentenced, 72 served 111 terms at the House of Correction, 73 were sent to the state reformatory 82 times; 22 to the penitentiary 25 times, 45 were sentenced to county jails 54 times. (These county jail sentences do not include the county jail detentions to which many were subjected prior to trial for which there was sentence as above.) If we total these figures we note that there is considerable overlapping—the same individual of the 157 was sometimes sent more than once to a penal institution and some received sentences to more than one institution.

This amount of social Failure regarded simply as sentences served or being served—short terms, long terms, life terms—a total of many hundreds of years inside prison walls, makes a ghastly picture.

at least could be registered and available at some central agency, to say nothing of the lack of development of identification methods, the accurate tracing of careers is often impossible. To do really thorough work, even going over entire institutional records, was beyond the resources at our command. But we have deemed the data, even so far as we have obtained them, ample to lead to reliable conclusions. The errors are those of under-statement.

The 47 males counted among the 256 Failures, but not known to be arrested, reveal a motley assortment of misconduct (Table 10). Some of them were involved in the most desperate misdeeds; thus 2 committed homicides—these disappeared; 14 others also disappeared after serious misconduct; 2 were killed in burglary; and so on.

Turning now to the 400 males of the first Boston series, it is found that only 25 served sentences as adults. Thirteen others were sentenced but appealed.[5] Of the 25 (Table 9), 14 were sentenced 15 times to the House of Correction, 10 were sentenced 12 times to the state reformatory, none to the penitentiary (state prison), 6 were sent 7 times to the county jail. Besides these, there were 59 other individuals who appeared in court for offenses other than mild misdemeanors.

The comparison may now be stated:

		With Adult Court Records	To Adult Correctional Institutions
1909 to 1914	Chicago (420)	209 (50%)	157 (37%)
	Boston (400)	84 (21%)	25 (6%)

In either city the number finally sent to an adult correctional institution is, doubtless, the fairest gauge of the extent of serious offense. In comparing disposition of cases in the adult courts it must be remembered that

[5] Concerning the adult sentences and commitments, it should be stated that the court procedure in Boston permits to a tremendously greater extent than in Chicago the opportunity to appeal from the court's decision. Indeed, this privilege is so stressed that one may say it is almost encouraged. For this reason we add to the figures on commitment those where sentences were appealed by the offender. Of those who appealed 10 had received sentences to the House of Correction, 1 to the reformatory, 2 to jail. (We have not undertaken to discover how many of the appealed sentences were finally served, but it is safe to say only a part of them.)

through the highly successful development of the probation system in Massachusetts there is a strong tendency to place on probation offenders not guilty of severe crime. The totals committed, 157 as against 25, show a tremendous contrast, which is accentuated by the fact that only 10 of the Boston cases received sentences of more than 6 months. Indeed, if it were possible to compare the total sentences in terms of years and months the contrast would be immense.

Although we believe these comparisons to be, if anything, over-balanced against Boston, we have enumerated similar facts for the group of 400 studied by us in Boston. While the post-war years make a situation not fairly comparable with the years 1909 to 1914 yet we know so well the careers of these young men that we include the findings here to satisfy the most critical who might feel that field work was imperative for fair comparative statements. But we must call attention to the fact that the court records and general follow-up for this 400 are very much more complete than any data we had for the Chicago series.

Summarizing the records for this second Boston group, we find the following: 103 (26%) had court records as adults for other than the very mild misdemeanors already discussed as appearing only in the Boston records—a proportion closely similar to that found for the first Boston series. But of the later 400, 63 (16%) received adult commitments. This is 10% more of the total than for the earlier years, although still much smaller than for the Chicago series (37%). While among the Boston series of earlier years barely 30% of those with adult records were committed, among the group of more recent years 61% were so dealt with. The question arises:

Were the adult offenses of recent years so much more serious or was there greater utilization of commitment for the same offenses?

We have records of the offenses of both groups and hence can answer this. In this last series there was one young man who after being several years in other parts of the country committed some terrible homicides. (For

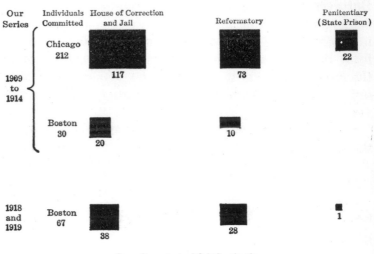

Commitments to Adult Institutions

CHART 2.

the remarkable story of this most inefficiently handled case, see Chapter IV.) The commonest offense was larceny, as in the first series; but there were 4 cases of robbery; 11 were sentenced for misappropriating automobiles or violating automobile laws, 5 for violating liquor laws. Short commitments were still made for very mild offenses, such as using obscene language, contempt of court, but not as many in proportion, namely, 18 out of 63, as against 10 out of 25 in the first Boston series. And while only 10 of the 25 received sentences longer than 6 months in the first Boston series, there were 43 who received such sentences of the 63 in the second series.

Thus it is fairly clear that there is a considerable increase in the seriousness of offenses, but at the same time there seems to have been a steadily growing tendency in Boston toward administering more severe punishments. But even so, the contrast with our findings for Chicago delinquents remains immense. Only one, the murderer in another state, received a penitentiary sentence. Aside from this, one was given 6 years, the longest term of the group. In entirety, only 6 of the 63 committed were serious enough offenders to receive sentences of over two years' duration.

The following figures show clearly the differences in the three series:

COMPARATIVE POST-JUVENILE RECORDS

	Total Individuals Committed	House of Correction	State Reformatory	Penitentiary (State Prison)	County Jails
1909 to 1914 { Chicago	157	72	73	22	45
1909 to 1914 { Boston	25	14	10	0	6
1918-19 Boston	63	25	28	1	13

What comparisons might reveal if we had such a study of a later Chicago group we would not presume to state, though it is generally recognized that delinquency and crime there has in recent years increased in quantity and virulence, as well as in many other parts of the United States.

Answering the question asked at the beginning of this chapter, we can safely assert that these comparative figures demonstrate that the immense proportion of Failures obtaining in the one series of cases cannot represent necessary outcomes.

CHAPTER VI

TREATMENT OF JUVENILE OFFENDERS CORRELATED WITH OUTCOMES

THE responsibility of the State when it takes charge of an offender, particularly the young offender, can hardly be over-stressed. The enormous significance of Success and Failure for the welfare both of society and the individual is seldom clearly envisaged during the routine of court and institutional procedure.

For the juvenile offenders whose conduct trends we have traced, what did the State do by way of treatment? And particularly, what was done with or for those who constituted the Success group, as compared to what was done with and for the Failures?

First, to determine this we may study the extent to which Success or Failure has followed commitment to juvenile correctional institutions. Strangely enough, very little material up to this time has been forthcoming from any source by way of critical or self-analytical study of the efficacy of such institutional régime or training.

A theory espoused in America perhaps more than anywhere else is that delinquents will be reformed by being sent to an institution, not for punishment, but where, housed with other delinquents, they are subjected to a supposed reformatory process. The institution may be named a correctional, industrial, or training school; the word "reformatory" being reserved in most states for the institution to which older offenders are sent and the term "reform school" having been largely abandoned. The truth of this theory can only be proved by patient gathering of data concerning subsequent careers of those who have gone back into the community after a period in such an institution.

The general policy of commitment to an institution, a matter worth much discussion, may perhaps be better studied by consulting court statistics, rather than figures for our groups. So for the moment we turn to such statistics, again making comparison of the two cities under consideration. Such comparison suggests a question that is bound to come up: Other than commitment what were possible solutions of the cases?

From Tables 12 and 13, we find that for a corresponding five-year period in Boston (the entire city) 9.5% of juvenile court cases were committed, in Chicago 40%, a proportion over four times as large. (Concerning whether the commitment figures for Chicago or Boston represent more nearly the usual practice in large American juvenile courts, we may state that the figures for commitment of juvenile delinquents to institutions in New York and Philadelphia much more nearly approximate the Chicago figures than those for Boston.) This policy appears to have been maintained—in 1921 we find the Boston Juvenile Court (the central court) committing less than one-fifth as many in proportion (Table 13) as the juvenile court in Chicago. So in Boston for a very large percentage of cases a solution other than commitment was found.

But we at once note great proportionate differences in the total cases before the juvenile courts—Boston with not more than one-third the population of Chicago having in the five-year period 1½ times as many, or in proportion to the population about 4 times as many. Either Boston had very many more delinquents in proportion, or heard in its juvenile court types of cases which do

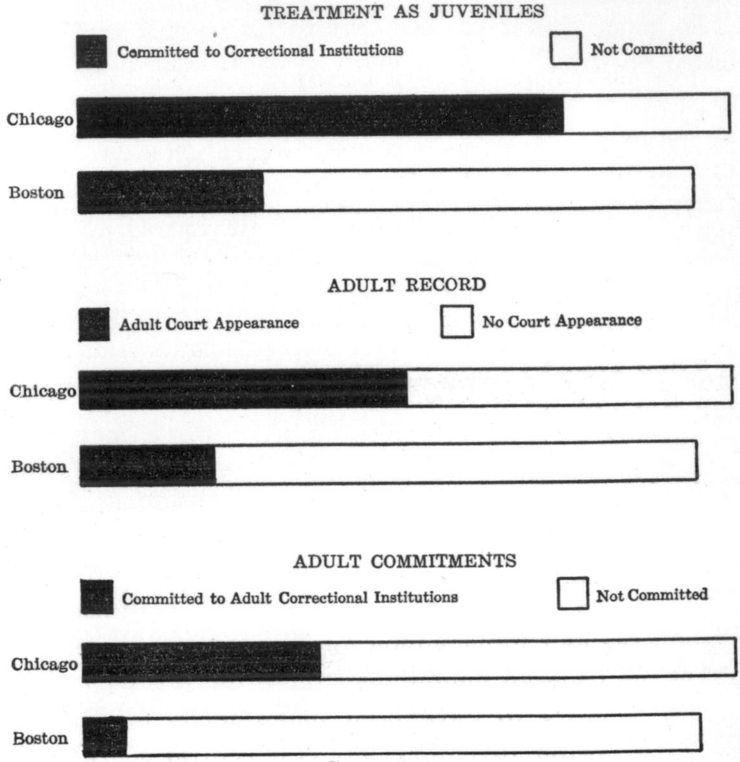

TREATMENT AS JUVENILES

■ Committed to Correctional Institutions   ☐ Not Committed

Chicago

Boston

ADULT RECORD

■ Adult Court Appearance   ☐ No Court Appearance

Chicago

Boston

ADULT COMMITMENTS

■ Committed to Adult Correctional Institutions   ☐ Not Committed

Chicago

Boston

CHART 3.

Comparison of Careers of Two Groups—Males
Who Appeared In Juvenile Courts 1909-1914.

not get into the Chicago court. The latter is the fact; in Chicago a vast number of delinquents have their cases disposed of by the police officers assigned specially to work with juvenile offenders. We find, for instance, when statistics are given, as in the juvenile court report of 1921, that 13,641 were so disposed of during that year.

The rôle this procedure plays in the continuance or non-continuance of delinquency cannot be answered here, but it is interesting to consider, and might be valuable for investigation and study.

So, since the above proportions for commitments are based on the total delinquents or total delinquent boys in court and the totals represent such great differences in the matter of selection of the offender for appearance in court in one city as compared to the other, it is much fairer to consider the proportions of commitments among the more serious offenders, those repeatedly delinquent. This we can readily do for our different series of cases. The figures utilized in this comparison are undoubtedly very accurate, since excellent records concerning individual juvenile commitments are available in both cities. We find (Tables 14, 16, 17) that 74% of our series of Chicago young repeated male offenders were committed, 29.5% of the Boston series for the same years, and 40% of the more recent series.[6] These differences, too, emphasize the very great contrast in policy, and this appears a matter of prime importance to us because of its possible relations to the great differences in outcomes in the two cities, as shown in the preceding chapter.

Suppose the reader asks here, But is not this contrast of policy due to difference in the seriousness of offenses

[6] Working in the Boston field we are greatly interested in the fact that only 24% and 14%, respectively, of the two series were committed by the central court, the Boston Juvenile Court. In Greater Boston there are different jurisdictions. There is, from the standpoint of understanding and dealing with the problem of the individual delinquent, an unfortunate overlapping of jurisdiction and probation, and frequently very little or no coöperation, so that, for example, recommendations made by us were not even known to the other courts in Boston. We ourselves are, thus, in some considerable number of cases left without means of judging of the value of our prognosis and recommendations.

even among repeated offenders? Are not delinquents in
Chicago guilty of worse types of offenses when they first
appear in court? Our statistics given later for juvenile
offenses tend to show that this is so.

But even if the Chicago delinquents were more heavily
involved in misconduct, does it necessarily follow that
the type of institutional treatment that was so largely

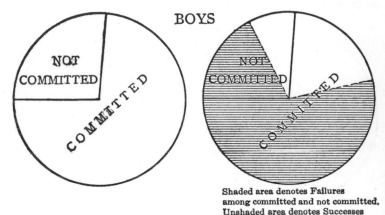

Shaded area denotes Failures
among committed and not committed.
Unshaded area denotes Successes

CHART 4.

Chicago Series: 1909-1914: 420 Cases
Commitments and Outcomes.

utilized, or, for that matter, institutional treatment at
all, was what was most likely to have brought success?
Has any large measure of success with such cases as yet
been demonstrated? The only answer to this can be
through observation of specific outcomes, a point we
may now cover in some detail.

Taking, first, the findings intrinsic to our Chicago
series: of the 420 boys there were **74** per cent or **311**
boys committed to juvenile correctional institutions, and
these 311 received 605 such commitments (Table 14).

Of the 255 girls 67 per cent or 169 were committed to juvenile correctional institutions, and these 169 received 245 such commitments (Table 15).

Now a point of vital significance concerns itself with the proportion of Success and Failure following such commitment to a juvenile correctional institution, as compared with outcomes among those not committed. Let us consider it.

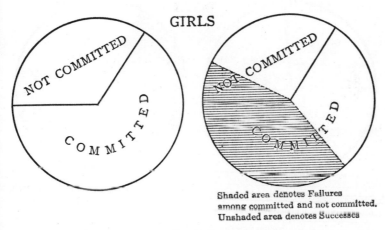

GIRLS

Shaded area denotes Failures among committed and not committed.
Unshaded area denotes Successes

CHART 5.
Chicago Series: 1909-1914: 255 Cases
Commitments and Outcomes.

Of the 256 Failures among the males, 86 per cent had been committed as juveniles (Table 14), and of the 164 Successes, 56 per cent had been committed. Or, putting it another way, of the 311 boys committed, 219 (70%) were Failures, while of the 109 not committed only 37 (34%) were Failures.

Similar facts for the girls show that of the 117 Failures, 79 per cent had been sent to correctional institutions (Table 15); and of the 138 Successes, 56 per cent had been so dealt with. Or, of the 169 girls committed, 92 (54%) were Failures, while of the 86 not committed, only 25 (29%) were Failures.

Such figures as these require pondering over; their interpretation may be many-sided, thus: (a) While undoubtedly there is great significance in the above very large proportion of Failures among those committed, it must, in all fairness, be remembered that presumably the committed represent the most difficult offenders.

(b) And then, the reader is not justified in concluding that the measure of Failure for the entire number of cases committed to these institutions is as large as the proportions in our series. We ourselves have reason to believe, however, from unpublished data that an astounding proportion of the entire cases committed later do badly in the community.

(c) And considering the argument that the most serious offenders are sent to correctional institutions, the rejoinder seems logical that if so large a number fail, it may well be that attempting their reformation by this type of treatment is a mistaken policy. Logically, the fact of the difficulty of their cases might lead one to suppose that there was need of very skillful efforts at cure, at intensive individualization of treatment, which is anything but what obtains in the ordinary correctional school. Case studies justify this reasoning.

(d) Then, while questioning the rationale of the belief that very repeated or very serious offenders will be remade through submission to a régime quite unadjusted to the specific needs of the individual case, it may be naturally asked what types of cases, if any can be named, do yield best to institutional care and training.

(e) Allowing for any or all of these points, we have,

however, to acknowledge that from actual data it appears
that this remedy, treatment in the institutions to which
offenders are sent by the Chicago juvenile court, had
remarkably little curative effect upon the members of our
group.

(f) In the light of the general figures, the question at
once arises whether the outcomes were better or worse
for one institution as compared to another. We offer
some facts on this in the next chapter, including comparisons with our Boston series.

We may next properly ask whether the percentage of
Failure was as great among our Boston cases (all males)
who were committed as juveniles. In the first series of
84 Failures, so designated because of adult court appearances, 34 (40%) had been committed as juveniles. The
second series shows 103 such Failures and 52 (50%) of
them had received juvenile commitments (see Table 16).

Or, looking at the facts in another way, as we did for
the Chicago series, we see that of the 118 boys who went
to juvenile correctional institutions in the first Boston
series, 29% (34 cases) had adult court appearances comparable to the 70% Chicago adult court records; and
of the 159 of the second Boston series, who received
juvenile commitment, 33% (52 cases) have appeared
in court as adults. All this shows clearly in Chart 6, and
simply stated is as follows:

			Total To Juvenile Correctional Institutions	Total Adult Court Appearances	Number in Adult Court Earlier in Juv. Cor. Inst'n
1909 to 1914	Chicago	(420)....	311 (74%)	209 (50%)	172 (55%)
	Boston	(400)....	118 (29%)	84 (21%)	34 (29%)
1918 to 1920	Boston	(400)....	159 (40%)	103 (26%)	52 (33%)

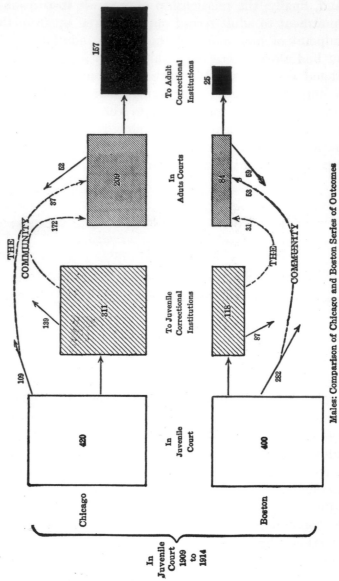

Males: Comparison of Chicago and Boston Series of Outcomes

CHART 6.

And, finally, the relationship of juvenile institutional commitment to adult record may be taken up from the standpoint of how many of those given adult commitment had already received "training" in a juvenile correctional institution. We have very complete data on this important point. Comparing these will do much to smooth out the inequalities in the facts that confront us when we deal with the already discussed great variations between offenses for which members of our group were brought into court in Boston and in Chicago,

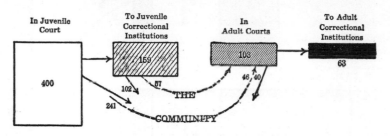

Males: Boston 1918 and 1919 Series of Outcomes

CHART 7.

because, in general, it will be only the more serious adult offenders we are dealing with. For either local situation nothing else will so clearly show whether juvenile institutional training, with all the possible hold upon the individual and upon his situation that it implies, had been given to many of those who later became such serious delinquents. Were those young adults who committed, for the most part, the more serious offenses and who were consequently sentenced, those, in any significant proportion, who had been in juvenile correctional institutions?

Our actual data show:

	Chicago	Boston 1st series	Boston 2nd series
Individuals Committed as Adults....	157	25	63
Number of the above who had been in juvenile correctional institutions	134 (85%)	11 (44%)	39 (62%)

More detailed facts showing the extent of institutional treatment that the Chicago cases have received are as follows: The 157 adult offenders served 272 known sentences. As juveniles these same individuals received 364 commitments to institutions. (A total, to the time of follow-up study, of 636 sentences!) Percentages are, looking forward, of the 311 to juvenile correctional institutions, 43% were committed as adults; looking backward, of the total 157 committed as adults, 85% had been in juvenile correctional institutions.

Adding the two Boston series in order to get figures of those committed more nearly of the same size—even though they cannot be fairly compared because not in the same year period—we find: Of 277 committed to juvenile correctional institutions, 32% were committed as adults; of 88 committed as adults, 57% had been in juvenile correctional institutions.

These figures are appalling, such a huge proportion having been at one time, for supposedly curative treatment, under complete control of the state. It is to be presumed that the more serious adult offenders are, in general, those in whose cases the strongest factors making for delinquency are at work; yet, granted that this is so, must we be content to allow such careers to continue?

If the causes making for delinquency and crime belong particularly to the personality make-up of the individual then surely efforts should be primarily directed toward modification of the personality or, if this is impossible, there should be control of the range of the offender's activities.

We believe that many more "cures" could be effected were stronger and wiser efforts made in more instances. We judge this by what we know of probable reasons for some successful outcomes in apparently very difficult cases.

And if the active causes for misconduct have been external conditions, it is a fair question to ask whether such conditions were met during and after institutional segregation. We know that with unfortunate frequency, (a) just the same sort of personal associations that made for delinquency outside have been renewed or recreated in the institution and (b) that very often the individual is after a period of segregation abandoned to exactly the old environment that played so large a part initially in the production of bad behavior.

Whether the Failures in the Chicago group represent those who appeared to be more irrevocably delinquent or whether they were the product of worse life situations is discussed in a later chapter.

Possible differences in the efficacy of the correctional institutions represented in this present study may be thought of in the light of the following: The boys of our Chicago group were sent to three institutions described in Chapter II. Referring for details to Table 14, it may be stated here that for our group we find very little difference indeed in the proportionate outcomes of the younger boys sent for truancy to the Parental School, those who went to the John Worthy School, a formerly existing walled-in institution (to which offenders were sent, usually for a few months, as punishment) connected

with the House of Correction, and those who went to
the modern industrial school at St. Charles. Many went
to more than one of these institutions. The range of
Failures is 68 to 74%.

The girls in Chicago were likewise sent to three institutions. There is somewhat more difference in the outcomes of those committed to one institution as compared
to another (Table 15), though all three have greater proportion of success than was found for the boys. The
state industrial school and "The Refuge" had practically
an equal amount of Failures, 51 and 52%, and the House
of the Good Shepherd 13% more.

The outcomes of those sent to the Massachusetts institutions may be of interest, not only for some comparison with the Chicago groups, but also because there is
classification by age, boys under 15 going to Lyman
School, and those between 15 and 17 to the state industrial school at Shirley.

Again, because of the smaller proportion committed
as juveniles, we have put together both series. Of the
800 (Tables 16 and 17), 98 were sent to Shirley, and of
these 38% were Failures on account of having an adult
court record; to Lyman 119, and of these 20% have had
an adult record. (To the discontinued Suffolk and Parental and other schools went a total in both series of
60, with 38% of these appearing in the adult court.) It
is likely that the court record of our last series would
be a little increased if the boys represented were as old
as the first Boston and the Chicago series, but the chances
are that with the youngest already two years above juvenile court age, the increase will be slight. The first
series, however, even up to date shows by far the smaller
number with adult court records.

It seems impossible to decide whether the much greater proportion of Success in Massachusetts is due to more effective institutional treatment, or to the fine parole work done afterward, or to both, or to the fact that through extremely serious early delinquency the Chicago boys had already a set which was harder to overcome.

But of two points we feel altogether certain: First, that since some proportion of Success is found in the Chicago series, and a much greater proportion in the Boston series, many Successes are possible. Secondly, a great responsibility rests on the state when it so completely takes the offender in charge and places him in an institution, and this responsibility includes consideration of his future social behavior. The obligations to society or to the individual cannot possibly cease with release from the institution, if, as we show above, in so many instances there is subsequent Failure. It is nothing short of foolhardy, after removing an individual for a comparatively short time from the situation in which he had developed undesirable conduct tendencies, to return him to the old conditions and expect him without very special help to withstand old influences and the reawakening of former impulses and ideas. It appears certain that one big element in greater success of juvenile delinquents sent to Massachusetts correctional institutions is skilled parole work with a great deal of placing after release, according to needs determined by the individual's entire situation. While we believe that treatment of juvenile offenders all along the line might be vastly improved, we also perceive that the soundest basis for ultimate success lies in adequate, efficient after-care, without which even the best institutional treatment is likely to fail when the individual once more must take up his life in the community.

There is very great difference in the treatment of the individual under parole from the juvenile correctional institutions in the two states. In the first place, such parole in Illinois was and still is for only a comparatively short period, and is only nominal as far as actual work with the delinquent is concerned. In Massachusetts, parole extends to 21 years of age and is supervised by two groups of capable officers, for boys and for girls. In 1916 Illinois had for boys one parole officer with mixed duties for the entire state; Massachusetts, that same year, had for its boys a superintendent of parole and 8 visitors, who had under their charge 795 boys—218 older boys from Shirley and 577 from Lyman, the institution for younger boys. Of the 577 boys on parole from Lyman only 241 were directly returned to their own homes; 336 were placed in carefully selected foster homes and visited. Much the same treatment was given Shirley boys.

To discuss in any thoroughgoing fashion all that the state should do and sometimes does for special juvenile delinquents one would have to canvass the situation in regard to those committed to institutions other than correctional schools, particularly what is done with those who are mentally defective or mentally diseased. But in our groups the numbers are too small to make such comparisons worth while.

Probation as a form of treatment in relation to Success and Failure in our series of cases is a subject we find so exceedingly complicated that we cannot in fairness present it in detail for the drawing of conclusions. Probation is a term that gives no clew to what is done by way of treatment; it may, on the one hand, be a name representing merely non-commitment of the offender, or at the opposite extreme, it may be the occasion of the delinquent receiving extraordinary personal attention and constructive help. Probation is not standardized; it varies according to notions about it in different courts, according to community resources for upbuilding of character, according to the interest and attitude and coöperation of different probation officers, even in the same court. From the standpoint of our present study probation is immensely different from institutional treatment, which offers a very special régime quite similar for all sent to the particular institution. It is obviously unfair to make comparisons of outcomes of probationary endeavor even in the same city, to say nothing of comparison of different cities. Nor can one fairly compare the results of treatment only under probation with the outcomes of institutional treatment, because surely each draws a selected group, namely those who are seemingly more promising individuals as set over against the severer offenders. Besides this, many of those committed have already been on probation. Then, in our Chicago group some of those on probation had earlier been in institutions, notably the Parental School—another complicating feature.

The fact is that treatment under probation is, or should be, highly individualized and involves subtleties and personality influences that do not lend themselves to statistical treatment, unless by very refined measures of quantity and quality.

Out of this complex situation in regard to probation

we may, however, offer the following statement of the simpler facts of our data.

Having probation only (Table 18) there were 12% of boys in the Chicago series, 50% and 43%, respectively, of boys in the two Boston series.

In Chicago a number were and are committed to correctional institutions without probation being utilized. From the annual court reports we find, for instance, that for the four years, 1909-1912, of all boys committed from Chicago to the John Worthy School or St. Charles, 38% were in court for the first time. This policy has been maintained; during the year 1924 about 20% of those who appeared in court for the first time were sent to St. Charles.[2]

In Boston the comparatively few committed tells the story of how extensively probation is used and it may be added that only very rarely is any one committed who has not been already on probation. But here again we must insist on the lesser severity of the offenses in Boston.

The outcomes of those who had as treatment only probation forms, naturally, a matter of interest, but the data do not permit of making sound comparisons. The number of our Chicago series, 51, is too small to be of statistical import; however, 15 became adult offenders, 30%. (See Table 19.) But the Boston cases have greater numerical value. In the first series 202 as juveniles received probation only. Of these, 34 (17%) appear as adult offenders. In the second series, 171 received probation only, and of these, 19 (11%) have appeared as adult offenders.

[2] We are indebted to the courtesy of Mr. Joseph L. Moss, Chief Probation Officer of Juvenile Court of Cook County, for the 1924 figures.

Without discussing the various complicated features of any detailed estimate of probation, because this in itself would require a special study, it may in general be safely asserted that young repeated offenders in very considerable numbers can be successfully dealt with through probation. Indeed, our figures demonstrate that where there is extensive use of probation, at least as it is conducted by the central juvenile court of Boston, by far the greater proportion, even of repeated offenders, do not become offenders after juvenile court age.

Concerning other methods of treatment of juvenile offenders, particularly placement in foster homes and commitment to institutions not specifically correctional, our figures (Table 18) are not large enough in the series under present consideration to warrant deductions concerning Success and Failure. Omission of discussion of foster-home placing does not indicate any lack of belief in this method of treatment. Chicago had developed so few resources that placing was seldom undertaken; in Boston this treatment is much more widely used through the several child-placing agencies, perhaps after a period of probation. Commonsense would suggest the advantages accruing from a better environment and wise guidance for the young offender; the question is which individuals are suitable for placing and what constitutes their proper management.[3]

[3] At the present time we are undertaking a detailed research into this method of treatment and its efficacy.

PART III

ANALYSIS OF THE OFFENDER AND HIS BACKGROUND IN RELATION TO OUTCOME

In attempt at possible differentiation of what makes for Success as opposed to Failure, we turn in this section to facts about the individuals themselves, their backgrounds, experiences, and offenses. First, we present figures giving the proportion of the sexes and the ages of the groups; next, facts concerning heredity, nationality and religion; then home and familial conditions; details about the physical characteristics and habits of the delinquents studied by us; their mentality; their offenses as related to Success and Failure and the experiences and features of their lives that we have considered as probably causative of their misconduct.

Does the explanation of outcomes—cessation of delinquency or continuance into careers of crime—lie in any one or any combination of these? Can the reasons for Success and Failure be found by analysis of such facts as those enumerated below, or can it be shown that such facts condition the effectiveness of attempted therapy?

For determining these facts we have utilized both the outcome series and the four groups, each of 1000 young repeated offenders.

CHAPTER VII

SEX AND AGE

(a) SEX

THE proportions of the two sexes in the main groups of young repeated offenders studied by us show a striking similarity.

Series		Boys	Girls
Chicago	I	694	306
"	II	692	308
Boston	I	758	242
"	II	686	314

The ratio of girls to boys in our Chicago series, about 1:2.3, is quite similar to the usual proportions heard in the Chicago juvenile court. But our figures for girls and boys in the Boston cases, 1:2.6, are considerably at variance with the Boston court yearly totals, which run about 1:9. (See Table 21.) This is due to the fact that many delinquent girls, even repeated offenders, have been brought to us for study by social agencies that have endeavored to help without bringing the girl into court. Whether proportionately fewer girls in Boston are delinquent would be altogether a hard question to answer— our own figures merely indicate the possibility that the court statistics may not represent the total facts.

(b) AGE AT TIME OF STUDY

Our statistics on ages would seem to bear on several points of general interest, and undoubtedly they do, especially as they demonstrate how early definite delinquent trends may appear. But it should be remembered that for our cases the ages given are those at time of first study by us; these ages represent merely the point

BOYS

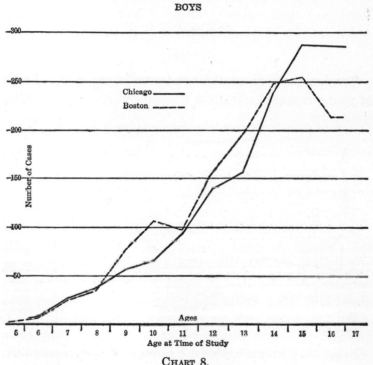

CHART 8.

Comparison of Chicago 1386 and Boston 1444 Cases.

in the career of a young repeated offender at which somebody thought the case was serious enough to be studied.

One finds by inspection of Table 22 that for all series there is a steady increase in numbers for every year from 6 to 14, and with the exception of one series, up to 15. For three series there is a drop for boys at 16.

For girls the drop comes one year later. We can compare our Table 22 for repeated offenders with the figures for repeated offenders in the Chicago court, Table 23. (Similar figures for Boston have not been published.) The yearly court increase up to 16 years appears for boys and then comes a drop; a decrease for girls also shows at the 16-year level. It is to be noted in Table

GIRLS

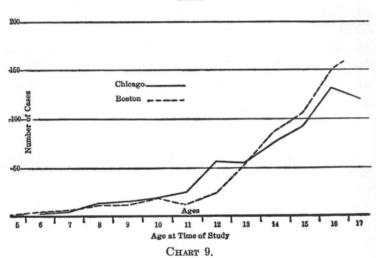

CHART 9.

Comparison of Chicago 614 and Boston 556 Cases

23 that this decrease does not obtain for first appearances in court. The explanation of this phenomenon is not obvious, and may be due to several causes. We are interested in the facts mainly because of the supposed steady increase of delinquency till it has reached its height at 18 to 20 years.

The median age for boys in our series is between 14 and 15, and the largest age increment is found in each series in passing from the 13 to 14-year levels. The court figures for repeated appearances show the largest increment at the age corresponding to our figures, but the median age is one year later. All this shows very clearly the great period of increase of delinquent tendencies, namely, early adolescence.

For girls the median age is between 15 and 16, both in our series and in the court statistics for repeated offenders. Our figures show no time of very great numerical increase, although the court figures for repeaters, Table 23, more than double themselves from the 14th to 15th year, and almost do so for offenders appearing for the first time in court. Undoubtedly the court figures are to be taken as more representative of the facts of age increment of delinquency.

(o) Age at First Court Appearance

A point that would seem to be of no little importance is the age of first appearance in court, but from figures given later it will be seen that this is not at all necessarily the age of commission of first offense. The earlier annual reports of the Chicago juvenile court gave ages both of first and repeated offenders, which we have transcribed in Table 23. But it is to be regretted from a prognostic standpoint that data on repetition of offense have never been correlated with age of first offense or appearance; thus, for individuals in court, for instance, for the fourth time at any given age, one would like to know the ages at time of first court appearance.

But with the data ascertainable, Table 23, how do the ages of those who appear for the first time in court compare with the ages of those who are repeaters in court? The median age for these first offenders is for boys, 14 to 15, for girls, 15 to 16. This, strangely enough, is identical with the findings for girl repeated offenders and is only one year earlier than for boy repeated offenders. Perhaps even more interesting is the fact that there is no decrease at any age for first appearances except for girls later than the 16-year group.

It might be of considerable value to study whether or not Success or Failure appears to be dependent in any degree upon the age at which the offender was first in court. This, because it might be argued that the juvenile court could not be expected to succeed with those individuals who, because of coming under its jurisdiction late in the period that the court covers, have had little chance to profit by its reformatory influences, while those caught young enough could be cured, as it were. Still, *a priori*, one might also argue that those delinquent enough to be in court young were naturally "difficult" children.

In the earlier reports of the Chicago juvenile court figures are given for the age of first and later court appearances, this evidently being regarded as a matter of probable importance. We may fairly take those years during which many of our cases were studied.

For convenience in comparing the figures with our own series we have grouped certain ages—those under 10 years, those 10-14 years inclusive, those 15, 16 and, in the case of girls, 17 years (Table 24). The first group represents children so young one would expect special adjustments to be made more or less readily, the second includes those who are older but yet have had the chance for at least three years of juvenile court effort to help them, the remaining represent those with whom the juvenile court has a shorter period for attempting reformation.

There are several curious points brought out by comparison of the figures for the court and for our group. Most striking is the much greater proportion in our series of those under 10 years, which is accounted for by several facts: (a) boys who were truant only were not reckoned in the court statistics among the delinquents, although such cases were heard in court at a special session; (b) some very young delinquents figured in the court records as dependents; (c) we were undoubtedly asked to see a larger proportion of those who were difficult as young children because this fact seemed to indicate that they were special problems. And perhaps requests for the study of the oldest ages were proportionately less frequent because delinquency at their age was considered less surprising.

Comparing Successes and Failures we note that among the males the percentage of Failure was greater than that of Success at all ages except for the 16-year group, where slightly more than half succeeded.

For the females there is no very great difference between the proportions at various ages. The showing for those first in court at 15 years is the poorest.

On the whole, then, there seems no ground for stating that the chances for reformation for our Chicago group and under Chicago conditions were to any great degree affected by the age of first court appearance.

(d) Age at Commencement of Delinquency

A significant study has been made for us of an unselected group of our Boston cases to determine from records of the juvenile court and from the statements of the parents and of the offenders themselves when delinquency actually began—particularly as related to its discovery. Data from 187 cases in which the requisite statements have been made show that delinquency in 40% had commenced one or more years before its discovery by the parents. In 24% of the cases delinquency had begun two or more years before the young offender appeared in court. In the 8 extreme cases delinquency had continued during five or more years prior to court appearance.

CHAPTER VIII

BECAUSE of the common belief that moral tendencies as well as many other traits are dependent upon inherited character or disposition and that prognosis, or possibility of moral recovery, in a case of delinquency is determinable in some measure by the record of behavior in the family, we may well examine outcomes in the light of what we know about the heredity.

(For our present discussion we have not used facts to be drawn from our records concerning 4000 young repeated offenders. This would be a big undertaking, perhaps worth such careful analysis as good research warrants. But one reason why we have not carried out such a work is that we feel we have no reason to believe that any different findings would be brought forth than were expressed in a former considerable research into the inheritance of criminalistic tendencies undertaken with the early Chicago material. That study led to the statement: Altogether there seems to be no proof whatever from our extensive material that there is such a thing as criminalistic inheritance apart from some otherwise significant physical or mental trait, which in the offender and his forbears forms the basis of delinquency.[1])

[1] "Inheritance as a Factor in Criminality," Edith R. Spaulding and William Healy, Bulletin American Academy of Medicine, Feb., 1914., or as summarized in "The Individual Delinquent," William Healy, p. 153.

(Making one exception, we may give our facts on alcoholism—drinking to the extent of at least occasional intoxication. Our figures concerning alcoholic parents are probably nearly accurate; they must not be confused with alcoholism in the home, which is included elsewhere as being directly influential upon the child, although earlier alcoholism of a parent may have affected the family finances or the compatibility of the parents and have had other secondary effects. We do not presume to interpret alcoholism as an hereditary factor, even though we give our findings. However, the figures have interesting bearings, for instance, in comparing Chicago and Boston and in comparing four series as representing a sequence of cases studied from 1909 to 1922, the last series being within the period of prohibition—although here again, we must note that some of the alcoholism recorded was in non-prohibition days, representing earlier habits of the parent. Our figures (Table 38) show Chicago 28.5%, Boston 45% alcoholic parents.)

It must be distinctly understood that we are not here considering heredity of delinquents as a whole in comparison with non-delinquents, nor are we discussing the inheritance of criminalistic tendencies as such; we are concerned only with the relationship of hereditary factors to outcomes designated as Success or Failure.

Our facts on heredity are those gathered at the time of the study of the case, facts usually given by the parents in personal consultation with us, sometimes checked by information from outside sources. So often have we found that the statements made in the consultation room are essentially truthful that we feel our percentages will not be far from correct. Concerning whatever errors there may be, it is to be noted that the most extreme facts and cases are best known, since mental disease requiring institutional care, criminalism with court appearance, excessive alcoholism, etc., are matters of public and other record.

Because other facts are more difficult to obtain reliably, we have enumerated only the direct heredity, that is, data concerning parents and grandparents; aunts, uncles, and all more distant relatives have been omitted. We have made three groups: (1) mental abnormality —mental defect, severe epilepsy, mental disease; (2) delinquency, including criminalism, desertion, gross immorality, or excessive abuse; (3) alcoholism, which means, of course, more than moderate use of alcohol— at least occasional intoxication. We have classified as normal those records of families in which facts belonging to the above undesirable categories were denied.

Turning to the collected data, we note in Table 41 that the group of 675 young repeated offenders shows 316, almost half, having normal heredity—there being in the family history no evidences of alcoholism, delinquency, or mental abnormality. If we take the other 359 cases and consider the items separately, we find among them alcoholism part of the story in 60%, delinquency in 45%, abnormal mentality in 31% (or 32%, 24%, 17%, respectively, of the total 675). There are, as shown, a considerable number of the cases where two or even three of these conditions obtain or overlap.

But of greater significance are the figures in the lower half of Table 41 which show more clearly the relationship between the family history and the outcomes in the case of the young offender. With the males, although there is a larger measure of Success where the family history is normal, yet the differences are not

very great between this and where the history shows
unfortunate traits. Irrespective of the family history
there is Failure in over half the males in every category.

Among the females there are not even as great differences according to family histories of good and bad qualities. Irrespective of family history there is similarity
of percentage of outcomes; under all categories except
one there is Success in over half the cases.

Thus there is no indication that traits found in the immediate forbears determine to any marked degree what
we have called Success or Failure. Taking the largest
figures for percentage of Failure we find it comes among
males where there is family history of abnormal mentality, but even these figures cannot be interpreted aside
from the context which shows that for the males there
was only 17% better measure of Success where the family history was normal.

(It can be clearly seen that in the above figures we
make no attempt to differentiate between the influence
of inheritance, as such, of certain qualities or conduct
trends and the influences that are brought to bear upon
a young individual through these qualities of his parents
playing upon his environment. Obviously if there is
in the home a parent who is delinquent or mentally
abnormal or alcoholic the effect upon the child may be
deleterious simply through the unfortunate social conditions created, and delinquency may ensue in consequence
of this alone.)

That Success occurred even when the family background seemed poor indeed is illustrated by the two
cases cited below. Failures from good stock can be accounted for by many other things besides heredity. It is,
however, Successes from bad family stock in which the

practical student of this subject must be interested as showing latent possibilities for reformation.   Even if it be thought there is little to learn from Failures from bad stock and Successes from good, the combination of bad background and good results represents neither the obvious nor the expected, and with the very positive data involved it offers an especially good basis for estimating some of the values of sound social effort.

A boy, 11½ years old, was seen first after he had run away for the second time from the dependent institution to which he had already been committed four times.   A year and a half later, having been at home in the interim, he was again in court, involved with several other boys in stealing wine, which they drank; he was truant; he frequently slept away from home, sometimes in a bath house to which drunkards went to get sobered.

Both father and mother drank; the former was excessively abusive and had served several terms at the House of Correction for fighting and abuse, he was said also to steal.   The mother had been under observation at a psychopathic hospital, but after rest and freedom from drinking was found normal mentally.   A delinquent sister of this lad was at the House of the Good Shepherd for a long period; a brother was at the state correctional school at this time.

The boy was sent to the correctional school.   On his release he returned to the mother, who was now living with the sister in a rooming house.   Soon the boy was in court on a charge of breaking into a store.   The probation officer now obtained work for him and gave him constructive supervision.   The father died, and home conditions improved greatly.   The boy worked regularly, was the main support of the mother and sister; then after a time entered the navy, where he has steadily had a good record.

Hattie M., when but 9 years old was brought to court by her mother, who stated that she was utterly unable to control the child.   The girl truanted frequently, begged money on the street, charged articles at the neighboring stores, remained out at night until eleven o'clock or later, was disobedient and destructive at home.   She had already been sent to an orphanage, but was soon excluded, the authorities saying they were really afraid of her influence—she lied, ran away, and was extremely troublesome in play with other children.

The account of heredity, given by the mother, included alcoholism, immorality, insanity, criminality, and possibly feeblemindedness. Details were as follows: Father, alcoholic and exceedingly immoral; his family negative, but not completely known. Maternal grandfather, a heavy drinker, died insane at 45 years. Maternal uncle, delinquent as a boy, in correctional institution between 10th and 14th years, regarded as feebleminded, now serving a term of three years for stabbing a man.

This little girl, normal mentally and physically, was sent to the House of the Good Shepherd. After a year she returned to her mother and step-father and lived at home for two years, giving no further trouble. Then on visiting her maternal grandmother, she found herself so happy there that she remained until the grandmother's death four years later. Soon after, she married a young farmer, and for years has apparently been a wholesome, healthy young woman, contented and happy.

If one may generalize from our data, and we see no reason why we should not, there is no basis for any preconceived notion that the chance of favorable outcome is necessarily very slight in the case of the individual with poor heredity. The chance of Success where there is good heredity is not enough greater, according to our findings, to warrant the assumption that on the basis of the heredity alone one can predict the likelihood of ultimate success. Hence there is no scientific justification for giving special attention and special opportunity only to those who are well endowed from the standpoint of family attributes.

CHAPTER IX

NUMBER OF DELINQUENTS IN THE FAMILY

A subject of perennial interest to sociologists is the extent to which delinquency runs through families, especially, how many of the children in the same family, presumably exposed to the same influences as well as having the same inheritance, are delinquents.

In the accompanying table the findings on 3000 of our cases are shown. Perhaps most significant are the following facts: Of families where there was more than one child, only one was delinquent in 62%. Of all the families where there was more than one child, all the children were delinquent in 4.4%.

The oft-recurring statement that the only child is in an unfavorable situation that might readily lead to delinquency finds neither confirmation nor contradiction in our figures, since the only comparison possible is with families of one child who did not become delinquent and about whom we have no statistics. At least we may say that only 10% of 3000 cases of delinquency are instances of one child in a family, and that does not seem an unduly large proportion.

And then in regard to the opposite contention, namely, that a large family conduces to delinquency among the children, the same absence of statistics of the general population for comparison blocks knowledge of true proportions. But even so, our larger families do very frequently show more than one delinquent; indeed, the

NUMBER OF DELINQUENTS IN FAMILIES. THREE SERIES, EACH 1,000 YOUNG REPEATED OFFENDERS

	Total Living Children	FREQUENCY OF DELINQUENTS					
		One Del'q't	Two Del'q'ts	Three Del'q'ts	Four Del'q'ts	Five or More Del'q'ts	Character of Others Unknown
CHICAGO I	1	119	..	..	..	..	..
	2	111	26	..	..	..	6
	3	117	21	12	..	..	12
	4	86	24	14	6	..	12
	5	86	22	11	4	4	11
	6	46	17	12	3	3	14
	7	32	10	5	6	..	4
	8	24	6	8	1	1	6
	9	16	5	4	..	2 *	5
	10	5	5	1	1	..	2
	11	2	..	4	..	..	2
	12	..	1	..	..	..	..
	13	..	..	..	..	..	1
	Unknown	..	..	..	..	..	42
		644	137	71	21	10	117
BOSTON I	1	63	..	..	..	..	..
	2	83	21	..	..	..	..
	3	112	43	6	..	..	2
	4	111	45	13	1	..	2
	5	91	35	16	3	..	..
	6	62	35	11	6	..	1
	7	61	24	14	4	2	2
	8	31	20	6	1	..	1
	9	21	11	2	2	2	..
	10	7	1	3	2	2	..
	11	1	1	..	1	..	1
	12	2	..	..	..	..	..
	13	1	..	..	..	..	..
	Unknown	..	..	..	..	..	12
		646	236	71	20	6	21
BOSTON II	1	114	..	..	..	..	..
	2	96	28	..	..	..	1
	3	85	30	10	..	..	5
	4	104	32	13	3	..	3
	5	92	36	15	3	2	1
	6	66	39	7	4	2 *	5
	7	43	15	9	7	3 †	..
	8	30	25	5	..	..	..
	9	13	9	3	1	..	..
	10	8	5	4	1	2 ‡	..
	11	1	2	..	3	..	..
	12	1	1	..	1	..	..
	13	2	..	..	..	..	..
	Unknown	..	..	..	..	..	10
		655	222	66	23	9	25

* In each of these there was one instance of 6 delinquents in the family.
† Here all 3 were instances of 6 delinquents.
‡ In one case there were 6, and in the other 7 delinquents.

bigger the family in our series the greater percentage of cases with more than one delinquent. This certainly is a fact significant for causation. But whether due to parental neglect, poverty, the play of bad environmental conditions, or the influence of one child on another, would only be determined by study of the individual case.

The reader may readily from the table work out other facts, but we hope always with recognition of the decidedly complex situations which must be duly regarded for fair interpretations. For example, the figures would seem to bear directly upon whether or not family and neighborhood conditions in and of themselves *necessarily* influence toward delinquency; if bad conditions are solely or mainly causative then all the individuals under such influences would tend to be delinquent. But any one familiar with good studies of cases knows that the influences which make for delinquency are frequently highly selective in their operation according to whether any member of the family has the personality or the interests or something else which leads him to be or not to be influenced.

One remarkable feature of this table, especially interesting to statisticians as bearing on reliabilities, is the similarities of the number of delinquents in families of different sizes, as found in each of the series and in both cities.

CHAPTER X

THE foreign elements of our population, it is very frequently asserted, are responsible for much that goes wrong in American social conditions. Especially has immigration been blamed for the extent of crime in our country. "Every authority agrees that immigration is a decisive factor in the crime situation," says a writer of to-day while reviewing the opinions of others about criminalism. And yet all this is quite contrary to the findings of the only careful study on the subject, that of the Immigration Commission, published in 1911 ("Immigration and Crime," a study by Leslie Hayford). From this we may quote:

"No satisfactory evidence has yet been produced to show that immigration has resulted in an increase in crime disproportionate to the increase in adult population. Such comparable statistics of crime and population as it has been possible to obtain indicate that immigrants are less prone to commit crime than are native Americans.

"The statistics do indicate, however, that the American-born children of immigrants exceed the children of natives in relative amount of crime."

What bearing have our data upon this question of delinquency and immigration? First, from our groups comprising 4000 young repeated offenders, what can be said about the relationship of the incidence of juvenile delinquency to nativity of the offender and of his parents? The facts for Chicago and Boston are shown in Table 28.

Taking Chicago first, we find among our series of 2000 that 83% of repeated juvenile offenders are native born, while 25% are of white American-born parents, 4% to 5% of colored parentage, leaving about 70% distributed among those of foreign-born parents. These are very like the proportions in the Chicago population as given in the statistics of the Federal Census of 1910 (Table 29). But when the figures for foreign nationalities are analyzed, differences between percentages of our groups and in the general population appear as follows: Among repeated offenders, Italians have about twice, the Slavs about 1½ times their quota. (The foreign Jewish also show to disadvantage, but our figures here are vitiated by the frequency with which their cases were directed to our Institute for study.) Then the colored showed twice as many repeated delinquents as was their proportion. Quite to the contrary, the Germanic group and the Scandinavian had only about one-half their proportionate number. Disproportions for other nations— Great Britain, Canada, Ireland, Bohemia—are very slight.

Similar differences appear also in comparison of the nationalities as given in Chicago juvenile court figures for repeated offenders in 1910. Of most significance is the following (Table 26): The Slavs, Italians, and in less measure the Irish, contribute to repeated delinquents a greater number than their proportion of the population, greater even than is found in our group; the Germans again appear to advantage, having not more than half their proportional representation. The foreign Jewish show here about their normal quota.

Turning now to the 2000 cases in Boston: We find that the number of our repeated offenders native born

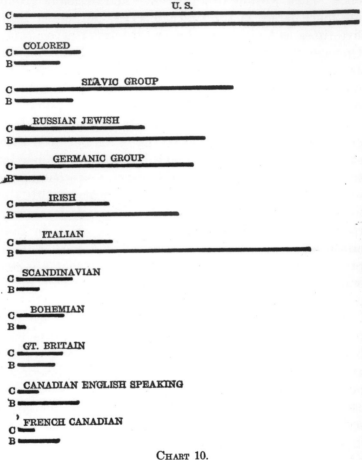

CHART 10.
Nationality of Parents
Comparison of Chicago 2000 and Boston 2000 Cases

and of white American-born parents is almost identical with the figures for Chicago—in each city almost exactly

83% and 25%. While those of colored parentage are somewhat fewer in Boston, there is no striking difference. Then, we note that the Slavic and Germanic groups are much larger in the Chicago series, the former being five times as large as in Boston, the latter seven times. Opposite findings in lesser proportions obtain for the Irish, Italian, and Russian Jewish, the most marked being the Italians with over three times as many numerically in our Boston series.

Thus immigration is about equally responsible in both cities for repeated delinquency, as far as our 4000 cases show. Our figures indicate the following in proportion to statistics for the general population: Boston showed only 23% and Chicago only 20% (Census of 1910) of inhabitants of native parentage. Although for several reasons we cannot closely compare our series in both cities with census figures, it may be mentioned that the proportions of nationalities seen by us correspond in general quite well with the proportions of nationality in the populations of Chicago and Boston (Table 29).

Turning to our followed-up Chicago series we find that 85% of the total group of 675 delinquents were born in the United States, the proportion for boys and girls being about the same. The parents of those comprising the group are native born in only 28% of the cases, thus coinciding with the findings from our larger series and being a little larger than the percentage shown in the census statistics for the general population of the city.

From our study of outcomes we can answer a very natural query, namely, how do delinquents of different nationalities appearing in the juvenile court tend to develop in regard to social misconduct, in regard to developing careers of crime? We mainly discuss males, since females so rarely become criminals.

Among our series of 420 followed Chicago cases (Table

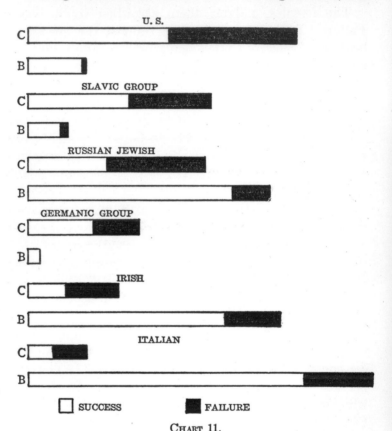

CHART 11.

Outcome Series: Chicago and Boston Nationality of Parents 1909-1914.

25) we find the differences of outcome according to nationalities so slight as to be negligible. With exception of the colored, which is a group so small as to have comparatively little reliability, the greatest difference in out-

come is only 8%. Delinquent whites of American parentage do no better than those in the several foreign groups.

The females, judging them according to Success or Failure (Table 25), show wider ranges, the lowest percentage of Success (32%) being found among the Slavic group and the highest (66%) among the Germanic group. Our American female delinquents stand just halfway between these extremes, with 49 per cent Successes.

Carrying this inquiry a little further, we note from Table 25 that the actually foreign-born delinquents, even those from non-English speaking countries, do as well in outcomes as those born in America. Indeed the females do better.

Our Chicago followed-up group of males appears to be very fairly representative of the proportions of nationalities of males appearing in the Chicago court, as shown in Table 26. There is one notable exception, however, the Jewish cases. This is owing to the frequency with which the Jewish social workers desired their cases studied, as mentioned above.

The second main point concerns itself with a comparison of the outcomes for males of different nationalities, considered separately, in Chicago and Boston. Our comparison is based only, for reasons given elsewhere, on whether or not the individual had a later court record. (See Table 27.) The number of those with adult court records in Boston as compared with Chicago is smaller for each nationality. We are particularly interested in this fact because not only do the majority of careers there of white males born in United States show such a fortunate outcome, but so do the nationalities, Slav, Italian, Irish, which are supposed to contribute so largely to American crime. Taking the Italian, the largest group of these three nationalities appearing in the Boston juvenile court, we find 79% of them not showing any adult court record, and the other two of the above three groups do as well or better. But in our Chicago series for the same three groups, we find percentages of those without court record ranging from only 41% to 56%.

Thus it is clear that nationality, as such, is not in itself

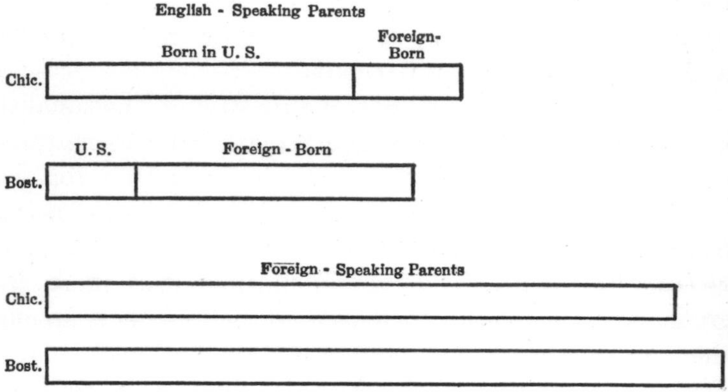

English - Speaking Parents

Born in U. S.   Foreign- Born

Chic.

U. S.   Foreign - Born

Bost.

Foreign - Speaking Parents

Chic.

Bost.

CHART 12.
Chicago and Boston Series—Males 1909-1914.

a factor which essentially precludes a measure of satisfactory outcome much greater than obtains in the Chicago series, even among the nationalities which are supposedly the most criminally inclined of our population. If, for example, the Italians in Boston make a 36% better showing (and these are Southern Italians, as in Chicago) then there is no reason to believe that there could not be vastly more delinquent careers checked among them anywhere, as, for that matter, among the other foreign-born.

Indeed, no figures on recidivism correlated with nationality, it must be insisted, can be interpreted as indicating any national potential unreformability, for, of course, many factors other than nationality play a part in determining outcomes. That something other than nationality conditions the delinquent career is shown by the fact that of the compared follow-up series of young repeated offenders in Boston no less than 92% were of foreign nationality, with only 20% having adult court records, while in Chicago 73% were of foreign nationality and 50% had adult court records.

The upshot of our findings in this study of nationality is: (a) Neither concerning the incidence nor the continuance in delinquency is there any better record for the children from native-born families than for those coming from foreign-born families, the latter taken as a total group.   (b) Among the foreign nationalities there are great differences—the incidence of delinquency among them is very much greater for certain national groups. Taking nationalities separately, some do much worse than the native-born stock, some do better.   (c) Most important is the fact that continuance in delinquency varies much more according to conditions operative in one city as compared with another than according to nationality. This would appear to have great bearing upon the whole problem of prevention and treatment of delinquency; it may well lead to greater hope and greater effort.

CHAPTER XI

THE comparative effectiveness of the activities of churches of different religious faiths in preventing or treating delinquency cannot be safely or fairly inferred from figures concerning the religions represented in our group, or among delinquents in general. Other facts are needed for interpretation, especially those which have to do with cultural norms, economic levels, customs and standards of national groups; all these are influences which affect original complaint, arrest, court statistics, as well as our figures. The extent to which individuals are brought into court, especially for certain forms of delinquency, notably sex delinquency, depends upon the group from which the delinquent comes. For example, some groups view sex irregularities much more leniently; the point at which such conduct is considered an offense varies according to racial or national standards. This must not be lost sight of, especially in considering girl offenders.

It is for such reasons that ordinary statistics do not afford safe bases for conclusions about the incidence of delinquency among special religious groups. However, our figures are fair as statements of comparative findings among registered offenders, and within their own limits are valid.

Our statistics are based only on family church affiliations. With Protestants and Jews this may not offer safe indication of religious practices—attendance at church, etc.—or of the belief of the individual members of the family, in particular, of the delinquents here under consideration.

We hardly need to warn that any fair conclusions about these proportions according to religions could only be made in the light of proportions of these same religious faiths for the total population of Chicago and these are not obtainable from census reports.

Because our series consist of such cases as we were requested to study, and such requests were more frequently made by some court officials than by others, we give for comparison the proportion of the different religions found among the entire juvenile court offenders. Table 30 indicates that the only large differences in percentages between yearly totals of delinquents in the Chicago juvenile court and our series is among the Jewish. We saw a much larger share of Jewish delinquents because of special requests from Jewish court workers, 19% of our cases, whereas they constituted only 7% of the court cases.

In this matter of religion our only aim is to show proportions of Success and Failure in the effort to see if any clear and trustworthy correlations of social value can be discerned. But here also we would be far from claiming that any findings are clear indicators of *causes* of outcomes; other factors enter again and again into the situation.

Perhaps most significant are the figures which show for the different religious groups the percentage of Success and Failure within each group. There are astonishingly small differences; the extent of Success and Failure is very similar irrespective of religious affiliation. In Table 30 we find that whether taking the Success and Failure groups or the religious faiths separately the difference is never larger than 10%.

CHAPTER XII

FOREWORD

FACTS concerning home conditions form data for a very important chapter in the study of causations of delinquency; the extent to which immediate surroundings in home life affect chances for reformation is always a very pertinent inquiry in the individual case and as a mass fact. Both for gathering scientific knowledge concerning the genetics of delinquency and for planning campaigns of prevention and treatment there is need for accurate information concerning these matters.

We have not attempted in this chapter to include the subtler features of family life which often are of extreme importance and which we greatly stress as formative influences in the lives of children. Parental attitudes, methods of discipline, emotional relationships between the children of a family, these are examples of matters concerning which we seek information in our studies of cases and attempt to evaluate in their relationship to misconduct; but they hardly lend themselves to enumeration, and hence we are obliged to confine ourselves here to the more objective features of family situations.

(a) ECONOMIC LEVELS

Poverty was formerly considered to be the most direct and forceful causative factor in delinquency and crime,

117

and this was to be expected, since it is the most objective and easily observed feature of the background. Fair estimates of its total relative importance in the production of delinquency are, nevertheless, very difficult to make, for here, if anywhere, it must be remembered that studies deal only with the caught (or registered) offender. Wealth frequently acts as a great protector and discriminator as far as arrest and punishment for crime are concerned.

In each of our cases a rough classification of economic status was originally made at the time of study. The measure being largely subjective, there seems, of course, chance for considerable inaccuracy. This probably obtained particularly in the first series of 1000 Chicago cases, for only with increasing experience could even subjective standards be formed. The figure for the second 1000 (Table 31) is likely to be more accurate; we are led to believe this especially because, having reviewed and re-estimated carefully the facts of home conditions in the 675 followed cases, we found destitution or poverty, defined below, appearing in 28%—closely similar to the 24% findings for the second 1000 cases.

Acknowledging some crudeness in our figures we give them, however, as having distinct value for depicting certain features of life in homes where delinquency arises, though we are far from stating the degree to which any causal relationship between the two exists. The statement seems fair that we have found poverty present in about 20% of all the cases.

Perhaps of more import is the endeavor to gain light on the extent to which economic status influences chances for cessation or continuance of delinquency. Hence our special attempt to discover whether there is any great correlation between outcome and economic level by painstaking comparative evaluation of original economic conditions in our Chicago followed cases.

It has not been possible to determine the exact income of the families, nor perhaps is that necessary. But it has been possible to do what seems entirely adequate for practical purposes—we have data which enabled us with quite fair accuracy to divide these home situations, from the point of view of material possessions, into five divisions, as follows:

Destitution; that is, there was often real want, for example, insufficient food and clothes; the meeting of barest needs sometimes was impossible without aid.

Poverty; that is, there was a constant struggle "to make ends meet"; not going hungry or without adequate clothing, but not having enough to live on without serious scrimping and denial and having no margin for anything outside actual needs.

Normal; that is, necessities in normal measure were obtainable, but not much beyond this; there was enough to meet ordinary needs and a small margin for very modest recreations or pleasures; thus the children might go to picture shows and have occasional other meager treats, but these were limited in number and in kind.

Comfort; that is, there was a margin for ordinary comforts, including recreations. The family could afford ordinary pleasures, such as occasional trips; the children could have spending money, could belong to clubs, and have wants supplied that were not extravagant.

Luxuries; that is the family could afford unusual cultural opportunities and even some extravagances.[1]

[1] Our belief in the validity and practicability of this five-fold classification is increased by finding, after the above categories were com-

The first fact of interest is the measure in which these degrees of physical comforts obtain for the group of 675 as a whole, irrespective of sex or of outcome. It is quite surprising that the findings concerning economic status resemble those for the population as a whole, that

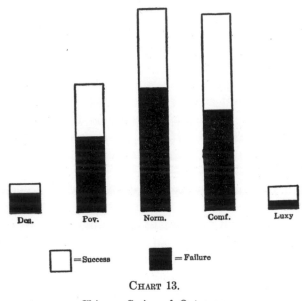

Des.   Pov.   Norm.   Comf.   Luxy

☐ = Success   ■ = Failure

CHART 13.

Chicago Series of Outcomes
Family Economic Status

is, statistically speaking, the curve of normal distribution is approximated. The figures for totals given in Table 32 show that among the group of offenders there is no preponderance of dire poverty, there is no over-weighting at the lower end of the scale.

pleted, that a very similar scale of values is utilized in "A Study of Women Delinquents in New York State" by Mabel R. Fernald and others.

FAMILY ECONOMIC LEVELS OF CHICAGO SERIES, 675 CASES.

Destitution	Poverty	Normal	Comfort	Luxury
5%	22%	35%	34%	4%

To find the rôle that early economic conditions in the family play in the determination of outcomes we may separate the percentages that obtain for Success and Failure. (See Table 32.) Or it may be of interest to show the relationship by finding the proportion from each economic level who succeeded and the proportion who failed, shown also in Table 32.

We find in the group as a whole that extreme poverty militates somewhat against Success, while cultural opportunities and economic ease somewhat favor moral recovery, but that less extreme differences in material welfare constitute no great determinant for or against reform.

Thus it is clear from the figures that great importance cannot be attached, in the case of either sex, to the effect of economic status on cure of delinquent trends. The majority of each sex is found in the section of the scale which includes homes graded as "Normal" and "Comfortable," and this is equally true for Successes and Failures. The most marked differences are in the sections of the scale at each extreme, and the relationship of economic status to outcome at these extremes is almost reversed, destitution seemingly increasing chances for Failure, two-thirds of the group at this level not succeeding; luxury to the same extent increasing chances for Success.

(b) PARENTAL RELATIONSHIPS

To what extent are so-called "broken homes" a background for delinquency and crime? Taking first our larger data, those on 2000 cases each in Chicago and

Boston, Table 31, we note that normal parental conditions (both parents alive and living at home) existed in only a little over half of the cases in each city. There was one parent dead in about 27% of the cases in both series, both parents in nearly 4%, parents were separated (living apart, divorced, or deserted) in 15%, a little over 2% of the offenders were illegitimate,[1] mother working out in 17%. (It should be added that included in the 15% separations there are desertions of at least one parent in Chicago 8.1%, Boston 2.7%. The extent of desertion in Chicago is corroborated by the court statistics, for example the year 1915 shows 6% of delinquents coming from homes with one parent deserted.)

For all these conditions we note a great similarity between the figures for the two cities, indicating, according to statistical probabilities, that if the four series of 1000 each showed such slight variations, such features of

---

[1] Much has been made abroad of the fact that many delinquents are of illegitimate birth. The figures in our larger series for Chicago and Boston are strikingly similar. We cannot compare them with the figures for the general population of Chicago because births are not accurately enough registered there. But the Massachusetts registration of births ranks as nearly complete; it has been used as the basis of the Federal Children's Bureau study of illegitimacy. The figures for illegitimate births in Massachusetts (4%) are nearly twice as high as in our Boston delinquent series, the facts for which have been obtained, not merely through court records, but through family histories and birth registration. The greater mortality of the illegitimate can hardly account for the difference. We wonder if the extensive placing by the children's agencies and the state and city authorities, most of which is well done and is undoubtedly a considerable preventive of delinquency, explains the situation. At any rate, our findings reverse the foreign statistics which apparently almost uniformly show a considerably higher percentage of illegitimates among juvenile delinquents than in the general population. (See the mass of statistics in proof of this point offered by Gruhle, "Die Ursachen Der Jugendlichen Verwahrlosung und Kriminalität." Heidelberg, 1912).

"broken homes" obtain very generally with delinquents. And we believe that most of these facts represent conditions not nearly so extensively obtaining in the family life of similar series of unselected children in the general population. Unfortunately we have no statistics concerning the latter; it is very unlikely, however, that almost half of all children of ages similar to those of our series belong to families broken because their parents are either not both alive or not both living at home.

In our series of 675 cases the facts of parental conditions are also quite reliably known. The situation for the group is given in Table 33.

Approximately the same proportions come from homes where both parents are living and living together, and from homes which in these respects are not normally constituted; and this is equally true for males and females.

Of more interest for our present study are data bearing upon the extent to which these features of the home conditions influence outcome, also shown in Table 33.

Among the males the percentage of Failure is greater than that of Success for any of the parental conditions enumerated, and does not differ much whatever the home conditions were. The normally constituted homes make little better showing than the broken homes. The females show more differences according to the separate categories of conditions, but the differences are hard to interpret and for all conditions except one small group, over one-half succeeded—normally constituted homes showed only 2% better than broken homes.

This is not altogether what might be expected; the facts are scarcely in line with the findings that delinquency so frequently originates in homes where parental relationships are broken. If our figures for Failures were

taken alone an assumption that broken families influence
outcomes would seem warranted; it is only when the percentages for outcomes in normally constituted families
are known also that the lack of significant correlation
in our group between outcome and familial status becomes clear.

It would seem that other factors in our Chicago group
outweigh whatever influences such family conditions
exert. And here it must be emphasized that the figures
can only be interpreted for the bare facts they enumerate; they do not deal at all with the probably much more
important factors of home life, such as harmony, parental
attitudes, home interests and all the subtler aspects of
family associations.

Conditions concerning step-parents, foster-parents,
orphanage upbringing are pictured by the figures in
Table 34, the data of which overlap those of the previous
table. These figures present nothing in home situations
that offers anything positive concerning the relationship
of parental conditions to outcome, the proportions of
Successes and Failures vary so much. But is there any
doubt that the mere fact of father, mother, step-father,
step-mother in the household is of minor consequence as
over against the significance of the character of parent or
step-parent?

It was possible to gather the facts about parental relationship in the first group of 400 male offenders in
Boston for comparison with the similar Chicago group
(Table 35). The percentage of normally constituted
homes (both parents living and at home) is 16% greater
in Boston, not a significantly large difference. But again,
the correlation of outcomes with parental conditions
seems to be more properly our concern. In Chicago of

those from "broken homes," 63% had a later court record;
of those from normally constituted homes, 59% had such
a record.   Figures for Boston for similar situations are
28% and 27%, respectively.   So even with a total
measure of Failure so dissimilar in the two cities, there
is little to indicate that responsibility for Success and
Failure rests on the fact of "broken homes."   The explanation of the after-record or outcome will have to be
sought elsewhere.

(c) Parental Neglect or Lack of Control

We cannot properly omit from consideration some
negative, very important aspects of home conditions, particularly those which bear upon lack of normal care and
discipline of children.   We have data on 4000 cases
(Table 31).

Extreme lack of parental control we have noted carefully on our records; we mean a state of affairs where
parents have not exercised even the minimum of good
discipline through incompetence, excessively large family,
both parents working away, etc., so that the child has
been allowed to go its own way, as would not be permitted under any normal conditions of family life.   We
found 40% of our total to come from families in which
this great lack of discipline was an unfortunate feature.

Extreme parental neglect we have had in mind more
recently as implying neglect, principally moral but sometimes also physical, as the result of extreme ignorance or
moral turpitude, moral indifference or overt bad example
on the part of parents.   We have enumeration of these
cases only in our Boston series where 22% appeared to
have suffered such extreme parental neglect.

Though not necessarily so, yet in some cases a mentally abnormal parent in the home is so plainly a bad influence that we are warranted in including it here. In 2000 Boston cases such a situation existed in 1% of the cases. We have figures for 1000 Chicago cases also; and here we strangely find seven times as many. We cannot believe that this difference represents a fact of heredity, rather it probably means that the well-known good public care of mental cases in Massachusetts has brought about a greater willingness to commit to institutions.

(d) Bad Influences in Family Life

In obtaining the stories of the family life of the delinquents studied some features have stood out prominently as being positively bad influences.

Excessive quarreling in the home is one of the conditions that has been cited both by delinquents and relatives as making directly for bad conduct. We have come to know (Table 31) that in 12% of our total 4000 cases there was excessive quarreling at home. Without any means of gauging in what percentage of families among our general population good temper gives way to quarreling in excess, we nevertheless feel that the proportion in our group must be unduly large.

We are in doubt about the significance of a fact that shows in both of our Boston series, namely, that girls come about twice as frequently as boys from homes in which there is excessive quarreling.

Alcoholism (meaning at least occasional intoxication), immorality or criminalism in the home are, of course, direct conditioning factors of delinquency in the children. Our figures on this for the total 4000 are 21%. There is no tremendous difference between the percentage for the two cities. Such differences as do exist would have to be most carefully interpreted and the influence of many factors, such as the effect of prohibition, would still be left in doubt. We offer below more careful studying of the effect of these conditions.

How many of our cases were so actually influenced toward delinquency by alcoholism, immorality and criminalism in the home is not to be determined except from the data of careful case studies. It seems likely that there is more to be learned, however, by discussion of outcomes rather than of the incidence of delinquency in families where such bad influences have existed.

For the purpose of studying these important background facts as related to Success and Failure we have thought it best to utilize only those cases where causative factors were carefully considered as such in the original study. Of our 675 Successes and Failures we have exactly 500 cases that were so studied originally. Of the 500 we find 169 (Table 37) with influences in the home which were estimated to be directly responsible, in part, at least, for the misconduct in question.

The outcomes are of particular interest: the girls' cases fall under the categories of Success and Failure in about equal proportions; the boys in 70% of the cases do poorly, particularly badly when there has been criminalism or sex immorality in the home, 44 of 52 such cases showed Failure (Table 39).

Wondering why the girls should do so much better, even when there were these same very bad influences in their home life, we have attempted a rather careful analysis (Table 40) of the treatment received by the 35 girls who came from homes where there was criminalism or sex immorality. Among the various adjustments we note that an equal number of both Successes and Failures, 14 each, went to institutions, but later adjustments of these girls show 13 of the 18 Successes and only 2 of the 17 Failures placed out and not allowed to return to a bad home, while at least 9 of the Failures were known to have returned to a home that was not bettered.

In the cases of the boys, few were placed; of the 44 Failures only 6 were removed from their poor homes, while of the 8 Successes, one-half were taken away from the influences of their family life. As shown in Table 39, the Success cases not placed show compensating facts and the Failures after placement were notably unpromising material.

For the treatment of delinquency the lesson to be learned from the above figures is very clear: the chances of good results through removal of a child for a long time from a bad home are very considerable, the expectancy of bad results if not so removed is even greater.

And then our findings afford very definite and very optimistic answers to two natural queries, (a) concerning whether or not early experiences with delinquency in the home leave ineradicable tendencies to delinquency, and (b) concerning whether delinquency showing itself in a child from a delinquent family necessarily represents hereditary and consequently ineradicable traits.

(e) Good Homes

In the homes, then, of how many of our cases have there been what might ordinarily be called really good family conditions? We asked ourselves this while working over the details of the obviously bad conditions in family life given above. To answer the question 1000 cases each in Chicago and Boston were taken. Specifi-

cally, if we ruled out the families in which there were
such clearly unfortunate features of home life, poverty,
great crowding or very insanitary surroundings, extreme
parental neglect or extreme lack of parental control,
excessive quarreling, alcoholism, obscenity, immorality or
criminalism, mother away working, mentally diseased
parent in the home, how many had we left? Enumerating the good homes thus by elimination, we found
(Table 31) the figures for Boston to be 10.3%, for Chicago 5%, numerically only a small difference. Among
2000 young repeated offenders, then, there were living
under reasonably good conditions for the upbringing of
a child, only 7.6%.

We have no other figures showing such high correlation between background conditions and incidence of
delinquency. Where to place a large measure of responsibility, where to direct a strong attack in treatment and
for prevention of delinquency stands out with striking
clearness.

CHAPTER XIII

MARRIAGE as a possible conditioning factor in reformation may very properly be discussed from our data.

Of the 420 males of our Chicago series (Table 41), only 37 (9%) were married at the time of our study, when their average age was about 25 years. The 9% represent 14% of the Successes and 5% of the Failures. These figures perhaps indicate that for males marriage may afford some anchorage, but that it entails responsibilities that only a few young male offenders are willing to assume. Or we may possibly infer that at the average age of our group comparatively few are adequately enough stabilized or adjusted in the community to marry, and that there would be a larger percentage of marriage among the Successes.

A very much larger proportion, 121 (47%), of the 255 females were married (Table 41). Of these 121, the Successes were 69%; of the 134 unmarried, 41% were Successes. Or, putting it in another way, 60% of the 138 Successes were married and 32% of the 117 Failures.

Of course, here too it is difficult to separate cause and effect; to know whether it was marriage that was responsible for "making good," or whether reformation led to marriage. We have no proof that marriage was the most potent stabilizing factor in these girls' lives, although we must consider it a very strong possibility. Marriage legitimatizes exactly the sex conduct which brought so many of them into court, and secondly, it usually offers the anchorage and security of a home— an economic as well as a social advantage.

In considering the marriages of the females, we are struck by the great number of sex delinquents who have married, and apparently done well. Of the 92 sex offenders who were Successes, 70% married. This Success outcome of sex offenders is not in accord with a belief, quite frequently expressed in older days, that an immoral girl is extremely unlikely to reform. We note that our case histories even show that many of the successful marriages were consummated while the individual was still on probation or parole, sometimes even while the girl was continuing conduct that was regarded by the court as unsatisfactory.

While among the male Failures, Table 42, at least half were deserters or legally separated, among the married women Failures there was only a small number of divorces, although the majority continued to be immoral.

CHAPTER XIV

In the history of criminology there was a period of firm belief in the close causal relationship between physical make-up and tendency to delinquency; even to-day this same idea is occasionally maintained. The physical examinations which have been made of our cases (many of them have also been examined by specialists in other medical clinics) offer extensive data which supply a critique for some of the older notions. Concerning any of the specific findings presented below, we should at once say that they are not offered in any sense as a brief for any physical theory whatever of causation of delinquency. We feel strongly that the implications of the findings for any one condition, be it enlarged tonsils, bad teeth, goitre, etc., would require checking up by determining the proportions in non-delinquent groups in the two cities we have under consideration. Of course we already have some standard norms, such as those shown on our age-weight charts, for certain facts of development.

Age-Weight Correlations.—With all the limitations that there properly should be in interpreting the physical conditions of any individual child by his weight for his age, our age-weight charts on large numbers of delinquents are of considerable interest. These charts may be fairly utilized as negating certain older ideas that delinquents and criminals were the malnourished, the

132

underdeveloped members of society, exhibiting, thus, the effects of poverty. Rather, the charts show surprisingly good conditions of development and nutrition for a very large share of our cases.[1]

It will be noted that there are closely similar findings of weight related to age for our large groups in the two American cities.

The median of the distribution in our group runs very close to the curve for the norm of the general population, but we note that the variation above the curve is more extreme than below, that is, there are more boys who show overdevelopment or overnutrition than there are boys who show underdevelopment or undernutrition. And in this the charts suggest a fact that exists in many a case, namely, a causal relation between physical overgrowth and the tendency to adventurous delinquency. Restlessness, poor adjustments in school and outside school, needs for larger physical self-expression, all frequently follow upon early great growth, and any of these may directly lead to delinquency as a form of activity which affords outlets.[2]

---

[1] For age-weight correlations we still feel compelled to use Burk's curve (Frederic Burk, Growth of Children in Height and Weight, Amer. Jour. Psychology, April, 1898), built up from data concerning 69,000 American young people of considerably varied nationalities and social groups. Nowadays, for interpreting the conditions of the individual in comparison with a really good American norm, such as obtains for a physically well-endowed and well cared for social group, we have the norms developed by Baldwin and Wood (published by the American Child Health Association). In making comparisons for our large groups it seems much fairer to compare them with averages of children found in the population at large. On each chart the curve of norms is that taken from Burk.

[2] In illustration of this fact Case-Study No. 2 and 3 of the Judge Baker Foundation Case Studies, 1923, presented a series of boys where such causations obtained.

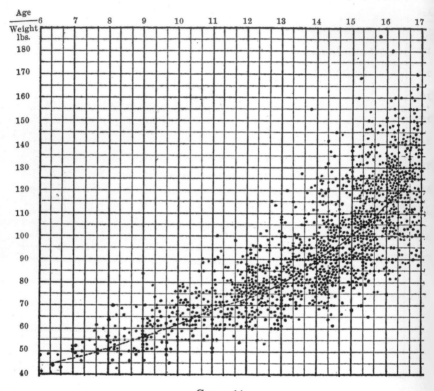

CHART 14.
Age-weight Correlations: Chicago Boys

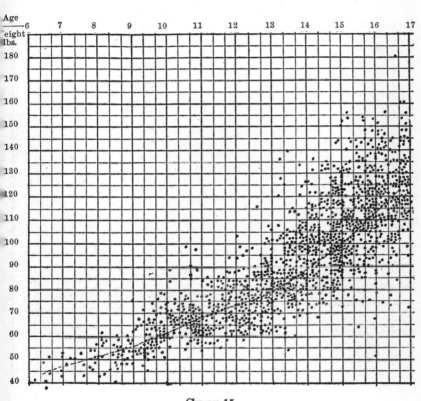

CHART 15.
Age-weight Correlations: Boston Boys

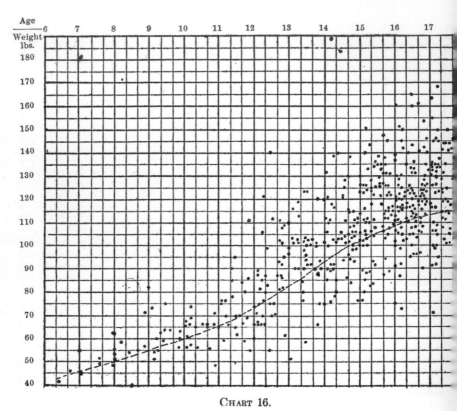

CHART 16.

Age-weight Correlations: Chicago Girls.

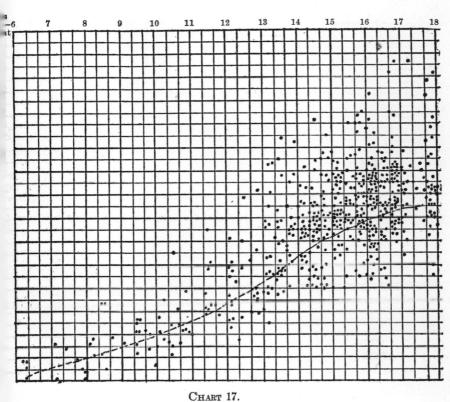

CHART 17.
Age-weight Correlations: Boston Girls,

Concerning the girls we may say that approximately 70% in each group is above the general age-weight norm. This is a significant fact, as we have many times pointed out before, and it falls in line with the common sense observations of many judges and others who note the frequent physical overdevelopment of girls who come before the juvenile court. There can be little doubt, by way of interpretation, that physical overdevelopment tends to draw a girl's attention early to sex life and that it leads her early to be attractive to the opposite sex.

Developmental Conditions.—In considering the matter of general developmental conditions, we have taken only the extremes, so that there can be little question about the facts which have been set down in Table 43 as data of judgment, rather than as physiological details. In the first place, we have found among boys very poor general development in about 15% of 3000 delinquents —not a very large percentage, to be sure, but larger than would seem to be indicated by the age-weight charts. The explanation is that great general overdevelopment (4.5% among the boys) does not mean the same as overweight for age; and weight and nutrition may not be specially poor when development of chest and strength, for instance, is very poor.

Comparisons of the sexes demonstrate that among delinquents girls much less frequently than boys are victims of very poor development; they are very much more often greatly overdeveloped—no less than 12% of the girls showing this condition, as against 6% very poorly developed. Overdevelopment of sex characteristics in girls is a matter of considerable importance, since it often leads the girl to be unusually attractive to the opposite sex or leads her early to pay special atten-

tion to sex affairs. Such overdevelopment was found in
7.5% of the girls. (Anything analogous was found in
only 3% of the boys.) A picture is thus formed that
reënforces the statement already made about the significance of the more-than-average physical development
found in a considerable proportion of delinquent girls.

Studying Success and Failure in relation to developmental conditions, we found (Table 44) that of the
very poorly developed among the 420 boys 61% showed
Failure, whereas of the very poorly developed girls 50%
were Failures. Of those showing marked general overdevelopment, about 50% of girls and of boys were
Successes. From any of these figures no safe conclusions
can be made or suggestions offered concerning the advantage or disadvantage of any of these conditions as they
might be allied to outcome.

Judging by our statistics for puberty it would seem
that the overdevelopment we enumerate for girls is a
general physical phenomenon and is not at all necessarily
allied to an early onset of puberty. Early puberty has
been considered by some an important factor in the
delinquency of girls; it undoubtedly sometimes is, more
particularly when it brings with it early attention to
matters of sex, but prematurity is not itself very common. Among the girls early puberty was noted in 5%;
among the boys in 12.5%. Very delayed puberty, often
a symptom of organic inferiority, was found in only 4%
of the boys and in less than 1% of the girls.

Good Physical Conditions.—In order to form an estimate of the number with good physical qualities among
the groups of delinquents studied, we have surveyed the
physical records of 1000 cases in each city. In good
physical condition, that is, free from significant physical

defects or ailments or abnormalities of any kind (Table 43) we found 27% in Chicago, 32.7% in Boston—a difference of no practical import. In order to compare this with the conditions of young people in the general population we turn to the study made in New York by Gulick and Ayres [3] and discover that from 75 to 80% of 7698 children examined had physical defects of the same order as those noted by us. So our series of delinquents appear certainly to no worse advantage physically than the general run of children.

For estimating the relation between outcome and good physical condition we took a considerably coarser measure and counted as normal (Table 44) those individuals who had nothing pathological of marked importance. That is, we did not count moderately carious teeth, slightly enlarged tonsils, etc., in this varying the procedure from our study of the 4000 cases so that comparisons between Success and Failure might stand out more clearly. Some of the findings are striking; of the 265 boys who showed nothing of a marked pathological character physically, no less than 71% were Failures. From this it seems clear that if future Success is the criterion, no advantage accrued to those boys who were in good physical condition. Of the 200 girls also in good physical condition only 44% were Failures. This figure, too, shows no great significance of healthy conditions for moral outcome.

Then, taking the opposite extreme, when distinct organic disease existed, as in the cases of 54 boys, the Failures (57%) were not proportionately so great as in those free from such disease. Among 20 girls the percentage of Failure, it is true, was greater than among

[3] Medical Inspection of Schools, Russell Sage Foundation, 1908.

healthy girls, but the total is too small to have much validity.

Sensory Defects.—Important defects of vision uncorrected by glasses were present in 14% of 4000 cases and of hearing in nearly 2%. Again, these figures are very similar to those found in school surveys and consequently, taken as totals, show no special correlation with delinquency. In rare cases, however, we do know that these defects have played a part in the determination of delinquent trends.

That marked sensory defect does not stand in the way of cessation of delinquent trends is shown by the figures of Success and Failure (Table 44), where for girls we find more with such defects succeeding than failing. The boys with marked sensory defect show 67% Failure, which is not quite as large a percentage as shown by those who did not have sensory defect.

Nose, Throat, and Ear Ailments.—Otorrhea, evidence of active middle ear infection, we found in 2.3% of 3000 cases, and nose and throat ailments of obvious significance in 22%. This, again, is similar to what is found in the general school population. But it has been a matter of no little surprise to us to find that in our latest series in Boston, with so many children having had tonsil and adenoid operations, our total remains so large. We have no explanation to offer. But, at any rate, from the fact that not a few of those who develop delinquent tendencies have had tonsils and adenoids removed, it stands out clearly that it is not justifiable to blame delinquency upon diseased tonsils and adenoids.

Nervous Diseases.—We have found a little less than 4% of 4000 cases showing evidences of disease of the nervous system, other than epilepsy and head injury, and, it should be added, neurological signs have been looked for as a routine measure. This has been a matter of some astonishment. Even hysteria is surprisingly rarely observed. The nervous disease found most often has been chorea. (Our recent experience with cases of encephalitis lethargica, that disease of the central nervous system which sometimes results in such difficult behavior problems, does not show in this enumeration of years past.)

Head Injury.—Evidence obtained from the developmental history and our examination of the individual shows a striking amount of severe head injury among delinquents and especially among some of the worst cases of conduct disorder. Nearly 4%, which is very large considering the rarity of such injury in general, show clear evidences of bad head injury, here enumerated only when serious symptoms ensued, sometimes with fracture of skull, sometimes with a considerable period of unconsciousness. (It should go without saying that very few indeed of these injuries occurred to girls.)

These figures, however, give small support to the extravagant claims of the two or three writers who, evidently on the basis of observations of a few selected typical cases, account for a large share of delinquency as due to head injury, and, indeed, have thereupon developed a theory of brain localization of centers of moral consciousness or control. Our own findings are not likely to be far amiss, because our examinations are fortunately strongly checked by carefully eliciting from the family the health history.

Concerning the outcome, that is whether or not the individual with severe head injury was able, after a period, to refrain from delinquency, we have our figures for 18 cases in Table 44; 7 of these, or 40%, were Successes as they passed through adolescence and to adult life. This proportion is about the same as for those who showed nothing pathological.

Venereal Disease.—On account of the development and availability of better methods of diagnosis of venereal disease in the last few years we offer figures for only the last 1000 young repeated offenders in Boston. Comparatively few of these boys up to the end of the usual juvenile court age, 17 years, have been immoral with girls, we find, and only about 1% had either syphilis or gonorrhea. On the other hand, very many of the girls have been immoral; indeed, that is the commonest complaint against them, and 14% had one of the two diseases.

Congenital Syphilis.—It would be very difficult, indeed, to estimate what proportion of any group of older children had been the victims of syphilis when born. In later childhood, even in cases of congenital syphilis, the ordinary blood tests are often negative and physical signs are not always present—the disease has probably been conquered by the individual. We found the ordinary somatic (structural) signs of probable congenital syphilis in about 4% of 3000 cases, and in nearly every instance the teeth constitute the distinguishing signs of probability. The small totals which we have for those who showed distinct evidence of congenital syphilis among our followed-up cases show about an equal number of males and females succeeding and failing.

Stigmata of Degeneracy.—Still as a matter of perennial interest we have those physical findings which point to "degeneracy" (the word made so popular by Lombroso, Nordau and others) being a factor in delinquency. In spite of the extreme assertions of some earlier criminologists, we can find among our young repeated offenders not more than 7% showing the well defined physical signs which were called stigmata of degeneracy. Of 23 boys showing marked stigmata and who were followed up for outcome we find 74% failing. But we should state here that since stigmata are much more apt to be found among the mentally defective it may well have been such defect which stands more directly in relationship to Failure.

Teeth.—We have had special interest in enumerating dental conditions in 2000 cases, not because we have accepted the recent theory that bad teeth, molar abscesses and the like are the real causes of delinquency (we believe that it would take much more than bare statistics to prove this), but on account of the great differences which we earlier noted between the teeth of children in the two American communities where we have studied. As may be seen in Table 43, there are immense differences; whatever the findings of an expert dental surgeon would have been, our rougher classifications show the variances. In Boston 80% of those we examined had fairly good dental conditions and in Chicago 39%. Or, to put it in another way, in Chicago 53% of 1000 cases showed one or more badly carious teeth, and in Boston only 8%.

It appears to us that the extreme difference between the cities is due to the very extensive use of the Forsyth Dental Clinic in Boston; the children being sent there by school nurses and families. A sort of community campaign has been fostered by this magnificent charity which together with other dental clinics has supplied the resources. Hence these most admirable results.

Goitre.—It is well known that Boston is not in a goitre

belt, whereas Chicago is in such a belt of moderate intensity, so it might be expected that there would be much difference between the findings in the two cities. Our findings of 1000 cases in each city show the very much greater frequency of the enlargement of the thyroid gland in Chicago. (See Table 43.) Medical men will naturally be interested in our statistics. But we would add at once that even though girls do show enlargement of the thyroid ten times more frequently in Chicago than in Boston, and though one finds boys showing enlargement in 4.6% in Chicago and 0% in Boston, we cannot safely attribute any of the differences in delinquency in the two cities to difference in extent of thyroid conditions.

SUMMARY

Summarizing briefly the main points based on the physical examination of delinquents, we may say that in general the delinquent group is closely similar to the general group of young people in so far as standards for comparison exist. Physically the delinquent does not form a separate group. Nor is any particular physical condition found to be significant in relation to the later career of the offender.

CHAPTER XV

EVERY student of delinquents knows that in some cases the habits of the offender are important in relation to the development or continuance of tendencies to misconduct. Indeed sometimes these habits have to be directly combatted before any success in treatment is to be obtained. Our numerical representation (Tables 45 and 46) of habits may not do justice to the matter because it is difficult to get the truth always.

Masturbation.—The habit of masturbation in a considerable number of cases is important in its relationship to delinquency. This is because of the break-down of morale which is often obvious where masturbation has been indulged in excessively. And in other instances where the habit itself is not so severe, undue thinking about it and over-conviction of its bad effects sometimes leads to a mental attitude that is conducive to the development of delinquency. On the other hand, of course, this habit is very commonly indulged in to some extent during childhood or youth and without production of delinquency. Irrespective of the question of whether or not the practice was specifically, especially in the less severe cases, a causative factor of the delinquency, we have enumerated (Table 45) the instances of excessive masturbation and find that a total of 10% of our young repeated offenders, boys 12% and girls 6%, were indulging to that extent.

From our early studies we have data on this habit that can be correlated with outcome. Of the 57 cases (Table 46) known to be excessive masturbators among our followed-up 420 males, we find 70% were Failures. But of the 27 girls, 63% were Successes—a reversal of findings for which there may be physiological and other explanations.

Smoking in Excess.—Without discussing smoking in causal relationship to delinquency, we may give figures, not for occasional smoking, but where it was a definite habit among children and young people. In our total series, 22% of the boys smoked to an extent that might well be considered excessive for their years. How difficult it is fairly to draw conclusions concerning any baneful influence may be seen from the fact that certainly many non-delinquent young people smoke to the same excess. Our figures are interesting in showing the great increase in recent years of smoking among juveniles, 10% of excessive smokers among our first series in Chicago, 33% in our last series in Boston.

Concerning outcomes, we may say that of the 45 excessive smokers whose careers have been followed, 62% have been Failures, a figure closely similar to the 60% of the total male Failures.

Other Bad Habits.—There was use of *tea and coffee* in excess in an average of 9% for the total series. We have enumerated the cases where *alcohol* was frequently used even in small amount, because the habit of taking any alcohol during childhood and adolescence is undoubtedly unfortunate. There is great variation again here among our series, the principal reason being that in Boston we have seen a greater proportion of Italians among whom giving wine to children, girls and boys, is common. So we have one series showing 7.5% of the children taking alcoholic beverages and another series showing 1.7%. But comparing the figures given here with the figures for alcoholic intoxication given under Offenses, it will be seen that while there is a greater amount of wine drinking in Boston there are more arrests for alcoholism of juveniles in Chicago. The facts which we are here discussing come to our knowledge during study of the family life. The use of alcohol, Table 45, among the juveniles in Chicago whose careers have been followed was too rare to afford any figures of importance. *Drugs:* As we stated under Offenses, the use of drugs during juvenile court age is very rare.

CHAPTER XVI

MENTAL STATUS

(a) FINDINGS IN 4000 CASES

OUR studies of the relationship of mental abnormality to delinquency and crime considerably augment the discussion of a subject which during recent years has been very rightfully much to the fore. Our findings are, perhaps, most worthy of note, firstly, because of the large numbers which our series present; secondly, because the cases have been unusually carefully studied; thirdly, because of the comparatively unselected character of our cases, quite unselected, indeed, except as they were young repeatedly caught offenders. (We would hardly want to call all juvenile first offenders seriously delinquent, and certainly to take merely delinquents who have been committed to an institution is hardly fair.) Then, our tracing of outcomes as related to mental normality and abnormality has afforded some significant material.

Appraising our data on the total 4000 cases of young repeated offenders (Table 47) we are at once struck by the great similarity between the main figures for the different series. It is all the more significant that the percentages for mental defect are so much alike since they have been arrived at through examinations made by different psychologists, so that any individual bias has been obviated.

Objective standardized tests have been used by us as they have been evolved. (Although we would insist always that mental diagnosis and even mental testing for practical purposes involves much more than establishing a mental age or intelligence quotient.) These facts and the size of the groups, making the largest collection of data that has been brought together on the mentality of offenders, creates for the percentages a scientific validity which should go far in answering the problem of the correlation of mental status with delinquency.

Many of the doubtful cases have been seen by us more than once and, like most of our cases, have been followed in their careers; not a few have been examined in other clinics and we thus have had the advantage of corroborative findings.

The figures for the four groups of those clearly *normal mentally* (see Table 47 and definitions) reveal a variation of only 3% from the average of the groups. The differences between the sexes is so slight as to be negligible.

On the one hand these figures show clearly that the mentally abnormal among delinquents constitute a much greater proportion than is found among the general population. Yet, on the other hand, those who have so stressed the part played either by feeblemindedness or mental disease in the production of delinquency will obtain from these most carefully developed findings small support for their extreme statements.

Stated in total, 72.5% of our 4000 repeated juvenile offenders were found to be definitely mentally normal.

The *feebleminded*, the group that has by some been so blamed for delinquency, also show close similarity in

totals in our four series. Sex differences would seem
to be of considerable interest because of the emphasis
that has been placed upon the feebleminded girl as a
potential sex offender. However, while a greater percentage of girls appear in each series, the differences are
small. The main fact is that the feebleminded appear
among serious delinquents from five to ten times more
frequently than in the general population, but, even
so, they form not more than one-fifth as many as the
mentally normal. Our total is 13.5% clearly feebleminded.

Subnormal mentally is a term we apply to a group
which is not to be recognized as either clearly feebleminded or within the limits of certainly normal mentality. It is the border-line class of some authors. (It
might better be called a border-zone—see definitions in
connection with Table 47.) It would be a fair guess
that if this border class were divided between the two
main groups (and it is for the sake of simplicity that
only the main groups are considered below in studying
outcomes according to mental ability) over half of the
total would be included as mentally normal. As subnormal or belonging in this border-zone our totals show
9.1%.

Suffering from mental diseases, *psychoses*, there was
found a considerable difference between the totals for
Chicago, 5.6%, and for Boston, 1%. Whenever there
is any question of mental disease the psychopathic hospital in Boston is utilized for study of our cases, so
there is corroboration of diagnosis in the figures given.
The lesser frequency of psychosis in the Boston series
may possibly be accounted for by the following:

Since 1912 Boston has had a fine psychopathic hospital (not a place of court hearings as in Chicago) in which the public has great confidence, so that many cases of mental trouble are taken there voluntarily. The treatment no doubt in some cases has prevented the development of delinquent trends.

It is a distinct possibility that environmental conditions, perhaps to be called the spirit of a community, which make for delinquency are particularly and early succumbed to by those who are poorly balanced mentally. At any rate no one, from general statistics available, would think of Massachusetts or Boston having proportionately fewer mentally diseased than Illinois or Chicago. Our figures would tend to show, then, that the mentally diseased in any considerable number do not become delinquent unless environmental conditions are morally unfavorable. And those who hold that a strong causal relationship exists between mental disease as such and delinquency or crime will have to meet the challenge of the figures of our very carefully developed case studies, in any of the four series, taken separately or comparatively.

Psychopathic personalities (see text of Table 47), a class of poorly balanced individuals most difficult when they show delinquent tendencies, are enumerated only for the Boston series, and there total 2.8%. (Particularly to professional readers we would state that we firmly stand against the diagnosis of psychopathic personality made simply on the basis of repeated misconduct without other signs of psychopathic trends—there are too many other causations of misconduct. But our original figures will probably be somewhat increased in the light of a special study now in progress concerning a better definition and diagnosis of abnormal personalities.)

In the above totals are included two groups: (a) *Constitutional inferiors*, those who on the background of a faulty biological make-up are great weaklings from the standpoint of character; these form 2% of the series; and (b) the *epileptics*, 5.5% in Chicago, 1.6% in Boston. For the epileptics we probably again have nearly accurate figures, and perhaps the greatest cause for the difference in the two cities is that for long there have been in Massachusetts special state institutions to care for epileptic children, so that there is a smaller percentage of them in the community. In Illinois there was at the time of our studies no such institution.

CHART OF DISTRIBUTION OF INTELLIGENCE QUOTIENTS

This chart represents the Stanford-Binet intelligence quotients of young repeated offenders seen in Boston. All cases are included since we began steadily to use this scale in 1917. (Once more we would insist, however, that this scale alone does not tell the whole tale of what these individuals are mentally, even from the standpoint of mental ability.)

The first point to note is that the chart for boys in its distribution of intelligence quotients approximates the normal "curve of distribution" of statisticians. Then, so far as comparison with intelligence quotients of the general population is concerned, we must remember that although, according to the Stanford-Binet scale, the norm is I. Q. 100 on a basis of 16 years as the average adult mental age-level, as a matter of fact the army findings show that for the general adult population the median or average age-level according to this

701 GIRLS

1625 BOYS

I.Q.

I.Q.

Distribution of Intelligence Quotients: Juvenile Repeated Offenders: Boston Series.

scale should be 14 years or less.[1]   Our I. Q. for ages higher than 14 would be increased if this modification were made.   Undoubtedly what on our chart is now reckoned as I. Q. 90 is near the median for the general population, instead of I. Q. 100.   So the apex of the curve on our chart is very close to that for American citizens in general.   We note, however, that the 13.3% of feebleminded in our group modify the lower sweep of the curve.

The distribution of females in the chart does not follow the normal curve of distribution; there are evidently forces at work that select girls that are brought into court and are brought to us for study.   We have noted this in our remarks on the incidence of delinquency as correlated with the appearance of the sexes in court.

(b) Findings as Related to Outcomes

What part does mental status play in determining the later careers of repeated juvenile offenders?   First, it may be of interest to know the general mental status of the entire group of Chicago cases utilized in our study of Success and Failure.

Classifying in simplest terms the facts of mental normality and unquestionable abnormality as these are recognizable if we merely follow wide distinctions, we find the following:

Normal intelligence	532	(79%)
Feebleminded	108	(16%)
Psychoses	35	(5%)
	675	(100%)

[1] For an interesting statement of the facts see "A Study of American Intelligence" by C. C. Brigham of Princeton.

But it is well known to psychiatrists and psychologists, and it should be much more generally recognized, that categories other than the simple ones given above are of great import for the practical ends of prognosis and treatment, even social treatment under the law. Irrespective of grading by mental tests into the groups of those of normal or defective capacity, we have other criteria which may classify the individual as being a psychopathic personality, an epileptic, a constitutional inferior, etc.

Organizing our data to such more practical ends the figures (Table 49) become as follows: Normal, 63%; Feebleminded, 14%; Psychopathic Personalities, 14%; Psychotic, 5%.   The Psychoneurotic and Constitutional Inferiors form comparatively small groups, each constituting 2% of the total.

Epileptics, who, of course, vary greatly in mental status, the disease being only sometimes the cause of mental disturbance or deterioration, are distributed in the above grouping.   Table 50 gives the mental classification as related to outcomes of the epileptics.

No important sex differences are revealed, except among the constitutional inferiors who as delinquents are almost all males.

Next, we may examine the figures which throw some light on the relationship between mental status and Success and Failure.   To what extent does normal mentality favorably condition future reform among juvenile offenders?   Is mental abnormality a handicap that bespeaks little likelihood of later law-abiding citizenship for those who are already repeated delinquents as juveniles?

Our data on outcomes indicate, of course, only the

Success or Failure following the specific treatment that our group received; one cannot safely infer what might have resulted had quite other social and punitive measures been accorded these offenders. We should particularly state that during the years covered by our study there was in Illinois no law enabling the judge of the juvenile court to commit the feebleminded to permanent custodial care nor was any colony for epileptics then in existence. We shall discuss later the specific social treatment administered the mentally abnormal of our group.

As one might expect, the outcomes for the mentally normal were better than for the mentally abnormal (Table 49). The percentage of Failure in the three main mentally abnormal groups was very large indeed. While among the mentally normal, Success and Failure is about equal, 50%, a bad enough showing, among the feebleminded, psychotic and psychopathic personalities the proportion of Success is not more than 33%. From these figures one may see that neither juvenile court nor correctional institutions, in their efforts to check delinquency, were cognizant of the difficulties the members of these groups presented, or if they were they did nothing adequate to control and reform.

The table which gives outcomes for the sexes separately shows that the males in all mental groups failed more frequently, except that the outcome among psychotic showed a small variation in their favor.

Taking (Table 50) the known epileptics in this series—and for this study we classify as epileptic only those who have had comparatively recent, plain manifestation of this disease—we find 24 cases, with 13 Failures as against 11 Successes. Should this seem very unexpected in the light of the well-known fact of the extreme criminal tendencies of some epileptics, we would again insist that this disease is greatly variable in its effect upon mind and character, although we confess to having been surprised ourselves at the good follow-up reports about some of these cases which seemed decidedly unpromising.

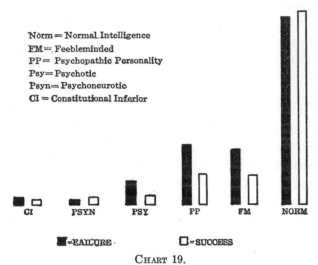

Nòrm = Normal Intelligence
FM = Feebleminded
PP = Psychopathic Personality
Psy = Psychotic
Psyn = Psychoneurotic
CI = Constitutional Inferior

CI   PSYN   PSY   PP   FM   NORM

■ = FAILURE   ☐ = SUCCESS

CHART 19.

Chicago Series: 1909-1914: 675 Cases Mentality Related to Outcome

The careers of individuals of exceptional mental capacity are of interest in connection with outcome, as always. Our earliest studies, before mental tests were as well developed as now, are hardly exact in total percentages for supernormal individuals. (See the chart of intelligence quotients ascertained in more recent years —I. Q. above 110 being generally considered as indicating supernormality.) But we have taken those who did demonstrate clearly on tests and in school work very exceptional ability and have tabulated their outcomes (Table 49). Among them there were twice as many (66%) Successes as Failures (33%). This is the highest percentage of Success found in any mental group— even though in and of itself it seems too low. Now, without detracting from the value which we believe inherent in supernormality as a basis upon which to try reformative measures, yet in fairness we must suggest that strong appeals were usually made for special individual aid for supernormal delinquents—and possibly this greater personal attention was a contributing factor in the better outcomes.

(c) Treatment of Mentally Abnormal Delinquents as Related to Outcomes

The many recent attempts to educate the public concerning the relationship of mental abnormality to delinquency and crime may have prepared the way for interest in any careful study of the conduct careers of a series of mentally abnormal juvenile delinquents. But in reasoning from figures and analogies there are various pitfalls against which we would warn the reader. Concerning, for example, our present study of outcomes: these are not figures for mental abnormality as related to delinquency and crime in general, but only as found in a local situation. Interpretation of the statistics can only be made for Chicago and for Illinois. What might have happened elsewhere, with a different social background and with different methods of care or treatment, cannot be inferred.

To any argument that mental abnormality and not environmental conditions is a predominating cause of crime, the only safe answer is a comparison of one city,

Chicago for instance, with other cities. For comparative purposes take London. Psychiatrists know of no statistics which even tend to indicate that there is less mental defect or mental disease there. Yet the vastly smaller amount of crime in London is a subject of constant comment by students of criminology. The murders in London as compared with Chicago are often quoted [2]—in 1920, 15 to 194, that is, 3 per million inhabitants as against 73. Similarly, great differences could be cited between other American communities and foreign cities, and Chicago itself varies from many other American cities in proportionate amount of crime. But there is not the least reason to suppose that Chicago leads other cities in the amount of mental abnormality among its inhabitants.

Indeed our graphic chart of treatment and outcomes in Chicago and Boston, Chapter VI, bears on this very point. We have shown earlier in the present chapter and in Table 47, that large series of juvenile delinquents in Chicago and Boston show surprisingly similar figures for mental abnormality—and yet there is a tremendous difference as regards the commission of later crime. If 420 juvenile repeated offenders in Chicago produced more than 14 homicides or murders and 39 professional criminals, and 400 repeated delinquents in the same years in Boston produced no homicides and only 2 professional criminals, is the difference likely to be due to mentality—or social treatment?

But we would not neglect abnormal mentality as a factor where it may be shown to exist—particularly in its bearing upon the necessity for adequate treatment of mentally abnormal delinquents. Especially is

[2] See, for example, Kirchwey's, Survey of the Cook County Jail, 1922.

there need to study outcomes as related to different types of treatment of different groups of the abnormal.

First, we may take our entire Chicago series of traced outcomes, 758 (Table 1), including those held in institutions. Of these, 283 were classified as mentally abnormal (Table 51). We found that only 38 (13%) of these were being held in appropriate institutions; 165 clearly abnormal either were never committed as such or did not remain in appropriate institutions. The additional 75 psychopathic were given no special treatment or social adjustment in accordance with their (or society's) needs.

Such facts as these are undoubtedly representative of what has been and is going on in most places with regard to the treatment of mentally abnormal juvenile delinquents. No better proof on this point can be found than the figures being given by many investigators, showing the large number of the mentally abnormal in our correctional institutions, figures arrived at by mental surveys of the inmates. The question, of course, is whether society gives proper therapy for the mentally abnormal individual in a correctional institution or properly protects itself by committing him there and allowing his release in ordinary fashion. (There is no gainsaying, however, that a highly developed parole and placing-out system can accomplish much with many who are not normal, whether it be by parole from a correctional school or an institution for the feebleminded. But to be successful this has to be a highly selective process, carefully carried out.)

Next, for the three main classes of the mentally abnormal we have undertaken to set forth two sets of facts for comparison, social treatment and outcomes

(Table 52). It is seen that of the 221 abnormal who have been adjudged Successes or Failures, only 32 were first sent to an appropriate institution, and only 8 were secondarily sent. We note that through poor institutional provisions for them, these 40 were not successfully held; many of them made escapes and have cost society a pretty penny. Only 4 are classified among our Successes. To correctional institutions were sent 133, or 60%, and of those 133 only 36, or 27%, were Successes.

Many other facts can be gleaned by the reader directly from Table 52, but this paltry 27% Success tells most of the story, with its implication of wasted effort and huge cost through placing a mentally abnormal child or adolescent under a régime which only too often does him no good (and perhaps much harm) and then allowing him to return to an environment that does not protect him from becoming a menace to society.

These findings concerning the treatment of mentally abnormal delinquents in relation to outcomes are worth much contemplation. When we remember that nearly all of these individuals after a term at a correctional institution or after escape or release from an institution for the abnormal returned to an unfavorable neighborhood or companionship situation, often an atmosphere surcharged with ideas of crime, can there be any doubt that it might have been foreseen that these mentally weak or unbalanced young people would be particularly likely to go farther in social misconduct? That even 71 of the whole 221 were Successes, according to our criterion of no further delinquency known, shows, however, that there is in this group some potentiality for reform. As is stated by those who are so successfully placing defectives from institutions and by those who observe children trained in special classes, the fact is that given simple and morally decent living conditions, many of the mentally abnormal will do well. Even here among our group of abnormals who are delinquents, environment, as judged by this follow-up work, has to a very considerable degree determined the outcome. The mentally abnormal properly cared for do not develop criminalistic ideas, and it happens that our follow-up proves that in some of them the earlier delinquent ideation and trends can cease to be a factor in their conduct.

Yet how much of a burden this group represents is suggested under the caption, "Adult Outcome," in Table 52. And perhaps we may say that, flounder as society does at present in attempts at moral reform and reconstruction of its delinquent members, at least for the mentally abnormal who early show delinquent trends, we know that definite social control is demanded. But there must be careful study in order to differentiate (a) those who probably need permanent custodial care, (b) those whose behavior tendencies may be greatly modified by training during prolonged enough segregation, (c) those who under control in good environmental conditions outside institutions may behave satisfactorily.

CHAPTER XVII

OFFENSES

(a) DELINQUENCIES IN 4000 CASES

THE figures for juvenile offenses among our four series should be of great interest because they represent, much more accurately than any court or institution records, the actual delinquent trends of large groups of young offenders. Our information has been gleaned from parents and the delinquents themselves, as well as from official records; and this means that a great deal is brought to light which is not officially charged in court.

But here, as with all statistics concerning delinquency or crime, there is great difficulty both in classifying and, after classifications are made, in interpreting the significance of misconduct which goes by the same name. There may be tremendous variations in seriousness, motivation, and other background features which are necessary foundations for sound judgment concerning the individual case. This complicates the situation in regard to figures for any group, and when, as in the present study, there is endeavor to compare one community with another the difficulties are magnified. Even the designation of offenses is not the same in the two cities where our studies have been undertaken.

Without a great deal of labor it would be difficult to

make many distinctions that might be worth much. If we could, we should like to separate out those instances where the delinquency seemed to show criminalistic ideation or intent, as distinguished, for instance, from the cases where the delinquency was much more in the nature of mischief or giving way to impulse or crowd suggestion. But since this is at present impracticable, we make our groupings according to ordinary classifications.

Our four series taken together give an adequate picture of the extent and kind of offenses in which the delinquent youth of two of our large American cities engage. Taken separately they are large enough to afford reliable figures showing the similarities and differences that may occur in urban communities.

We may preface comment on the statistics by the following general impression: We are thoroughly convinced, and we must again call attention to this point, that the delinquencies of Boston juvenile offenders are vastly milder in nature than those committed by juvenile delinquents in Chicago. This, however, is a matter that is most difficult to show in bare statistics that follow the usual classification of offenses. But some few of our data indicate clearly something of the true facts, notably our figures for burglary and for robbery with violence.

In an earlier section it was shown that the Chicago later careers were often extremely desperate, including the commission of many extremely serious crimes, almost none of which were found in any significant measure by tracing an analogous group of Boston juvenile delinquents. In the light of this it becomes a matter of great importance to note what, if any, differences exist between the offenses of juvenile delinquents of the two cities.

(In making our categories of offenses we have not included the more indefinite group of either the Chicago or Boston courts. In particular we have avoided the vague term "incorrigibility" as used in Chicago, and "waywardness" and "stubborn child" as used in Boston. Statistics of the total series are found in Table 54.)

Offenses Against Property.—It is clear that the most common offense committed by boys is *stealing*. Of course stealing includes some very petty offenses as well as some serious larcenies. Practically it is difficult, however, to fix a line of demarcation between stealing and larceny, and we have not attempted this except when, as shown in Tables 54 and 55, we have analyzed the nature of the offense and have made the classification along commonsense lines into petty and serious stealing and larceny. The finding that among juvenile male delinquents stealing in general is the offense of most frequent occurrence is in keeping with facts indicated in other studies dealing with this subject. It will be noted, too, that the percentages for stealing in Chicago and Boston vary only slightly, 68% and 70% respectively.

Burglary—major breaking and entering—often a most serious offense because indicating a trend toward professional criminalism, is much less frequent than stealing; the average for our four series has little meaning because the variation between the separate series is large. That it is as great as 17 per cent for one series of boys indicates that burglary may be found among juveniles in proportion large enough to warrant serious concern. This is one of the types of delinquency that characterizes offenses of boys in Chicago as opposed to Boston; in each of the two series it is found in much larger numbers in the former city, 8% and 17% versus 4% and 3.3%.

Automobile stealing has, of course, increased in recent years and figures gathered for the years our Chicago series cover have now little comparative value. Indeed, so rarely did such stealing occur then that no figures were kept. Our Boston data can only be compared with statistics given in the Chicago juvenile court reports which indicate that for the years 1918-1919 automobile stealing constituted 4.4% of the total offenses of boys; for 1920-1921, 9.6%, while our Boston comparable figures are for our series 2.6% and 2.4%.

Other forms of offenses against property occur among male juvenile offenders much less commonly and their significance depends both on the extent to which the individual is guilty and on the motivation of the act. Thus *picking pockets*, found in about 1.5% of the cases, may be undertaken with an attitude bespeaking professionalism or may be committed on impulse in the face of an obvious opportunity. *Forgery* (2%), though comparatively infrequent, is always serious because intent and planfulness are involved; whereas *arson*, averaging about 1%, though always dangerous, has not the usual motivation of adult fire-setting; it is practically always done either for excitement or in attempted reprisal. Differences between the two cities in regard to any of these offenses are slight.

Offenses Against the Person are infrequent in our group compared with some other delinquencies. However, the figures for our Chicago series give no fair picture of the extent to which the more desperate offenses of this character occur there. While it might be supposed that in studying repeated offenders we were likely to see the more serious cases, often we did not receive for study young fellows who committed *robbery* or "hold-ups," for reasons connected with the exigencies of police service and of detention and with holding over to the grand jury. Our proportion of such cases is no greater than is found in the Chicago juvenile court reports; our totals are small. The 1.5 per cent and 4 per cent, respectively, for our Chicago series represent 11 and 28 individuals; in the Chicago juvenile court there were more than 150 and 450 cases of robbery during approximately the same periods. In our Boston series there were no cases of robbery or "hold-ups." That the great difference in our series is not due to selection of cases for study is shown by totals from the court records. We may cite juvenile court statistics as follows: In Chicago during the five years, 1909-1913, an annual average of 31 cases of robbery appeared; in the Boston Juvenile Court an average of 2 cases appeared during the same period. Then during the next five years, 1914-1918, in Chicago the yearly average increased to 95, while in Boston for the same years the average remained only 2 or, in terms of percentage of all juvenile male offenders for five-year periods, we have the following:

1909-1913 { Chicago; 6301 boys; robbery 2.5%
          { Boston;   4741   "   "   0.2%

1914-1918 { Chicago; 11410 boys; robbery 4.1%
          { Boston;   4217   "   "   0.3%

We also note that during the period in which the Chicago situation in regard to robbery was getting worse (and after 1919 it became still worse) cases of robbery in the Boston Juvenile Court remained almost nil.

Assault and battery is a term that is so ill defined that we have no figures in our series that can be used safely for comparison. This in itself is a comment upon the difficulties of classification of offenses. In both Chicago and Boston the term is loosely used in court charges. If, however, we do care for comparisons, we may note that for the years 1909-1913, totaled, the percentages as charged in court for this offense were:

	Boys	Girls
Chicago	5.7	1.2
Boston	5.7	2.3

In Table 54 it is seen that under the general heading "Offenses Against the Person" the largest single figure is for *"fighting with weapons,"* 42 cases, in our first Chicago series. This is a very serious offense. Because of lack of enumeration we cannot give figures for the second Chicago series, and we cannot make comparison with the court statistics because there the offense is not separated from what is merely called assault. But there is a very surprising difference from our Boston series where we have it carefully enumerated and find altogether among 2000 cases only 4 boys guilty of this offense. If any one thinks this difference due to exhibition of national traits, our statistics for nationality should be consulted.

Other offenses against the person are so slight in number that figures in percentages are not worth recording. There were 3 instances of *homicide* at the time of study of the cases among the Chicago series and 1 instance in Boston. Attempted homicide is recorded against 1 boy each in Boston and Chicago.

Offenses of a sex nature, among boys, are rather infrequent, heterosexual interests beginning for the most part later than the juvenile court age, while abnormal sex misconduct, usually of a homosexual nature, varies in importance, the young participant being often passive though some already at an early age show marked homosexual trends. Immorality with the opposite sex is committed by about 4.5% of boys; homosexual affairs by about 4%. The increase of boys engaged in heterosexual affairs in the second Boston series is interestingly due to probation officers, after the ascertainment of facts, having made a special effort to bring in others involved in group situations in order to prevent further spread of the misconduct.

The extent to which sex offenses such as obscenity and exhibitionism are tolerated before complaint is made varies so with possible complainants—school people, neighbors, parents—that figures do not represent the real incidence of such offenses. So far as we have knowledge we find no significant difference between the two cities. Concerning actual *rape,* we may say that it occurs very rarely among our group, but the juvenile court statistics for five years, 1909-1913, show a very great difference between the two cities:

Chicago .... 31 cases (0.49% of the total delinquent boys)
Boston .... 1 case (0.02% of the total delinquent boys)

The succeeding years show in Chicago an increase to 51 cases in the five years, 1916-1921, but no cases at all in the Boston Juvenile Court.

Offenses Against Social Regulations cover a number of delinquencies varying widely in import. It is under this general classification that we find *truancy* and *running away from home* second in degree of frequency among all offenses, each being engaged in by about 40% of boys. Naturally the two offenses largely overlap, for nearly all boy runaways are truant during the time of absence from home.

Under truancy are counted only those cases in which school non-attendance has been more than slight and for unjustified reasons. Our figures represent truancy as we have learned of it in the study of our cases and do not tally with court statistics, partly because often we find truancy existing where unknown to the court, and partly because truancy is handled so differently in the two cities. A special study of this problem would be necessary to make comparisons that are fair and would need to take into account widely divergent facts. Thus Boston manages its truant problem very well without a parental or truant school, but truancy is a court charge on a par with any other offense. Chicago relies on its special institution for truants, but while juveniles are committed there by the court, truancy is considered a special problem and statistics are not recorded among the regular offenses given in the annual court reports. The large extent to which truancy obtains among boys of both our Chicago and Boston series gives food for thought concerning the school's frequent inability to interest and control a number of its charges. The causes of truancy vary greatly; they constitute a problem aspects and intricacies of which need special research.

Running away from home, according to our interpre-

tation, means more than merely staying away from home
overnight, although it may indicate being away a few
days in the home city or going great distances and remaining months. The specific causes that lie back of
it, of course, are varied; perhaps one might interpret
it most broadly, however, as expression of desire for
new experiences. We can offer no explanation of the
decrease found in the Boston second series.

Sleeping out at night, which indicates merely sleeping away outdoors or in places other than in a home,
is charged more frequently in Boston, the figures indicating 22% as against 12% in Chicago. *Vagrancy,* on the
other hand, is found in larger numbers in Chicago, as
one might expect, since that city is such a great railroad center. It probably occurs in larger proportion at
a somewhat later age.

Staying out late at night appears rarely as a court
charge. We have learned of it usually while obtaining
the histories of delinquents. We have no good figures
for comparison. That the percentages in the Boston
series show so large an amount, 19%, is possibly due
to the fact that so much more is made even by parents
in Boston of milder offenses and of preventive work
for children. Perhaps it is partly due to more careful
inquiry on our part in taking family histories. We consider being "out late nights" an important form of misconduct, especially betokening that treatment is needed
in the case, but the offense does not appear in the classification of either court. When charged it is called incorrigibility or waywardness.

One of the most serious offenses, *carrying concealed
weapons,* is not common until after juvenile court age.
Our figures indicate this; even the largest percentage,

2.5% for one series in Chicago, represents only 21 cases.

Excessive idleness, recorded as occurring in an average of 10% of the boys' cases, and *excessive lying,* found in about an equal number of cases, also represent facts incidentally obtained. Complaint is nearly always made by the family, and standards vary tremendously regarding what are considered offenses of these kinds. We include lying because it is a form of misconduct that has great significance for character development and in relation to other forms of delinquency.

The larger figures for *gambling* and *begging* in the Boston series, for the former offense 4% as against 2% in the Chicago group, for the latter 2.5% versus 1%, represent, perhaps, more a difference of policy in the two cities than differences in conduct among boys. In Boston arrests for very petty street begging are common and court action is invoked not only for "gaming" and "gaming on the Lord's Day" but also for "being present at gaming." We may also mention "selling without license," as a delinquency charged only in Boston, to demonstrate the fact that arrest of juveniles there is sometimes for offenses so mild in character that there is nothing analogous charged in the Chicago court.

Alcoholic intoxication is rare among juveniles, our total being 2.2% among boys, with somewhat larger figures in Chicago than in Boston. *Use of drugs,* in spite of considerable public impression to the contrary, is extremely rare during juvenile court age. We have seen only three or four cases in Chicago and two in Boston.

Delinquencies of girls as differing from male offenses are always of interest. *Immorality* of girls with the

opposite sex is a charge representing a larger percentage
of cases than any other offense except stealing by
males. We are sure that it would not be safe to draw
any conclusions concerning the somewhat larger figures,
60% and 73%, appearing in our Chicago series as compared with 52% and 55% in our Boston series. The
seriousness of the situation in either city is plain.

Stealing by girls shows the next largest figure. It
includes shoplifting. Perhaps because in Boston a
definite campaign against shoplifting has for long been
undertaken, girls being brought into the juvenile court
for this offense to a much greater extent than they were
in Chicago, the figures for Boston are larger, about 40%
as against 30% of girls' cases in Chicago.

Running away from home, appearing as a delinquency
in some series more frequently than among boys, is commonly connected with girls' sex delinquencies. *Out late
at night* is naturally more frequently reported or
charged as a delinquency of girls than of boys, and often
is incidental to sex charges.

Excessive lying is an offense more frequently complained of among girls and perhaps this may be explained by its relationship to sex offenses and because
of the natural desire for self-protection in these matters.
At least the possibility of such an explanation indicates
that our figures of themselves offer no proof or suggestion that lying is an offense or characteristic that in
general differentiates the sexes.

False accusation, a very important delinquency when
it occurs, and one which we have observed in most
extravagant forms when it sometimes creates a vast
amount of trouble, is rarely charged in the court complaint as such. Those guilty of it usually appear in

court on some other charge, oftenest of a sex nature, hence it is more common among girls than boys. We have seen no instances of it among boys in Boston and very few in Chicago. Among our series of Chicago girls the 5% and 9% in the two series represent a total of 42 instances. In Boston we have enumeration of one series only, 2.8%, 9 cases.

For all other offenses, the percentage among girls is small. *Forgery* and *arson* are about as common as among boys. *Attempted suicide* was somewhat more frequent than among boys, there being 2% averages in the four series, with a somewhat greater proportion in Chicago than Boston. *Truancy* is much less frequent among girls, 8% contrasting markedly with 40% among boys. *Begging* by girls is very rare.

Alcoholic intoxication occurs in the Chicago series for girls as frequently as for boys, while we have no cases recorded among girls in Boston. This same contrast is shown in court figures for the two cities, the juvenile court reports for five years, 1909-1913, show for Chicago a total of 47 boys, 11 girls, and for Boston 36 boys, 2 girls. Somewhat different are figures for Chicago 1916-1921 with a total of 12 boys and 23 girls.

The more violent types of offenses among boys, such as burglary, robbery, carrying weapons, naturally are not found among girls; we have seen no accomplices in "hold-ups." There was one attempted homicide among the Chicago girls.

(b) Delinquencies as Related to Outcomes

Turning now to the group of Chicago followed-up cases, it would be of great value to determine, if possible, any differentiation of Successes and Failures on the basis of offenses committed. It might be thought likely that outcome depends in some measure on the type, as well as extent, of offense engaged in by the young delinquent; that commission of certain delinquencies indicated irremediable traits, or proved the individual vicious, hardened, or insensitive to fundamental requisites of social life. Can any such theory be substantiated by correlating the delinquencies with later Successes or Failures?

One great difficulty in drawing conclusions lies in the fact that at the time of the study of the case a large majority of the young delinquents had already committed more than one offense. As indicated in Table 56, there were only 111 boys out of the 420 whose delinquencies though repeated were confined to one kind of offense, and except for larceny, 43 cases with 70% Failures, there are too few cases of any one kind of delinquency to give proportions of Success and Failure any great significance.

From Table 55, with data relating to large numbers, we find it well nigh impossible to draw conclusions, especially for the Failures, for if these individuals are guilty of more than one offense, one can hardly dwell on the significance or outcome of any single type of offense. Still, suggestions of salient facts are to be obtained from scanning this table; for example, even with comparatively small numbers, the 82% of Failure for homosexual cases appears tremendous and decidedly significant. Perhaps a somewhat more definite statement is permissible for the Successes, since they always prove the possibility of a favorable outcome in spite of the various offenses in which they have been engaged, and sometimes despite indulgence in some form

of delinquency which may supposedly be extremely unfavorable to a good outcome. Thus we may say that
3 out of the 5 boys who forged succeeded, irrespective of what other delinquencies were engaged in, and
so forgery, although a delinquency and crime that easily
invites repetition, does not in and of itself indicate irrevocably delinquent trends.

The most important fact revealed by Table 55 is the
small percentage of Success outcome for any special
category of delinquencies committed by the boys.
Roughly, for offenses committed most frequently, that
is, stealing, truancy, running away, only about one-third
were Successes in Chicago. For other delinquencies committed often enough to make percentages have meaning, the figures, with the exception of homosexual
offenses, are very similar. Thus, just about the above
ratio of Success obtains for burglary. None show Success outcome in more than 50% of the cases.

From such facts we may conclude that the outcome
rarely has any relation to the type of offense committed,
but rather is dependent upon some other factor or factors. It should carefully be noted that there is no type
of offense in which some one did not succeed; hence none
absolutely precludes possibility of Success.

Whether the greater severity of the offenses in Chicago, even though the offenses come under the same
classification groupings, has anything to do with the relatively unfavorable outcome would be a problem for a
special study.

Among the girls there is a showing of 50% Success
both for sex offenders and for those guilty of stealing.
Only a small number of cases are found under other
categories and we cannot therefore draw valid generaliza-

tions concerning them, though certain data are interesting as, for example, 5 of 8 girl false accusers appear among the Successes.

It must be remembered that this particular study of cases over a long period pertains only to Chicago delinquents. While we have no other such carefully studied and followed-up series for comparison, we know that the general outcomes, as sketched elsewhere in this book, of an analogous series of delinquents in Boston appear much better and consequently that engaging in the same types of offenses, as they may be grouped according to ordinary classifications elsewhere, does not necessarily mean that the outcomes of cases are similar.

CHAPTER XVIII

CONDITIONS DIRECTLY CAUSATIVE OF DELINQUENCY

THE only possible way to know the immediate and essential causes of delinquency is to study intensively the nature and conditions of offenders individually. There is a great variation from individual to individual, not only in regard to separate causations but also in the combination of causes from case to case. In order to give some picture of the various probable causes which over and beyond the background features of physical and mental and environmental conditions already given may conspire to produce delinquency, we have enumerated them, Tables 57 and 58, as they appear in our summary analysis of each case.

Bad Companions.—A large share of all delinquency among juveniles is a companionship affair. Realizing that frequently the companions were not worse and perhaps even not so much to blame as the offender we have studied, yet we may safely conclude that in many cases if it had not been for the companionship the offense would not have been committed. It is important in planning effective preventive work with delinquents to know that in 62% of 3000 cases companionship could fairly be regarded as a causative factor in the delinquency, a figure that varies little for the sexes and is practically the same for the two cities.

Adolescent Instability and Impulses.—Nobody who studies juvenile delinquents with emphasis on the genesis of their misbehavior can doubt that adolescence frequently plays a very considerable part. Among 3000 cases we decided that the instabilities and impulses of adolescence were directly causative in 18%, being more active in the cases of girls, where this cause figured as 25%.

Early Sex Experiences.—Unfortunate early improper sex experiences, encountered in very many instances before 10 years of age, are important factors, we find, in development of delinquent trends. The delinquencies produced may not be sex affairs at all—misconduct tendencies in other directions may be largely the result of the experience. In the total 4000 cases we came to learn of such unfortunate experiences as dynamic forces in a total of 12.5% among girls, in 18%.

Mental Conflicts.—Those who would know criminalistic beginnings, even of some of the most marked careers reaching far into adult life, should be acquainted with the phenomena of mental conflict. There are forces and urges in the inner mental life, sometimes called mental mechanisms, which, unsatisfactorily functioning and at cross-purposes, lead to the development of most definite and deep-set delinquent tendencies. We were able to discover such conflicts in 6.5% of 4000 cases, and it is likely that probably many a conflict was undiscovered. It seems very curious that the percentages have remained closely similar for all the four series. The existence of mental conflict to this extent is one of the findings that demonstrates the absolute necessity for special studies being made of the dynamic mental life of delinquents if prevention of further delinquency is to be accomplished.

Extreme Social Suggestibility.—This is a personality

characteristic that must be known and reckoned with
in the treatment of delinquents. It was found as a really
well-marked characteristic in 4% of our cases.

Love of Adventure.—The disposition that craves adventure may find outlets in delinquency, sometimes in
misconduct of a severe sort. Enumerating cases where
there was an inordinate love of adventure and excitement which very evidently led to the delinquency in
question, we found about 2.5%—the boys, naturally,
showing this type of causation much more frequently
than the girls.

Motion Pictures.—It has been our regular practice to
make inquiry concerning the indulgence in and effect
of such amusements as moving pictures. Starting with
ideas somewhat to the contrary, we have been surprised
to find that moving picture shows seem to have very
little effect in the production of delinquent tendencies;
we could discover no reason to attribute more than 1%
of the cases to this cause.

Other Direct Causations. Studying our Boston series
of 2000 cases at a period after we had gained experience
by much discussion and analysis of possible causations,
we made closer scientific inquiry into causes for our main
purpose of trying to steer the individual offender toward better living. Enumeration of what we then dis-
covered discloses the following: *School dissatisfaction*
appears as a major cause in 9%, the girls, however,
showing only 2%. *Poor recreations,* meaning by this a
conglomerate of all sorts of poor amusements, such as
clubs with bad practices, frequenting low resorts, and
dances of a bad sort, cheap movies in excess, were found
in 20% of the cases. *Street life* in excess appeared as
a very bad feature in the life of boys in 15%, for girls

in 2% of the total. *Vocational dissatisfaction* as a cause was disclosed in about 3%. Formation of a *habit of delinquency* appeared in 6%. Recently we have ourselves been more alive to the meaning of this last cause and to certain other features of the offender's mental life as productive of delinquency: in our last series we enumerated *sudden impulse,* particularly in cases of shoplifting, in 7%; recurrent or obsessive *ideation or mental imagery* in 6%.

Considering *physical conditions* of all sorts as apparent actual and direct causes of delinquency (though, of course, never the sole cause) we counted 5.6% of 2000 cases, and *premature puberty* in 3%.

It is out of the wealth of such findings as these that suggestions must most validly come concerning how to check effectively a beginning career of delinquency.

CHAPTER XIX

ANALYSIS OF GENERAL BACKGROUND

WHAT can be the reasons for the great differences which are found, comparing Chicago and Boston, in the seriousness of juvenile delinquency and in the after-careers of youthful offenders? This is a question which we have time and again put to ourselves.[1]

Especially do we feel impelled to discuss any forces which probably make the one city so unlike the other in matters affecting delinquency because we have found nothing satisfactorily to account for the dissimilarities in studies of the human material itself, whether viewed from the standpoint of national or racial population groups or of the mental and physical types of the offenders. With nothing sufficiently explanatory, then, in the nature of the individuals involved, it is clear that there must be dissimilar conditioning factors in the environment or in the treatment given.

There are many phases of civic life and achievement in either or both cities which do not appear to be directly relevant to the quest for explanations, although far be it from us to proclaim our ability to evaluate the significance of all features of civic life, even as they bear upon our problem. We must content ourselves by trying to set forth, side by side, certain items which

[1] In the following analysis and comparisons, as well as elsewhere, we deal with conditions and situations only as they relate to the Boston Juvenile Court itself (the central court). We are fully aware that the same facts do not obtain in all juvenile court jurisdictions of Greater Boston and vicinity.

seem to us possibly and probably causative of the differences of which we have spoken. But we do not commit ourselves in the least to the statement of any opinion in regard to the degree to which any one feature is responsible.

It will require on the part of the reader boldness not at all countenanced by critical thinking to pick out of our array of facts any one or two items as having more importance than all else. It is undoubtedly much safer in such a complex problem to consider a number of elements as interactively responsible, realizing, however, that there are outstanding signs of some influences being major.

In offering the following data we have tried to make comparisons of the conditions which existed when the cases were studied, although in most respects the changes since that time in both cities have been slight.

Logically we could begin analysis almost anywhere, but our point of departure may well be the juvenile court, because of its official relation to delinquency. We realize full well, however, that there are many public influences of importance affecting the child long before it reaches the court and that there are agencies for prevention and treatment of delinquency at an earlier stage, including not only the school, the church, welfare agencies of all kinds, but even the police.

THE JUVENILE COURT

Chicago	Boston
1. Court serves Cook County, a large area.	Court serves a small and mainly a congested area, though some offenders come from outlying districts. Overlapping of probationary work with that of courts in other districts.

(*Chicago*)

(*Boston*)

2. Judge selected yearly by the Circuit Court bench from among its members (but see comments below in text). Election term six years.

Judge with permanent appointment by Governor.

3. Hearings in public room, except girls' cases.

In conformity with statute, hearings with only directly interested persons present.

4. Court administers cases of delinquent, dependent and neglected children, mothers' pensions, truants for commitment, and feeble-minded for commitment. Yearly average (1912-1917): delinquents, 2442; dependents, 2333.

Court administers cases only of delinquent and neglected. Yearly average (1912-1917): delinquents 865, neglected 135 (figures for the central court only).

5. Delay from filing of complaint to court hearing ordinarily 7 days, often longer.

First hearings quickly follow complaint or arrest, same day or next.

6. Probation officers about 125 —of these about 30 police probation officers.

Probation officers 4.

7. Very little utilization of child welfare agencies for supervising or placing.

Much utilization of child welfare agencies for placing and supervision.

8. Department of complaints, including neglect cases—Assistant State's Attorney for this service.

Complaints of neglect, etc., very largely handled by Massachusetts Society for the Prevention of Cruelty to Children.

9. No appeals from decision of court.

Delinquent and family informed at hearing, according to statute, of right of appeal.

The above items are by no means arranged in order of importance, which itself would be hard to determine.

Concerning (2), we are not aware that the difference in the manner of the judges' acquiring office is of any significance, because in Chicago there has been an admirable retention of good judges. But we know what might, and in fact does, occur in communities where judges have to consider politics.

Point (4) we feel to be extremely important in its possible relevancy to the treatment of delinquency. The judge in Chicago, even though he has a woman assistant, now herself an elected judge, who hears the cases of delinquent girls, carries a vast burden that makes it impossible for him to give to cases anything like the amount of time that is given in Boston. A crowded court calendar necessitates hearing and disposing of even very serious cases with comparative rapidity.

It is less easy to interpret the facts under (6) because the system in Chicago is so complex, some probation officers there being assigned to duties other than probation work with delinquents. It might be felt that the number of delinquents assigned to probation officers would be the significant story, but this seems doubtful because of varying conditionings of their work, one example being the tremendously different distances to be covered in one city as compared to the other. We would refer the reader to the studies of the Federal Children's Bureau, particularly to the monograph 141, *Juvenile Courts at Work*, for some comparisons of the work. Probation in Boston can only be understood by keeping in mind the supplementing of its work as mentioned under Point (7). Some details are given later in this chapter under the heading Child Placing Agencies.

DETENTION

Chicago	Boston
1. Detention Home with capacity for 125 or more, and much used.	No detention home. Exceptional cases held in special private homes; nearly all cases taken directly to own homes; occasionally older boys held in jail.
2. Yearly average of delinquents detained was 2,780 (1911-16), *con-*	Yearly average less than 100 delinquents detained; one in every

(*Chicago*)	(*Boston*)
siderably more than are heard in court; daily average 66. Days of detention a year, 21,218.	3 days. Days of detention a year, 100.
3. Average of boys' stay, 7 days; girls', 11 days.	Average detention of the few cases, one night.

The rôle that the detention home plays in relation to creating a tendency to delinquency is undoubtedly very important. The real dangers inherent in the situation are (a) the unavoidable hazard of moral contamination, (b) the great likelihood of developing unfavorable attitudes toward the law, the court and society in general. These influences are almost inevitable, even under management as excellent as that which obtained in the Chicago Detention Home. Indeed we may quote from an annual report the words of a most efficient superintendent, ". . . whether it is a lad of ten held for truancy, or a boy of sixteen held for burglary or forgery, they are all housed together. . . ." Speaking of girls she says, ". . . they never leave the Home without a thorough schooling in every particular pertaining to immorality. . . . It is impossible to keep the children from talking to each other." Standards of delinquency are established among those detained. The petty offender is almost ashamed of his lack of prowess; the desperate delinquent sets the pattern.

In Boston only one delinquent is held at a time in a family.

One wonders if the difference in methods concerning detention is not a fundamental feature in the whole delinquency situation in the two cities. There is much more that could be said to this point. We have in our case records many evidences of moral harm received by children in the Chicago Detention Home.

POLICE

Chicago	Boston
1. Under control of city government and in close touch with politics.	Not under city government. Commissioner given long term appointment by governor.
2. Police detailed as probation officers to juvenile court.	Police immediately, even at night, turn over practically all cases to regular probation officer.
3. Police not only receive complaints but adjudicate many thousands of cases yearly.	Police adjustment of cases obtains to only a slight extent.

It is just such intangible assets as intelligent attitudes on the part of the police that may very particularly influence young people for the good, and such attitudes, very evidently, are more to be expected under good leadership and freedom from hampering political influences.

We have known (3) of police officers themselves holding minor juvenile courts in Chicago. Earlier there was no regular enumeration of this in the court reports, but in 1919 we note that the police were settling yearly 15,000 or more juvenile cases out of court. For discussion of this matter the reader should consult the Federal Children's Bureau report No. 104.

This police work gives indication of how minor offenses similar to those that come into court in Boston are dealt with in Chicago. In the Boston practice of bringing minor cases to court and dealing with them through methods of social investigation and court hearing, we see possible partial explanation of the apparent greater effectiveness in the prevention of delinquent trends and careers.

INSTITUTIONS

Chicago	*Boston*
1. Many institutions for orphans, dependents, and semi-delinquent children.	Few such institutions. Most work for such children done through placing in private families. State Department of Public Welfare alone has under placement 6000 children.
2. Juvenile correctional institutions extensively used by the Chicago Court for commitment. (See Chapter VI.)	Proportionately very few commitments to the industrial schools from Boston Juvenile Court.
Very little classification in the institutions.	Separate industrial schools for delinquent boys under and over 15. Youngest boys of the junior institution are on farm colony some miles away from the others.
A parental school to which many truants are committed.	No parental school.

PAROLE

Chicago	*Boston*
1. Slight amount of good parole work from state institutions—almost none for boys, very little for girls. Comparatively little placing.	Excellent staff of parole visitors doing very active and effective work under trustees of state schools. The large majority of girls and many boys are placed out in carefully investigated homes. Their own homes are also investigated for fitness for child's return. *All those committed are legally under control of the trustees until 21 years of age.*

CHILD PLACING AGENCIES

Chicago	*Boston*
Five agencies, institutional, court, and private, through which delinquent children may be placed. No state or city department for this.	Sixteen agencies, institutional, court, and private, also large state department and city bureau through which children may be placed.

The above statement tells but a small fraction of the story. The long-established policy of placing children in good foster families, the number of agencies doing this work over a long period, the good support of the same, the developed expertness in investigation and care are most noteworthy in Boston. This explains why the Boston Juvenile Court is able to function so well with only four probation officers. We cannot here state all the advantages accruing to the children through the staff conferences, formulation of constructive plans, expenditure of considerable sums, and the persistence with which difficult problems are followed up by child placing agencies. Since even very difficult cases are taken for placement, this means that much thought and highly individualized treatment is given them.

Spirit of the Community

We have long been thoroughly persuaded that one of the most important phases of the situation with regard to delinquency anywhere is the spirit of the community, difficult as this may be to define. This spirit is itself evolved from many forces in the life and the cultural history of the community.

It is certainly neither a matter of wealth nor of civic pride in material things, even of the better sort, for of the two cities under discussion, Chicago in these respects outdoes Boston. Nor can we conceive that it is altogether a matter of age of the community, because no one can doubt that, given a strong impulse, a most distinguished service for the prevention of delinquency and crime could be accomplished in a very few years. Social welfare activities depend less upon wealth, material civic pride or age of the community than upon mental attitudes and interests, the sense of values, and a vision which sees what is possible and practicable and what is right to do.

The moral spirit of a community is easily reflected in the conduct of its children. Where such general spirit is poor there is very ready imitation of the predatory tendencies of public officials and of other adults who are allowed to persist in evil doing. The knowledge of graft in connection with a city hall, of laxity or venality in a public prosecutor's office, of loose administration of justice in a court (and one of the shrewdest policemen we have ever known has assured us the last point is of vast importance) are all influences that determine trends toward delinquency and crime. One may note this directly exhibited in individual and group lawlessness, and even in youthful self-justification in misdoing. Where community spirit in such matters is better, certainly delinquencies are commensurately milder.

Then the good spirit of a community directly concerning child welfare is inevitably proportionate to the feeling of responsibility on the part of adults. This expresses itself by personal service in preventive and remedial agencies or in the support of such agencies and in the creation of favorable public opinion toward all good efforts in behalf of childhood and youth.

Believing that appreciation of what is necessary to the betterment of conditions might be furthered through appraisal of pertinent features of the background of life in the two cities as it bears on the production or prevention of delinquency, we have asked two well known leaders and students of civic activities in these cities to contribute respectively their ideas. Each of these men has long resided in the city of which he makes some appraisal, but has had experience elsewhere to give basis for comparative judgment. Each has had intimate acquaintance with the stronger forces, personalities and institutions which have been making for the public weal. We are indebted to them for their conceptions set forth below, minor changes in wording and arrangement being chargeable to us as the authors.

Mr. Joel D. Hunter, Director of the Associated Charities of Chicago, writes:

In attempting to account for any set of social facts in Chicago the youthfulness of the community and its marvelously rapid growth must be kept in mind.

Chicago was incorporated as a city in 1833. Less than one hundred years of age, it is the second largest city in the United States. In the span of one lifetime it has become one of the greatest industrial centers of the world. Rapidity of growth in every line is a striking fact in the history of the great mid-western metropolis and of the state of fertile areas and mineral wealth, a corner of which Chicago occupies. Naturally with this have come economic, transportation, health and all other problems as complex and as difficult of solution as in any other urban center.

Chicago and Illinois did not just grow. There came men with ability for leadership who had heard of wonderful opportunities for development in the middle west. They were satisfied, "hung up their hats," and stayed. Tens of thousands who were not leaders followed from the four quarters of the globe. They came so fast, with so many different racial and cultural backgrounds that Chicago became and still is a city of people whose beginnings are elsewhere than in the middle west and who have not been long enough away from their original homes to have established common interests with their neighbors. Chicago's population is so mixed that it has no native group in the sense that older communities have, no group with generations of traditions that form a steadying background from which different phases of civic life develop.

In the field of social work in Chicago and Illinois there are at least three outstanding facts in the asset column. The main one certainly has been a group of leaders, several of them great names in the history of general social welfare quite beyond the limits of Illinois, all of them brave, fine spirits working amid difficulties, their eyes always toward the great possibilities of the future. The second fact is that from their influence came the early recognition of social needs and the resulting and logical creation of public and private organizations to meet the needs. This is shown in the early growth of the settlement movement in Chicago, the passage of progressive laws and the training of professional social workers.

In particular there have been, among the special forces for good in the field under discussion, Hull House, the Chicago Woman's Club, Cook County Juvenile Court (the first juvenile court in the world), the Juvenile Psychopathic Institute, the Juvenile Protective Association, the United Charities, the School of Civics and Philanthropy, the extended development of the playground system and the first Mothers' Pension Law.

The third asset is the lack of tradition. Not feeling bound by what has gone before, Chicago has been early conscious of mistaken effort in the social field and has sought for measures and means by which to improve. There has been among social workers a sound willingness and desire to learn from the successes and mistakes of other communities.

On the liability side there is the fact that development of social welfare resources has not been as rapid as growth of the city's needs. Often the words of the prophets of Illinois have fallen upon deaf ears in their home state. As this book concerns itself with children, a general statement of liabilities in children's work should be given. Efforts in behalf of children have not been commensurate with the seriousness of their problems.

Some of the weaknesses of work for children have been:

(1) There is no public body in Illinois which takes guardianship of children and places them in families. The Cook County Juvenile Court is an exception, but the number placed by the court is so small that it is almost negligible. Children who must be removed from their own homes are largely placed in private institutions, many of which are built on the congregate plan. There was no law in Illinois providing any public money for the care of children in private families until 1923, the year that marks the beginning of this much needed policy.

(2) The State of Illinois has not taken as much responsibility in efforts related to social welfare or in actual social welfare work as have some other states. The theory of the relationship of the state government to local government has been different. There is no centralized authority such as has functioned well elsewhere. In the different counties of Illinois the standards vary widely and will vary until there is more central control.

(3) There has been frequent political interference in practically every State, County and City Department that has to do with social welfare. (It should be stated that the Juvenile Court of Cook County and the Institute of Juvenile Research are notable instances of public depart-

ments that have been strong enough to withstand political influence.) How much worse this is in one state than in another is not clear, but because of its existence in Illinois there has been a lack of desire among some social workers to develop public activities in the child welfare field. There has not been a united demand for the establishment of the functions named under (1) and (2). However, now the Council of Social Agencies is bringing about much better feeling and closer co-operation between public and private agencies.

(4) There has been rapid growth and strong adherence to the policy of child care in private institutions. This was largely because public subsidies were available under laws passed in 1879 and 1883. Appropriations have been regularly made under those laws. Cook County in 1923 appropriated $280,000 for the care of children in private institutions, as against $30,000, its first appropriation for their care in families. Because of the money invested in institutions, because of the established habit of institutional care for children, and because of the laws of the state, it will be difficult to change the practice of caring for normal dependent children in private institutions. The record of many of these is of course splendid, but it is agreed that institutional life should not be the only way provided.

(5) The private child-placing organizations have not been adequately financed, and hence could accept for placement relatively few children other than those who were received for adoption or permanent placement. They have not met the community need for temporary family care undertaken in connection with scientific and intensive treatment. More opportunities for such placement of children is one of the greatest needs in Chicago and Illinois at present.

Mr. J. Prentice Murphy, Director of the Children's Bureau of Philadelphia, former Executive Secretary of the Boston Children's Aid Society, states his views thus:

Any attempt to understand the background of social work in Boston and Massachusetts calls for review of many factors which at first glance seem to have no bearing on the situation whatsoever.

There is a peculiar grouping of welfare traditions about New England communities—traditions that go back to the social concepts of the early settlers—and while materialistic things in their lives came to the fore day after day, there was a hard-mouthed idealism that, it would seem, gave a bent or attitude which has had an increasing effect on the way succeeding generations have approached and handled their social welfare problems.

Far-sighted planning, really big thinking, has characterized New England in almost every field of thought and walk of life, and this is true of her social work. There has been for the last seventy-five years much more reason and less emotion in Boston and Massachusetts social welfare work than can be said for any other city or state. The welfare traditions of the city and of the state are rich in names and achievements of the utmost importance. There is little reason for questioning that for its size no other city in the country can be compared with Boston for the amount of its contributions, bequests and legacies to private welfare work and that no city or state has expended in relation to population greater sums for public welfare work. This is so much the case that outside states frequently cite Massachusetts public expenditures as being too generous. Moreover, work taken up is considered a serious matter and is pursued year after year, and this tends to security and standards.

The social and cultural life of Boston have been enriched by rare groups and rare liberalizing movements. The Abolitionist group certainly because of its New England leaders had a profound effect on the whole field of social welfare as New England viewed it. When the Civil War was over, this same group plus the leaders of New England youths who had been in the war turned toward many local and neglected welfare needs. Many of the fundamental steps looking to the care and protection of children in Massachusetts were instituted during the period 1860-1870.

There was a response to all this from many church groups. The church leaders in the community took an active part in all welfare work and especially in child welfare.

Then, one of the peculiar and valuable possessions of Massachusetts has been the type of lay people who became interested in social work. They had leisure, they were educated and cultured, and they acquired such an understanding of the methods of social work as to be fully able to counsel with any group of leaders, some of them being in positions of great influence so that they could assist largely in giving form and structure to the plans agreed upon. There are many who might be cited as having clear understanding of what must be done for the welfare and guidance of children.

The effect of Harvard College in the earlier days on the social work backgrounds of Massachusetts can hardly be fully stated. President Eliot in particular took an active interest in broad social welfare measures, whether in public education or health work or in work for children.

The Boston School of Social Work as a more recent agent has more directly affected its home community than can be said of any other professional school of social work. For almost two decades the School has been sending out into the community splendid people who put into practice the best principles of social work. The School has enough graduates in agencies in the city and state to be said to have really given a caste to the whole situation.

Coming to governmental aspects, we may say that there has been almost a uniformly high type of governor, many of them socially minded. The public welfare service, while not continuously good, has averaged so, particularly since 1900. Civil Service has been conducted well, so that good people have entered public departments and have been protected. The social welfare workers in state service compare well with private groups. In the matter of social planning and statesmanship it has certainly been an advantage that the capitol has been in Boston. The more alert and trained groups were here and they have because of their proximity kept in closer and more effective touch with state officers and work. In the children's field the state public agencies have developed so extensively that it has been possible for the best private agencies to do a more detailed and thorough piece of work with the fewer cases.

The Division of Child Guardianship of the State Department of Welfare is unique among all similar bodies in the United States. The quality of its work is such as to definitely influence the conditions that make for delinquency. The State Department of Welfare had as its first secretary, Frank L. Sanborn, beginning in 1863, who wrote into his first five reports the death knell of almshouse care of children in this country, the first clear statement of the possibilities of family care for dependent and neglected children and a prison and reform school plan. The different steps can easily be traced from the placing of children in state almshouses in the earlier part of the nineteenth century to the big development of placing children directly in families under state care, which began about 1880.

The Boston city government has not been on as high a plane as the State Government. But appointments by the governors to certain positions in Boston have been high. The quality of social work, as done by the City of Boston, has not equalled in the past that of the State (the exception possibly being the Overseers of the Poor), yet it has not been venal or corrupt and it has been superior to similar work elsewhere. The Trustees for Children of Boston were of course subject to inspection by the State Department of Welfare, and this acted as a check and kept out abuses.

There is in Massachusetts in general a tradition of law enforcement which has had a vital effect on the life of the community. In Metropolitan Boston for at least twenty years there has been almost no charge of police corruption; police commissioners, generally of a splendid type, appointed by the governor, have been in charge. The attitude of the Boston police now and before the police strike has, on the whole, been distinctly one of respect for law enforcement. The public itself is very considerably sensitive about early delinquency and neglect.

Concerning the courts: The judges throughout the state are appointed, not elected, and this has made for better membership of the bench. The juvenile court does not deal with dependents as such. While there is a sensitiveness to early delinquencies, and serious consideration is given by officials to such, there is no wholesale loading of all sorts of child problems on the courts. There is what might be called a proper use of the court.

Judging by conditions elsewhere, Boston has benefited from having a non-centralized court system. The Boston Juvenile Court, while handling a considerable volume of work, has been able to dispose of it in accordance with reasonably good standards. This would not have been the case if, right at the beginning and with no adequate staff, all juvenile cases in Boston had gone through its hands. The non-centralized court has aided in keeping the city from building a central detention home.

With regard to the detention of delinquents there has been offered to the courts in Boston by the Children's Aid Society a special type of family detention care that, so far as the Boston Juvenile Court is concerned, is quite satisfactory. The Society meets the cost of operation and of finding homes; the court that of board.

The probation service of Massachusetts is much above the service of most other states. It has several features that are of great value. There is a State Commissioner of Probation, and the officers are protected by good Civil Service laws. The central registry of offenders maintained by the office of the State Commissioner tends to make the work much better coördinated and intelligent.

Massachusetts has an admirable system of industrial schools and a parole department which has reached a very high standard indeed. The close supervision of the industrial schools by a special board of trustees who also have full authority in matters of parole is a very important part of the plan and one that is really conducive to the welfare of the child.

It has been of enormous significance in relation to delinquency that for years a large public in Massachusetts has been educated to the importance of feeblemindedness, and, more latterly, of psychopathic conditions. This has been accomplished by the devotion of such men as the late Dr. Walter E. Fernald. A whole generation of social workers, judges, legislators and other public officials has come under his influence.

The quality of social work in the community has been excellent. The

Associated Charities (Family Welfare) heads have done much to expound good case work. The Confidential Exchange, established in 1876 and the teaching of people to use it have been a tremendous help. The training of volunteers by the Associated Charities and the acceptance of the idea by others permeated the community with informed people. The Children's Aid Society of Boston, through its directors and staff, made a contribution to the understanding and care and protection of children that has had a national effect. The most advanced Society for the Prevention of Cruelty to Children is a big force in the community.

These agencies in many instances have practised limitation of intake in order to keep the quality of their work high. They have tended over a long period to the making of fewer distinctions between dependent and delinquent children. They realized that all children present some problems. They early saw the evils attending much institutional work and the possibilities of good foster family work. Cases when accepted have not been surrendered lightly or tossed about. The private agencies have been pace makers, assisting the public groups in the improvement of their work. The result of good agency standards has been long tenure of workers, and this in turn has maintained the agency standard.

Of course these analyses are not complete, as the writers thereof would readily acknowledge. Were we to add anything it would be some statement concerning the work of the settlements which in both cities has much direct bearing upon the prevention and treatment of delinquency. Perhaps the chief difference is in the greater number of settlements in the smaller area covered by Boston. This means that with the close contact which these settlements have with families and neighborhood problems, there is in Boston a proportionately much greater covering of the field and consequent earlier awareness of signs of trouble.

PART IV
CONCLUSIONS

CHAPTER XX

THE long array of data gathered in this book offers convincing evidence that the treatment of juvenile delinquency by some prevailing methods is followed by an amount and extremity of failure that is appalling.

Tracing the lives of several hundred youthful repeated offenders studied long ago by us and treated by ordinary so-called correctional methods reveals much repetition of offense. This is represented by the astonishing figures of 61% Failure for males (15% being professional criminals and 5% having committed homicide), and 46% Failure for girls (19% being prostitutes). The whole group of 675 shows 55% Failure. Thus in over one-half the cases in this particular series juvenile delinquency has continued into careers of vice and crime.

A corollary to the above is readily deducible. The opinion offered by various observers that adult criminality in a very large proportion of cases has its springs in juvenile delinquency finds ample support in our figures. There is no reason to suppose that the picture the above facts present is not a fair sample of what frequently happens in the development of delinquency into crime. Our data show clearly the early life period at which a very considerable number of careers of crime begin.

201

Continuing as offenders there appeared in adult courts no less than 209 of 420 boys whom we knew when they appeared in the Chicago juvenile court. And of these, 157 had charged against them offenses so severe that they received commitment 272 times to adult correctional institutions, a considerable number for long terms. Taking criminal statistics by and large this is an immense proportion to be coming from any series of consecutive cases studied merely because they were repeated offenders in a juvenile court. It represents a most disconcerting measure of failure.

But the data of other series show the possibility of Failure being much less extensive and less severe. In terms of adult court appearances a comparable group of males in Boston resulted in 21% Failure, in contrast to 50% in Chicago, and there was no case of homicide and only one known professional criminal.

Another index of severity, commitment to adult correctional institutions, shows for this same group less than one-sixth the Chicago commitments and no very long terms and no penitentiary sentences.

A second Boston series, of the post-war period when delinquency throughout the country was more prevalent and sentiment in Boston was stronger for commitment, show, as compared to the Chicago series, considerably less than half the number appearing in adult courts and less than a third committed—only one of these, having committed homicide, was sent to a penitentiary.

Contrary to traditional expectations, more of the females than of the males do well enough in their later careers to be classified as Successes. It appears clear that personal effort with them has counted; for example, we find that a much larger percentage than of boys were removed from vicious homes.

Important findings concerning the facts of treatment of juvenile offenders as related to outcomes can be formulated as follows: At some time in their careers a very large proportion of the males in our Chicago series received commitment to juvenile correctional institutions, and of these a very large share became adult offenders. For several reasons it is unfair to compare the 70% committed who later appeared in adult courts with the 34% non-committed who appeared in adult courts. But it is a valid conclusion from these figures that the treatment undertaken by the state accomplished very little of its avowed purpose; in any large measure it did not prevent recurrence of offending, and this holds true in the Chicago series for each of the several juvenile correctional institutions utilized.

We have proof, on the other hand, that such results are not necessary because they do not obtain for series of cases dealt with elsewhere. We found that from the Boston Juvenile Court a much smaller proportion of cases is regularly committed to juvenile institutions, and of those committed a very much smaller percentage appear as adult offenders.

Court statistics and our own findings concerning Boston as compared to Chicago bring us face to face with one of the most important socio-legal contrasts with which we are acquainted.

In Boston we find:

(a) A very much larger number of cases in proportion to the population are brought to the juvenile court.

(b) Frequent appearance in both the juvenile and adult courts for much milder offenses.

(c) Undelayed hearings after arrest, always on the same day or the next.

(d) Avoidance, largely through this, of detention of the juvenile offender, except in a very small proportion of cases.

(e) Commitment less than one-fourth as often.

(f) Through the central juvenile court having jurisdiction over only one section of the city and through the court having fewer functions, much more time given to consideration of individual cases.

There can be no doubt that much in this procedure counts as comparatively beneficial in its influence upon the offender, inculcates respect for the law and, in turn, redounds to the protection of society.

We cannot in fairness read into figures more than they denote. Thus we cannot infer that it is difference in institutional régime that is solely responsible for all the great difference between outcomes in those sent to juvenile institutions in the two communities—there is, in particular, a marked difference between the work that is done under parole from these institutions; often in Boston this means placing in foster homes, or applying other constructive measures. Nor can we infer that the fact of non-commitment alone signifies a better procedure and hence is an explanation of the greater success of those not sent to juvenile institutions. It is not the bare procedure that counts; the fact is that for the non-committed very often much personal work is done by a wide variety of social agencies.

Surveying our data on age of first court appearance, nativity of parents, religious affiliation, whether or not families are normally constituted, family economic status, physical and mental conditions of the offender, character of the offenses—in none of these to any large extent do we find significant differentiation between the Success and Failure groups.

Among the smaller numbers that constitute some of the sub-groups we do find conditions that correlate more highly with outcomes. For example, family "destitution" increases the chance of Failure and "luxury" seems to increase the chance for Success. Among the groups of the mentally abnormal there is a larger showing of Failure than among the group as a whole, but even here a third have not proved to be adult offenders. One group of offenders, namely, those who have been engaged in homosexual offenses, have a lower proportion of Success than any other group. Failure in excess appears from homes where there is criminalism, alcoholism or vice.

Our data indicate that it is an unwarranted assumption that outcome is dependent on heredity. Poor traits appearing in the family backgrounds of our cases do not correlate highly enough with outcome to afford a reliable criterion of potentialities inherent in the individual.

With the figures before us we cannot fail to discern that Success did occur under any and all categories of conditions. Many mentally abnormal, properly cared for, do not develop criminalistic ideas and if already started in delinquent ways their misconduct tendencies may be checked. We are surprised to find no great contrasts between the outcomes of those who have and have not engaged in harmful habits; we are equally astonished to find such a large number of successful marriages among girl delinquents. So to whatever group of facts we turn, some measure of Success is found; even among the groups with the most extreme figures of Failure there are enough who do not become criminals to warrant the conclusion that no conditions, whether of mind or body or life situations, preclude the possibility of checking the development of a criminal career.

The above findings are corroborated, in so far as we have data, by comparing the Chicago and Boston groups. Matters to which one would attribute a determining part in outcomes, prove to be of very little import. In racial stock there are certain variations that would only seem to make for the probability of less success in the city where, however, there were better outcomes. Mentality groups in the two cities, judging from our large series, in the main comprised about equal numbers. And indeed there are no substantial differences in the human material [1] that comes into the two juvenile courts to ac-

[1] Comparison of specific physical findings, see Table 43, show a marked difference with respect to teeth conditions and to goitre. The latter is due to the fact that Chicago is in the goitre region; nobody would allege, surely, that delinquency is more severe or outcomes worse in the goitre regions as compared to the non-goitre regions of the United States. Explanation of the dental findings are given in Chapter XIV. Concerning a certain theory that a considerable relationship exists between abnormal mental reactions, including delinquency, and focal infections arising from carious teeth, it might be interesting to point out that the institutional cases in Chicago among whom there was such a large measure of Failure, are the very ones that more generally had dental care as part of their institutional treatment.

About the differences in mental findings we may remark that though for the epileptic and psychotic the percentages seem to vary significantly between the two cities, yet the actual number of cases represented is too small to bear greatly upon the general conclusions.

count for the vast discrepancy between the after-careers
of two similar groups of juvenile offenders.

Some conclusions concerning the conditions under
which delinquency begins and flourishes may be readily
formulated from our data:

Delinquency has definite age correlations. Misconduct
tendencies may begin very early; accessions to the ranks
of delinquency increase rapidly from the age of nine or
ten years. Just when decrease begins could only be
shown by further researches; it is not clear that there
is any decrease for the period when good statistics are
available, the juvenile court age.

In regard to the proportions of the two sexes, there are
such selective forces bringing boys and girls into court
for different offenses, and there is such natural protection
of girl sex offenders that no safe deduction can be drawn
about their comparative tendencies to delinquency.

Following much that has been said earlier, it appears
hazardous to offer any conclusions concerning the possible
relationship of heredity to delinquency. Among the
difficulties of interpretation is the fact that there are
so often, surrounding youth, bad social situations created
by socially unfit parents, the effects of which are not
those of biological inheritance.

Statistics of the relation of delinquency to the size
of the family shows nothing of marked causative
significance.

Some foreign races show an undue proportion of delinquency springing up among them, others show less
than an average amount. But these are facts of incidence
only—that environmental influences count tremendously
even for the races contributing to delinquency pro-

portionately more than their share is shown by the contrasting outcomes of different nationalities in two communities.

The opportunities that wealth and social position give for covering up delinquencies make the prevalence of delinquency at different economic levels hardly worth discussion.

Certainly broken home conditions exist more often in the background of delinquency than is average for the general population. This points to the many deleterious influences resulting from lack of normal parental super-vision, guidance, companionship and control. The exten-sive effects and contamination of specially poor family behavior are readily to be inferred from the number of homes catalogued as defective in these respects, and also from the discovery that so few delinquents come from really good home life.

No physical findings except overdevelopment of girls appear at all significantly correlated with delinquent tendencies.

Among delinquents the mentally abnormal, both de-fectives and psychopaths, appear very much more fre-quently than in the general population; yet this must not be stressed too greatly in the light of the fact that for large series even of repeated offenders, about 70% appear and continue to appear quite normal mentally.

The compared offenses as committed in two American cities show great differences, not so much in classifiable types as in degree of severity. And it is for some of the most extreme and severe offenses that, though the actual numbers are small, the most striking contrasts are shown. Only a few of the above possible factors of incidence seem to be responsible for this contrast, and these only partially; there must be other influences at work.

In all these negative conclusions from statistics of conditions and make-up of offenders we find little satisfactory explanation of delinquency. It is clear that there are many factors that are not so easily enumerated, particularly factors concerning inner mental life (attitudes, stabilities, ideas, urges), concerning the subtler influences of companionship and of various features of environmental conditions—these can only be disclosed and enumerated through careful study of what has initiated and continued the individual in the ways of delinquency.

It is evident that statistical studies cannot readily present the complete picture of delinquent causations, particularly since causations exist never alone, but in such different combinations in different individuals.

A corollary of this, again, is that the individual must be well studied if his needs are to be known in order to be met, if society is best to protect itself from his further developing criminalistic tendencies. In treatment no great generalizations about dealing with delinquents in groups are possible. The complexity of causative forces and factors leads logically to the conclusion that to meet them there must also be a wide range of resources. Very commonly, particularly in institutions, set forms of treatment are supposed to be adequate for meeting all types of individuals and great variety of causations. Ascertainable facts make it evident that in our group the separate needs of individual offenders were not and could not thus be met. And this is doubtless a major cause of the large percentage of Failure.

Concerning prognosis, our data lead to the conclusion that continuance in or cessation from delinquency does not depend on any single factor in the individual case. Nothing in the mental or physical make-up entirely conditions the outlook, nor do any of the facts of causation or continuing environmental conditions. How society meets the issues that the individual case presents is always a large part of the dynamic situation.

It can be predicted with reasonable certainty that some individuals by virtue of their mental characteristics, plus their acquired delinquent trends, under ordinary living conditions will continue in delinquency and crime. Our data show this and demonstrate in these cases the urgent need for permanent segregation, for more stringent protection of society than a court ordinarily undertakes.

While some conditions and some personalities may be more difficult of correction than others, and while some few combinations of conditions and personality present almost insurmountable obstacles to reform of the individual, yet data tend to show that there is no type of personality, no physical or mental condition, no social situation or causation, that alone does not show some Successes as well as Failures.

From all this it is a fair deduction that as a whole the treatment of delinquents is unwarrantably inefficient, particularly in the light of the fact that there is an abundance of evidence that careers of juvenile delinquency are in the main swervable. In both cities from which our data are gathered, the extent of Failure is such as could not be tolerated in business, industry or science.

It seems perfectly clear that there was a time in the lives of the criminals we have studied when, if intelligent, forceful treatment had been undertaken, there would have been a fair, or even better than a fair chance that the delinquent career would have been checked.

The possibilities of drawing practical conclusions are by no means exhausted; there are many we have not attempted to cover, but of these we would select two generalizations of great import:

Inherent in our data is the implication that there are many intangible, imponderable elements in community life that influence the ideas and mental attitudes of young people in ways that are productive of delinquency and crime. The general standards and community atmosphere in regard to law breaking must play an immensely important part.

From our analysis of comparative community backgrounds it is evident that social resources and agencies as they exist for recreational, educational, foster home placing and other child welfare measures have very vital relationship to prevention, causation, and treatment of delinquency and crime. The much greater proportionate development of such resources for child welfare in the one community as correlated with the much better state of affairs in regard to delinquency and crime betokens a relationship of cause and effect.

CHAPTER XXI

GENERAL CONCLUSIONS

THE plain facts presented in this study have less significance in their immediate import than in their deeper meaning. Below their surface they clearly show that as a people and in our separate communities we are going about one of our main duties to ourselves in a very lax and indifferent way.

It is of no little moment for our civilization that the great majority of us are so taken up with material affairs and pleasures that human conduct as such has little meaning for us. Even when conduct is exhibited in one of its crudest and most disastrous manifestations, namely delinquency and crime, we take no special pains to set about the task of even understanding the true facts of the situation, either for the sake of the offender, or of his victims, who make up society at large.

It may be our American abundance that in some measure makes us so peculiarly indifferent to the wastage implied in delinquent deeds and careers. By way of example one might cite the attitude of those city department stores which perhaps correctly consider that they will lose more financially by prosecuting and following up shoplifters than by merely letting them go with no great fuss made about the matter beyond some attempt to retrieve their own goods. And out of the nation's total monetary loss through crime, amounting to many hundreds of millions a year, big business corporations as a matter of course charge off huge sums to profit and loss, as in the case of the unchecked enormously extensive stealing from railroad and express companies, without any consideration of the moral issues involved, particularly the moral detriment to the offenders.

If our lack of capable endeavor to lessen delinquency and crime is attributable to comfort and indifference, we may as well acknowledge it. Material advantage with us is valued, then, more than the promotion among our citizenship of right conduct trends and the development of better personalities.

When crime becomes unusually frequent or spectacular, the zest with which the remedy is discussed is not at all out of proportion to the importance of the subject, though such sporadic debate does not represent much sound knowledge of the situation and accomplishes nothing constructive to offset the ordinary lack of interest in causes and prevention. Many facts which it is not our business to present in this study can be adduced to prove the dearth of appreciation of the tremendous extent of criminalism. From our own studies, and hardly so much expressed in our statistics or mass figures as in the tragedies of human beings and their families, we would strongly assert that delinquency and crime do indeed form one of the greatest burdens which in this country organized society carries.

And whether we continue along the old path of allowing criminalism to flourish among us very largely uninterfered with in its inception and growth or whether we proceed along a path of progressive control, depends upon the spirit brought to the situation. Modification and control we believe from our comparative studies to be possible to an immensely larger degree than now exists. But it needs a new attack, based upon prolonged scientific and experimental research, utilizing more professionally trained workers with offenders, utilizing new techniques and providing new environmental situations. To neglect such attempt at progress is to maintain the standpoint of the old-fashioned agriculturist who refused to learn scientific methods of increasing his crops.

With everybody saying this or that about the causes of crime and attributing the failure to control it to this or that department of public effort—the parole or probation system, the district attorney's office, the police, the courts, the institutions—we may well in our own work turn in all commonsense to the study of data concerning beginnings of careers and to the problem of prevention. With modern science we feel that the prevention of trouble everywhere is vastly more important and often vastly easier than the curing of the trouble. We have in mind bending the twig and early shutting of the barn door.

But it is often said that the immediate and practical problem is the handling of criminals just as they are met every day in the courts. It is all right to talk about causes and youngsters growing up, say some who consider themselves eminently practical, but the real issue that has to be met is crime as it exists. They keep on saying this year after year, while under existing conditions ever new armies of recruits to the criminal ranks rise up to challenge society.

One is reminded of the old medicine treatment of tuberculosis as a disease first recognized when well established. Almost nothing was accomplished until another type of attack was made upon it, namely, investigation of how the disease earliest begins and how it spreads. From these standpoints the problem of prevention was attempted, and behold, within a few years such progress has been made that we are largely rid of this affliction. To make an analogous advance is the practical way out of our crime scourge.

The most evident facts concerning crime are first, its usual beginnings in early youth and, second, the frequency of recidivism. The latter, baldly stated, signifies that under our legal system we do something to an individual because he is an offender, perhaps even severely punish him, and then he proceeds to offend again.

There are many factors and conditions involved in these phenomena of early beginnings and recidivism and they should signify much for us. Such matters as habit-forming, recurrent suggestion from the environment, the development of anti-social attitudes, obsessive impulses toward delinquency, success in avoiding unpleasant results, and other plain and understandable elements come into play. And we can clearly see that if such bases of delinquent tendencies are allowed to persist, outcomes are such as appear in our statistics and case studies of criminalistic careers. Our findings, by this time in hundreds of cases, show the tragedy of continuance in delinquency, as well as the fact that by really good treatment many an impending career can be headed off.

The matter of prevention might be stated in another way. Such investigations as have been made tend to show that if an individual gets to young adult age without the development of criminalistic ideation and tendencies, the job of prevention in nearly every case is done. It might be difficult to specify what such an early adult age is, but probably it is not beyond eighteen to twenty-one. If by that time decent ways of living have been established in thought life and in social life, there is very little chance of turning aside from desirable conduct.

Our records show how a vast deal of crime has its roots in tendencies established during the years of youth or even childhood. In our series we see hundreds of juvenile delinquents with careers unmitigated, unswerved, headed straight for a longer or shorter career of crime.

It is just this common observation that leads us to state that unless the stream of delinquency is checked at or near its source, its progressive flow represents a cost to society, vast in its negative and positive aspects, in non-contribution to society by the offender as well as in actual outlay for his arrests, trials, attempted reformation and safe-keeping. Others have attempted some estimate of this cost in monetary terms; we have not, but from our figures, graphs, and charts, the magnitude of the expenditure may be partly inferred.

The futility of laying most stress either in discussion or treatment upon adult criminality becomes clear when we realize the length of time that bad standards, ideas and habits have existed in the individual case and how delinquent trends have become deeply set by the time adult life is reached.

The easy way with which such considerations of a commonsense psychology are ignored in ordinary court handling of offenders is most astounding. It is because of lack of recognition of relative values in the whole situation, the beginnings, recidivism, the inefficacy of late attempt at prevention, the establishable failure of much correctional treatment in reformatories and prisons that hardly a dent in the situation has been made. At meetings of bar associations and at prison association conferences the discussions, perhaps also by reason of neglect to consider the scientific aspects of the situation, have led almost nowhere.   The essentials of causation and prevention have not been made the subject of scientific and businesslike study, and no really scientific experiments are carried out on which to base possible accomplishment in reformation of offenders and prevention of criminal careers.

Our studies particularly throw light on the problem of the efficacy of correctional institutions, especially important because of the strongly developed notion in modern times that such institutions are really very definitely correctional and reformative.   To be sure, there are frequently present in the minds of those in authority several reasons that form the basis of decision to commit the individual.   It satisfies the offended; it gets the offender out of the way, that is, for the time being it prevents him from being a delinquent in open society; it may be regarded as retribution; it supposedly deters others from committing offenses; it offers some chance for reformation; and, then, very frequently it appears to be the easiest solution of the case.

But are such justifications for commitment sound? Perhaps in this treatment there is "just deserts," though many an individual we have studied has regarded the life in some institutions as not being altogether undesirable. But in any case, is retribution a worthy end in itself? In some cases punishment may be.

The fact of segregation is obviously real though only temporary; the individual while in the institution cannot be an offender outside.   But taking in this country the number of offenders as a whole it may readily be seen that the practical problem of segregating them even for a comparatively short time is most difficult.   Many more institutions would have to be built; the cost would be excessive. And to protect society effectively detention would have to be much longer, which again would entail enormous increase in our present institutional population.

Undoubtedly the strongest claims that can be made for institutional commitment are that such commitment is either deterrent or reformative. So far as the latter is judged by later careers, we have abundance of evidence that the results do not justify the claim. As for deterrence, that, too, is doubtful in view of the increase of crime in recent years during which commitment, as we have shown, has been considerably more frequent.

If in rejoinder it is insisted that the many Failures among those committed simply means that the worst offenders are the committed, we may offer the argument that, even so, the correctional institution is masquerading falsely if it fails to correct large percentages. It is as if one argued that some hospital showed very poor results in cures because all the people who went there were sick people. With correctional institutions, as with hospitals, the recovery rate should be constantly checked and correlated with the nature of the trouble, the treatment given, the after-treatment, and all other points that may be important factors, including above everything else the amount and kind of scientific effort that is put forth by way of attempt at cure. Failures in any event certainly bespeak ineffectiveness of treatment. Delinquents are sent to institutions to be cured.

According to the best scientific knowledge of the present time (we do not at all know what this will be fifteen or twenty years from now) certain individuals are practically incurable in the sense of their being made nonoffenders in society. After most careful studies for classification, so that there can be little or no attempt at excusing poor therapeutic endeavor, such individuals should be held apart. It is an intelligent and clearsighted provision that has led to the establishment of colonies or institutions where such individuals may be segregated for indefinite periods.

So far as the presumably reformable are concerned, one might next ask what there is in the current régime of an ordinary institution that is particularly or directly or scientifically calculated really to reëducate or reform the offender. If in private practice a specialist in behavior problems studies an individual who exhibits misconduct tendencies, he sets about obtaining a knowledge of the individual and an understanding of the causations of his behavior, particularly in the dynamic aspects of mental life, and in the light of what he finds he undertakes treatment, none of which, neither examinations nor understandings nor therapics, are represented to any very appreciable extent in institutional work. And to compare institutions again to hospitals, we might suggest that in hospitals not only is work done as well as in private practice, but very generally much better.

Obviously there are certain disadvantages in institutional life that even the most progressive and favorable management must offset. In particular, the herding together of delinquents or of criminals, with all the chances that this represents for contamination by bad communications, is deplorable. The worst that the worst offender knows is likely to be one of the main topics of consideration. Then there is the retaining of the offender over a varying period in an artificial atmosphere where he has little opportunity for developing normal social contacts.

This leads to the danger of institutionalizing the individual; in large measure he is prone through the set régime to lose initiative and the capacity for self-direction. To a certain extent among juveniles, and more especially among adults who have many hours of cell life, there exists the menace of solitary thought, so well known as dangerous from the standpoint of mental and moral hygiene.

Then a subtler but very real danger arising through commitment and institutional life is the frequent development of a sense of inferiority rooted in the simple fact of the institutional record. Because of the emphasis that inferiority feelings have received in recent years there has been some little recognition of this fact by superintendents themselves. We have even had young offenders say to us, speaking of institutions, "You're never the same if you go there."

The failure of institutions in both juvenile and adult life appears to be great, whether used for a long period of training and reformation or for short term sentences with a purpose of punishment and deterrence. Since the scientifically unselective use of institutional commitment meets with such a minor measure of success in just the cases that one looks to the institution to cure, the efficacy of such commitment must be doubted.

In all fairness it should be added that while our comparison of two communities has demonstrated much inefficacy in institutional commitment, it may be that the weakness is not altogether in institutional work as such, but rather in the after-treatment represented by the release of delinquents and criminals without adequate supervisory care or placement, allowing old associations, ideas, and habits to be reawakened through return to bad environmental conditions.

Indeed if one is specially interested in the differences in after-careers following institutional life in the two communities cited, differences exhibited in our figures and charts, it may be stated that the after-care, namely the parole system and its workings, forms one of the most striking contrasts between the two.

We recognize fully the need for institutional treatment for some offenders; there is nothing to substitute for the control and disciplinary education which can there be carried out. But scientific study should form the basis of selection for such treatment. The régime and management should be scientifically adapted to the needs of the human material received. How special groups can be most successfully treated in institutions is a matter as yet unsatisfactorily formulated; the different degrees of success attained in various institutions would seem already to offer some data for a valuable study.

Here we deliberately limit our discussion of the efficient treatment of offenders to what is done through correctional institutions, because in most places this is the standard form of treatment and because such large numbers are committed. Treatment by other methods is too complicated for present discussion; it is almost impossible to compare the work done by probation officers in different cities where methods and conditions vary greatly. Other forms of treatment are not represented in our study in sufficiently large numbers to be worthy of analysis. And we shall not here be tempted to say anything about the part that churches and schools and other social agencies might and should play in therapeutic endeavor when the very earliest signs of delinquent tendencies are observed.

But taking it altogether, since in our studies the groups of Failures differ in no essential way from the groups of Successes, it seems clear that a vast amount of delinquency and many a delinquent career is preventable. The very differences we have found to exist so plainly between the outcomes in the two communities indicate the potentialities for reform among juvenile offenders.

From one point of view even some of our worst findings need not cause pessimism. If, for example, in one of the institutions included in our study, 72% of our series were Failures, we might ask why 28% were Successes. The latter are to be accounted for as well as the former; they, too, show potentialities. Then if there are factors in the general life of one community which are helpful in the prevention and treatment of delinquency, such factors represent nothing, so far as we can see, that it is not practicable for other communities to develop. Though method and means may vary, the principles involved are applicable anywhere.

It is true that certain statistical comparisons of offenders, offenses, background, as well as of treatment given, are often difficult, many conditions with the same name being essentially quite different. But apart from statistics, our case studies over and over again give ample proof that if certain situations and indications had been met, the probability of success would have been great.

In so many instances one can point exactly to what is needed, beginning with such simple issues as those presented by the mentally defective or the mentally diseased with delinquent tendencies. A well-conducted study of the individual would bring to light companionships, home conditions, elements of mental life, and scores of other factors which without any question might be met constructively and with a successful outcome if only more ingenuity and more devices were operative in an endeavor to check the rising tide of delinquency and crime.

Comparatively little is known about the treatment of delinquency because definite experiment has not been carried on as it has in other fields. But as it stands, we find that many of the Failures found by follow-up study were predictable and many of them actually predicted. Other individuals showed much promise but went on living under circumstances that were known to be inimical, circumstances that should have been altered, and the result was predictable, namely, inevitable failure. Still others without any particular promise evidenced in their personality make-up have, following alterations of their life situations, done well. There can be no doubt that if a bad outcome under unaltered conditions seems inevitable, it is well within the power of organized society to expend enough effort to change the circumstances so that a chance of good outcome may follow. It seems almost certain that of the 61% of Failures shown in one of our main groups many would have turned out differently if they had been understood and their individual needs met. Such a large percentage of Failure demonstrates fully that we are not doing what is right and possible.

With our data showing that for the most part there are no peculiarities in delinquents that set them off as a group, or even that radically distinguish those who have a good outcome after having started in delinquency, from those who are Failures, and with our knowledge of much that can be modified in external conditions and in mental life, the future seems to have great possibilities. We may rationally believe that if a reasonable part of the enthusiasm, energy, and funds devoted to other forms of civic and social improvement, or if a tithe of the present-day genius and ingenuity that is displayed in invention or that is at the service of banal entertainment were applied to a constructive program for the prevention of delinquency and crime we might have just as large returns as in these other fields.

CHAPTER XXII

BECAUSE the common background of all human beings includes wishes and urges and drives that do not always accord with the formulated desires of organized groups of society, combat will always be necessary against delinquency and criminality. The price of law enforcement is constant effort, eternal vigilance. As stronger or special causations of crime may at times develop, or as more powerful suggestions or aids to delinquency appear in our civilization, for example in the recent growth of means of rapid transportation, just in proportion shall we have to evolve social machinery to counteract these special incentives or opportunities.

Self-protection, which is the duty of society, includes a program of well-being for all members of the community, including offenders. The offender must be aided to mend his ways and the potential offender directed toward a better course of conduct. The expanded altruism that is concerned with the welfare of the offender is really an essential part of a larger egoism.

The unplanful and almost chaotic procedure of the present in dealing with delinquency and crime is perfectly obvious to any student of the subject. Very frequently and at any stage what is done has strange irrelevance to anything that has been done before, or, in many cases, to what is likely to be the outcome. One is tempted to find some analogy in industry and think

225

of what might happen if in some process of manufacture practically no attention were paid to the nature or potentialities of the material which was being worked with, and if there were no consideration of the results of what had been done in earlier steps of the manufacturing procedure. Analogously, here is the offender, human material received at a certain stage—manufactured just so far—what is he fit for, what are his needs, what has been done with him, what is the result of what has been done, what further can we do to modify his conduct, what is the outcome likely to be if we undertake such and such treatment? No sound judgment is possible without such a practical, longitudinal view.

A notorious young robber has recently figured much in the newspapers; every one wonders, now that his record is put together, how he has been able to continue to be a pest so long; normal or abnormal, it would seem that he could easily have been taken care of. The main trouble has been that at certain critical stages no true picture has been constructed of him that might have been provocative of right treatment, as a young boy pursuing a career that was bound to lead to criminalism, or as a young man, a living example of the futility of short jail terms, over and over having immediate offense largely placated through pleadings of his weeping mother, or the interference of a local politician, and through a system of appeals allowing previous, well-considered findings of a court to be arbitrarily overruled.

Since presentation of a complete picture of the offender's career is not allowed in the trial, it may be that other interest, perhaps of newspapers, in showing up beginnings and careers of criminals is what in the long run will most effect a better program of legislative and ad-

ministrative procedure.   Only through picturing individuals as they are, made what they are by a combination
of external causes and their own natures, and partly by
the treatment that has been given them, can adequate
impetus be given to a demand for the application of
scientific method in this field.

Without scientific practice the situation that embraces
the needs of the individual and the needs of society is
not met when he is handled as an offender, and very often
indeed he turns and rends society.   This result as reaction can be read between the lines of many a criminal's
life history.   Again, the first requirement of self-protection is that society make every attempt to understand
the offender, to deal with him in ways that do not de-
teriorate him, but rather that build up in him a better
mental attitude, by methods that make for him a fair
opportunity after release from institutional life.

A program is needed.   To reduce delinquency mate-
rially in our complicated civilization the development of
a thoroughly conscious and constructive plan is indispensable.   And this must be based not on the theories
or proposals of treatment that so many seem to feel
themselves competent to uphold, but on the results of
experiences and the constant measuring of conditions and
efforts by observed outcomes.

Nor can a plan be safely founded except upon recognition of the large variety and complexity of causes that
any careful student of cases of delinquency and criminality can demonstrate.   The theories earlier set forth
voluminously by continental writers and the narrow,
one-piece explanations of some American and English
theorists must all be discarded for a larger vision.   We
must perceive the individual and his environment re-

acting back and forth on each other, each being changed as each is reacted on.

We can easily enumerate a grist of criminological theories: possession by the devil; economic and sociological theories of causation; theories accounting for crime by imitation, degeneracy, heredity; crime as a disease; the somewhat later absurd attempts to account for a very large share of misconduct as manifestations essentially of epilepsy, feeblemindedness, injury of a hypothetical "moral brain center," immigration, physical inferiorities and irritative conditions, such as imperfect vision or focal infections from abscessed teeth, psychopathic inferiority, innately defective emotional make-up, mid-brain lesions, poverty, the unclear conception of dementia precox, inadequate personality, neurotic compensations for inferiority. These are enumerated to show, not that there is no truth at all in them, but rather that the very multiplicity of theories proves the danger of setting about any program that is based upon the idea that all or a large share of delinquency and crime is attributable to any one cause.

The same warning may be given against following any such simply founded theory of treatment. Any expectation of accomplishing all or nearly all in the way of effective treatment by some particular plan of using force, punishment, kindness, religious appeal, medical care, or by any set form of reformation, is doomed to disappointment. The varieties of human beings and the varieties of causes of delinquency are too many to be met by a unitary conception of what it is possible to do in the therapy of delinquency and crime.

In general terms it may be insisted that a hard-headed, entirely practicable, but scientific, social and legal plan, far-seeing and far-reaching, is the great primary necessity.

In a chronological sense, the plan may begin with the pre-delinquent aspect of child life, by developing specific and locally directed efforts for diverting children's energies and ideas away from delinquent trends.

In a case first known after delinquency has shown itself, the scheme of treatment must have flexibility and variety of resources enough adequately to cover the very considerable range of conditions in the individual and in the environment which lie back of and are causative of misconduct. There should be vigorous, non-sentimental handling of juvenile offenders, having in mind that what is done for childhood is done for a lifetime and that the efforts made for childhood yield the best returns for society.

Also in later youth and with adult offenders the possibilities and effects of dealing with human material must be reckoned up if there is to be successful outcome. Although by this time many more experiences and habits have been added there is no reason to believe that there are any different general causative principles of conduct than are active among younger people.

There still seems to be a lingering notion among those who are poorly informed that punishment such as can be given under modern conceptions of humanitarianism forms an adequate program for older offenders. The hard facts of recidivism completely disprove this. Whether we speak of the juvenile or the adult offender we may fairly state that punishment in very many cases is no more reformative or deterrent than when it is utilized in family life. And there can be no doubt on the part of those of us who have occasion to study many instances of family life that where punishment is the only corrective the most unfortunate delinquent trends and mental attitudes are created.

We may best regard the field of delinquency and crime as one for human engineering, and the work to be done very analogous to that required for any other engineering project. But no work of modern engineering is carried on with so little ascertainment of fundamental facts about conditions and results that there is always opportunity for acrimonious dispute concerning the barest essentials of procedure; with almost no professional literature upon matters of treatment and accomplishment; with except in the rarest instances no professional training for what should be highly professional work; with very little study undertaken of the materials involved, so that there is practically no scientific estimate and formulation of possibilities and difficulties prior to deciding what is to be done; with, in general, no modern scientific approach, so that what is done is carried out under a traditionally developed theoretical system of meeting situations.

Stated briefly and in principles rather than in details, a plan is given below. Variations of detail are necessary for different communities, but the essentials remain the same.

THE PLAN

Awareness of the Facts: Much of the collecting of essential facts about delinquency and crime is too simple to be called research; rather it is surveying, taking stock of more or less readily ascertainable data, first of the incidence of delinquency under comparative conditions enumerated as completely as possible, and of the very important facts of recidivism as related to comparative conditions. Then it may be of much value logically to consider gathering the facts under two heads: (a) those which show society's behavior in its efforts to meet delinquency and crime, and (b) those which show the behavior of the delinquent or criminal, following, or in reaction to, the treatment given by society.

For practical purposes there should be avoidance of mere compilations of figures, most of them valueless, which have characterized so many laboriously gathered criminal statistics, including those published in the year-books of foreign governments and the academic collections of facts which sporadically appear in this country. A clear-headed view should be maintained—the really vital facts are those that indicate causes that can be met and those that throw critical light upon treatment as it fails or as it produces profitable results.

A campaign for better and centralized records, to begin with, for the purpose of registering offenders and the dispositions of their cases, is a prime requisite of the larger program; and this, particularly because of the interstate activity of criminals, will necessitate a federal bureau of identification and registration of facts, such a bureau as is so effectively maintained in the older countries.

But local systems of recording data should include much more about the offender, his arrests, his periods of detention, trials, findings through scientific studies of his case, judgments pronounced, record on probation or under commitment and parole.

As in business or industry only the gathering of such facts will determine what deeper facts are necessary upon which to base better success.

Less superficial facts are demonstrably essential, particularly those concerning the causations of social misconduct in the individual case, causes as they exist in the personality make-up of the offender, or as they are reflected from his earlier experiences or are subtly created by present environmental influences. And this includes the facts of reaction to treatment either by way of preventive work, or after the delinquent is recognized as such, undertaken by the police and court officials, under reformative and correctional régime, by any agencies in the given community supposedly working for the purpose of helping the offender or protecting society.

Research: No forward-looking project of human engineering can be carried on without research any more than can other forms of engineering or industry. This entails thoroughgoing studies into the indications for and the deeper meanings of various forms of treatment as they are given by society to different varieties of human material, and as related to different types of causes. And perhaps above everything we need carefully conducted and well-followed attempts by the experimental method to develop other and more successful ways of influencing human individuals to adhere to the norms of social conduct. So far indeed very little resource and ingenuity has been exercised in meeting the various kinds of problems that delinquency presents.

Development of Professional Literature: Requisite is the progressive growth of a sound, open-minded, scientific, technical literature dealing with the many classes of facts concerning delinquency and crime, particularly as these are directly related to practical treatment and its results.

Education of Personnel: The importance of a special equipment of knowledge and personal technique on the part of those who deal with offenders has been much emphasized at international and other conferences concerning work with delinquents. Judges and all others who have to make decisions about offenders, or who work with them in any way, must develop a professional attitude that includes the acquirement of the best of scientific knowledge, as in any other profession. What is required for the successful dealing with delinquency and crime is not knowledge of legal procedure nor of criminological theories of the past, but of the more modern scientific attitudes such as accomplish most in other fields. Modern students of behavior problems are developing facts and methods that are practical and comprehensive enough to be denominated a new, partially developed science. To reckon with the psychology of conduct, to be familiar with the motives and conditions of behavior is fundamental to understanding the young offender, his needs and the chances of altering his conduct trends for the protection of society.

Study of the Individual Case: Indispensable requirement for dealing intelligently with the human material as it comes to hand is understanding of the individual case. Instances of misconduct which on the surface appear much alike and are designated by the same terms may be actuated by conditions and motives so dissimilar that successful treatment must be based upon such study of causes and diagnosis of the make-up of the individual offender that the most essential facts may be brought to light. A mere so-called examination of the offender, including even a short psychological or psychiatric examination, is insufficient to bring out just the subtleties that very frequently form the very essence of the situation. In professional terms we speak of study from etiologic, diagnostic and prognostic standpoints; in nonprofessional language we may state that what should be known are the causes of the delinquency, the individual's limitations and his possibilities, his special needs, how he is to be steered toward becoming a non-offender, and all this in terms of how society is best immediately and in the long run to protect itself against this offender's delinquent tendencies.

The variations in causes of offense are so great in detail and in combination that very considerable time and skill are required to reveal them. For this a department of diagnostic service in courts or in connection with treatment on probation or in institutions is imperative. The cost of a well-rounded study, perhaps twenty-five to fifty dollars, is very little indeed compared to the tremendous expense of trials and of subsequent work with offenders.

That it requires expert service and a very judicious correlation of findings in order to evaluate physical and mental facts as they are dynamic elements in the offender's trends, and the social or environmental features of his life as they bear upon his conduct, should be no bar to securing such service—the task is so important.

Better Administration of Treatment: A host of cases could be given, pitting Failures against Successes, to show that the economics of the general situation, society's protection, and the offender's welfare are all involved in able administration of treatment, the main principles of which must be characterized by the following:

(a) Treatment that meets the needs and utilizes the potentialities of the offender, that tends to build him up, and that secures for him such a place in community life that, particularly if he is released from an institution, he is not almost bound to be again an offender. This latter can strongly be furthered through a finely-developed parole system. For this, as well as for the possibility of readily removing from the community the paroled offender if he gives evidence of more misconduct, we are led strongly to advocate constructive lengthy parole for all offenders, for even those who have served their maximum sentence.

(b) Treatment by the businesslike method of attempting at every stage, or at frequent intervals, to estimate outcomes, for example, the results upon the individual of being handled under authority of the law, from the first arrest and detention in a police station, or in a juvenile detention home, to the last efforts under parole. The real effect upon the offender, and consequently upon society, of industrial school commitment, of county jail detention, of prison sentence, of the practices of criminal lawyers, and many other matters as parts of treatment, are to be considered and balanced over against other possibilities.

Punishment, as a purposive part of treatment, should, in particular, be so planned that it does not bring in its wake personal deteriorations which, in turn, tend to produce further delinquencies or other problems burdensome to society.

(c) Treatment that combats sources and conditions which originate or foster wrongdoing and which continue to create delinquencies and generate new delinquent careers in spite of what is done by way of supposed deterrence, either through inflicting punishment or otherwise.

There must be agencies definitely engaged in the work of prevention, including especially the police. Our experience leads us to know that there are many opportunities for stamping out sources of moral contamination, many chances for friendly contacts that would tend to prevent wrongdoing.

(d) Treatment after judgment of guilt, by considering the whole situation, following careful study of the individual and his case. The plan of treatment may perhaps best be formulated and decided on by a commission, members of which are trained to genuine expertness, as other boards or commissions are qualified in business or science. Such a commission is already virtually in existence in the best juvenile courts where the judge and the experts who study the case confer about the type and sometimes the details of treatment. The commission should include representatives of the correctional institution, of the probation and parole departments, each of these to pass along information concerning the needs of the case to those who will have charge of treatment.

(e) Treatment that gives more power over situations. We are convinced by observation that much can be accomplished by more years of control of juvenile offenders, either after commitment or under probation. Results are much better where the state has control of committed offenders until they are 21. And we see advantages in raising the age of the jurisdiction of the juvenile court, and in placing a family relations court under the same jurisdiction. The court then is in a position to accomplish much more by way of prevention and checking of delinquent careers. Criminologists rightfully call attention to the great advantages of a court which, with a proper conception of the unity of the problem, deals with family situations wherein so frequently are embedded the roots of delinquency.

Building Up Resources of Treatment: In order to meet the extremely varied conditions found in different cases it is necessary to build up a variety of resources for treatment. These will necessarily vary in different communities, depending upon local needs and conditions. In principle the following are generally applicable:

(a) Since the most important resource is always the human element, the first requisite concerns itself with building up personnel, in personality and education very specially fitted for the work, judges, probation officers and all who have to deal with offenders. Effective probation and parole require a staff adequate to develop constructive work for the offenders in their charge.

(b) In institutional treatment the main resources are not buildings and material equipment, but rather workers who appreciate that it is the conditions of inner mental life which affect the offender most vitally. The need everywhere in institutions is for experts who have the understanding and the skill to modify human lives.

(c) Resources include organizations and social agencies for taking up the various tasks of readjustment— for developing better interests and recreations, for re-education of members of families, for providing foster homes and adjustments other than return to old bad environmental conditions, for relieving economic stress, etc. Organizations that might meet the needs are too numerously varied to list, but the two that exist practically everywhere, churches and schools, interest themselves all too little in offsetting and curing tendencies to delinquency. Resources for psychiatric treatment, some day to be of great importance in this field, await education of a larger number of qualified professional people.

(d) Building up resources for prevention demands organizations whose function it is to look after the sources of contamination and conditions that are stimuli to bad conduct.

(e) Treatment that in its administration has power enough behind it to make effective what is proposed; that is not interfered with by too easy right of appeal from court decisions, as in some communities; that can properly hold adults, including parents, legally responsible when they contribute to the delinquency of the offender; that has authority enough over probation officers or other officials to insure their carrying out of the constructive measures that have been planned.

(f) In America, there must be built up a much more effective police service, if not to the extent that exists in Europe, yet strong enough so that the chances for escaping detection and punishment are not as great as they are at present, so that crime does not offer its present chances for profit and adventure. We agree with some of the keenest European observers who have commented on the very real fact that with us crime seems worth committing because of the considerable chance of success. And we have noted in many cases that delinquency appears to the delinquent as a game—to best the efforts of the police is part of the satisfaction sought. Indispensable to betterment of the whole situation is lessening the chance for the successful commission of crime.

Coördination: A program to be effective must provide for businesslike coördination, analogous to that between the different departments of a large industrial concern. Working together for the same end, namely protection of society and reforming the individual's tendencies, all agencies and departments that play any part whatever in connection with the offender must coördinate. Actively coöperating must be the police, agencies for scientific study of the individual, upper and lower courts, probation officers, the public prosecutor's office,[1] institutional personnel, parole boards and officials, a central bureau of information. This would make possible a passing along of information and consultations so that at every stage of an offender's career there would be available a longitudinal view rather than a mere cross-section picture of conditions at any particular time.

Coöperation must also exist between different communities and states; already mentioned is the importance of a federal bureau of information concerning criminals.

Education of Public Attitudes: Certain public conceptions concerning delinquency must be vastly changed. According to our observation, the attitude of a portion of our public has influenced many a youth to believe that the criminal is a kind of hero, and that a criminal career offers great possibilities and great adventure: this whole point of view must be keenly combatted. That criminality offers escapes and compensations for personal inferiorities and for many of life's humdrum occupations is an interpretation that public opinion must dispel.

Society should be specially concerned with the influences of newspaper presentations of criminal matters. The story of the crime, the almost invariable practice of dealing merely with the details of the immediate offense and with the transactions of the police and of the lawyers in the courts, must either be modified or offset by life stories of criminals, of the disagreeable aspects, the deprivations and dissatisfactions of their lives, and of what lies back of their careers. These, told in very specific

[1] This department often exercises arbitrarily greater power over larger numbers than do many courts themselves.

ways, offer possibilities of developing a much stronger public attitude towards criminal matters, without detracting from the human interest of newspaper writing. Through such methods the public would become interested in causes, and would acquire knowledge of what exists by way of contaminations and sore spots and ineffectualities in handling offenders. The public would become much more in a mood to participate in efforts to better conditions. We discern it to be a matter of vital importance that newspapers should strive against even indirectly and unintentionally picturing crime as exciting, alluring, a means of getting unfortunate ego satisfactions, so that delinquency and repetition of delinquency is stimulated. It is most undesirable for delinquents to obtain enjoyment from being "written up"; their pleasure in notoriety is based on the same psychology that leads other people to find satisfactions in published recognition of their activities, even in philanthropies or civic service.

The main points for a program are, scheduled, as follows:

PROGRAM:
- AWARENESS OF THE FACTS
- RESEARCH
- DEVELOPMENT OF PROFESSIONAL LITERATURE
- EDUCATION OF PERSONNEL
- STUDY OF THE INDIVIDUAL CASE
- BETTER ADMINISTRATION OF TREATMENT
- BUILDING UP RESOURCES OF TREATMENT
- COÖRDINATION
- EDUCATION OF PUBLIC ATTITUDES

We offer the opinion, based on our long years of observation, that such a program as the above, hard-headed and scientific, is entirely practicable were interest and effort elicited at all commensurate with its importance as a program for the development of right conduct among a citizenry.

PART V

APPENDIX I

APPENDIX I

For explanation of the several series concerning which statistics are given, see Chapter II, Material and Method.

TABLE 1
CHICAGO SERIES OF OUTCOMES
GENERAL FIGURES

	Total		Males	Females
Group estimated in terms of Success and Failure	675	73.4%	420	255
Indifferent Success	29	3.2%	20	9
In Institution for Feebleminded	23 } 4.1%		} 12	11
In State Hospital for Insane	15 }		} 7	8
Dead	16	1.7%	11	5
Total traced cases	758		470	288
Not found	162	17.6%	96	66
	920		500	354

TABLE 2
CHICAGO SERIES OF OUTCOMES
GENERAL FINDINGS OF SUCCESS AND FAILURE

	Males	Females	Total
SUCCESS	164 (39%)	138 (54%)	302 (45%)
FAILURE	256 (61%)	117 (46%)	373 (55%)
	420	255	675 (100%)

245

TABLE 3

CHICAGO SERIES OF OUTCOMES

Males

13 KNOWN HOMICIDES

Age	Nativity of Parents	Mentality	Circumstances
15	Irish	feebleminded	street hold-up
15	U. S. (white-colored)	normal	burglary
17	Norway-Germany	"	"
17	German	"	robbery
18	Polish	psychopathic personality	"
18	German	psychosis	"
18	Finnish	feebleminded	burglary
18	Irish-German	psychosis	robbery
19	U. S.	normal	"
19	Polish	"	burglary
20	German	feebleminded	jealousy
21	U. S.	normal	burglary
24	Italian	"	hold-up

TABLE 4

CHICAGO SERIES OF OUTCOMES

Males

39 PROFESSIONAL CRIMINALS

Of these:—34 born in United States

30 normal mentally
5 feebleminded
1 psychotic
3 psychopathic personalities

RACE OR NATIONALITY OF PARENTS OF 39 PROFESSIONAL CRIMINALS

Parents		Burglars	"Hold-ups"	Swindlers	Thieves	Sex Perverts
U. S.	white	2	2	1	3	..
	colored	..	..	..	1	..
Irish		3	1	..	2	1
Slavic		4	..	..	2	..
Jewish		1	..	1	3	..
English		2	..	..	..	1
Italian		2	2	..	..	..
French		1	..	..	1	..
German		1	..	..	1	..
Scandinavian		..	..	..	1	..

TABLE 5

CHICAGO SERIES OF OUTCOMES

Females

CRIMINAL RECORDS

1 chronic thief
1 swindler and forger
22 definitely prostitutes

16 have 21 illegitimate children

TABLE 6

CHICAGO SERIES OF OUTCOMES
Males

VIOLENT DEATHS
Killed in committing crime
1 during burglary
1   "   hold-up
1   "   brawl

Suicides
2 after careers of crime
2 during juvenile court age

TABLE 7

CHICAGO SERIES OF OUTCOMES

POST-JUVENILE RECORDS

INDIVIDUALS AND COMMITMENTS OR COURT APPEARANCES

Records of 209 Males

	House Correction		State Reformatory		Penitentiary		County Jails		Other Adult Court Appearances	
	Ind's	Com's	Ind's	Com's	Ind's	Com's	Ind's	Com's	Ind's	Tot'ls
One time	50	50	64	64	19	19	40	40	58	58
Two times....	13	26	9	18	3	6	3	6	13	26
Three times.	4	12	..	..	..	..	1	3	8	24
Four times...	2	8	..	..	..	..	1	5	3	12
Five times.... (or more)	3	15	..	..	..	..	..	..	8	40
TOTALS:										
Individuals .	72	..	73	..	22	..	45	..	90	..
Commitments	..	111	..	82	..	25	..	54	..	..
Appearances	..	..	..	..	..	..	..	..	..	160

Records of 25 Females

	House Correction		State Reformatory		Penitentiary		County Jails		Other Adult Court Appearances	
One time....	5	5	..	..	2	2	..	..	14	14
Two times....	2	4	..	..	..	..	..	..	3	6
Three times...	..	..	..	..	..	..	..	..	2	6
TOTALS:										
Individuals .	7	..	..	..	2	..	..	..	19	..
Commitments	..	9	..	..	..	2	..	..	..	..
Appearances	..	..	..	..	..	..	..	..	..	26

(Since some individuals were committed to more than one institution, the 157 male offenders (Table 8) who received one or more commitments appear here as the 212 individuals committed 272 times to the different institutions.)

TABLE 8
CHICAGO AND BOSTON SERIES OF OUTCOMES
COMPARABLE MALE RECORDS

	To Juvenile Correctional Institutions	Comparable Adult Court Records	Homi- cides	Profes- sional Crimi- nals	To Adult Correctional Institutions
Years 1918-1919					
Chicago cases (420).	311 (74%)	209 (50%)	13	39	157 (37%)
Boston cases (400)..	118 (29.5%)	84 (21%)	0	1	25 (6%)
Years 1918-1919					
Boston cases (400)..	159 (40%)	103 (26%)	1	?	63 (16%)

TABLE 9
CHICAGO AND BOSTON SERIES OF OUTCOMES
COMMITMENTS OR SENTENCES AS ADULTS

Boston 1909-1914 Series

	House of Correction		State Reforma- tory		Peniten- tiary		County Jails		Totals
	Ind's	Com's	Ind's	Com's	Ind's	Com's	Ind's	Com's	
One time.........	7	7	5	5	0	0	3	3	
Two times	1	2	2	4	..	..	1	2	
One time appealed	6	6	3	3	..	..	2	2	
TOTALS:									
Individuals	14	..	10	..	0	..	6	..	30
Commitments ...	..	15	..	12	..	0	..	7	34

Chicago

	House of Correction		State Reforma- tory		Peniten- tiary		County Jails		Totals
TOTALS:									
Individuals	72	..	73	..	22	..	45	..	212
Commitments ...	..	111	..	82	..	25	..	54	272

(Again we must speak about overlapping;—the same individuals sometimes being committed to more than one institution. As the Chart in the Text shows, 157 and 25 individuals in the Chicago and Boston series, respectively, are involved in the above table.)

Boston 1918-1919 Series

	House of Correction	State Re- formatory	State Prison	County Jail	Totals
TOTALS:					
Individuals	25	28	1	13	67

(63 individuals received the 67 sentences. Of course too few years have elapsed to make the figures for this group comparable with the older groups.)

TABLE 10

CHICAGO SERIES OF OUTCOMES

FAILURES BUT NOT ARRESTED

16 disappeared following offenses, thus:
  2 disappeared after homicides
  1   "   " wounding a policeman by shooting
  3   "   " burglary
  5   "   " running away from juvenile institutions
  5   "   " doing poorly in general
11 chronic loafers—most with other vicious habits, alcoholic, etc.
 8 extremely immoral sexually
 3 nonsupporters and deserters of family
 3 definitely vagrants
 2 semi-vagrants
 2 killed in burglary
 2 criminalistic feebleminded at large

47

DISHONORABLE SERVICE RECORD

Of the 256 male failures we learned 21 had received dishonorable discharges from the Service. (Of course there may have been more.)
 9 received adult commitments
 4 had court appearances
 8 not known to have been arrested

21

TABLE 11

BOSTON 1909-1914 SERIES OF OUTCOMES
ADULT COURT APPEARANCES WITHOUT COMMITMENT

(These figures are not at all comparable with similar Chicago statistics, as indicating equal seriousness of offenses. To make them thus comparable, 32 cases would have to be subtracted from the Boston figures as being instances of arrest and court appearances for offenses so mild that we have no similar record of arrests in Chicago.)

	Individuals	Appearances
One time	53	53
Two times	23	46
Three times	6	18
Four times	7	28
Five times	1	5
Six times	1	6
	91	156

TABLE 12

CHICAGO AND BOSTON COURT STATISTICS

JUVENILE COURT CASES, FIVE-YEAR PERIOD—1909-1913

		Delinquent cases heard		Juveniles Committed to Institutions
Total Chicago juvenile court....	....	8,852	....	3,557 (40%)
Boston juvenile court.........	5,214	....	542	....
Other Boston juvenile sessions	6,868	....	615	....
Total Boston	....	12,082	....	1,157(9.5%)

TABLE 13

CHICAGO AND BOSTON COURT STATISTICS

YEARLY COMMITMENTS TO JUVENILE CORRECTIONAL INSTITUTIONS

	Total of Delinquent Boys in Court		Committed	
	Cases		Per cent	
	Chicago	Boston *	Chicago	Boston *
1909	1352	1146	30.0	3.6
1910	1161	942	38.0	5.2
1911	1320	920	44.0	6.0
1912	1105	859	30.0	9.6
1913	1363	874	33.0	11.0
1914	2258	906	23.0	9.8
1915	2326	627	18.0	11.0
1916	2192	599	17.3	6.0
1917	2328	940	19.5	4.2
1918	2306	1145	21.4	4.0
1919	2647	1223	32.0	5.5
1920	1912	902	33.3	6.6
1921	1754	735	36.0	6.5

* Boston Juvenile Court; not including juvenile sessions in other courts in Boston.

TABLE 14

CHICAGO SERIES OF OUTCOMES

JUVENILE RECORDS—MALES

	To Juvenile Correctional Institution	Not to Juvenile Correctional Institution
Of the 164 Successes	92 (56%)	72 (44%)
Of the 256 Failures	219 (86%)	37 (14%)
Of 420 Males	311 (74%)	109 (26%)

(Not sent to correctional institution means on probation, or placed, or in dependent institutions, or a combination of these.)

INDIVIDUALS AND NUMBER OF COMMITMENTS

Successes

	Parental School (for truants)		John Worthy School (since abolished)		St. Charles	
	Ind's	Com's	Ind's	Com's	Ind's	Com's
One time	26	26	25	25	38	38
Two times	8	16	5	10	4	8
Three times	2	6	5	15	1	3
Four times	0	0	1	4	0	0
Five times	1	5	0	0	0	0
TOTALS:						
Individuals	37	..	36	..	43	..
Commitments	..	53	..	54	..	49

Failures

	Parental School (for truants)		John Worthy School (since abolished)		St. Charles	
	Ind's	Com's	Ind's	Com's	Ind's	Com's
One time	49	49	63	63	80	80
Two times	22	44	26	52	28	56
Three times	6	18	9	27	4	12
Four times	1	4	3	12	0	0
Five times	1	5	0	0	3	15
TOTALS:						
Individuals	79	..	101	..	115	..
Commitments	..	120	..	154	..	163

SUMMARY

To:

Parental School...	116 boys.	Of these	32%	Successes	68%	Failures
John Worthy School	137	" " "	26%	"	74%	"
St. Charles........	158	" " "	28%	"	72%	"

Table of Total Male Juvenile Commitments

92 Successes; 163 commitments; average commitments per individual, 1.7
219 Failures; 442 " " " " " 2.
311 Males 605 commitments (12 of these were commitments of the same individuals to an institution too little utilized to be compared with the three institutions listed above).

TABLE 15

CHICAGO SERIES OF OUTCOMES

JUVENILE RECORDS—FEMALES

	To Juvenile Correctional Institution	Not to Juvenile Correctional Institution
Of the 138 Successes	77 (56%)	61 (44%)
Of the 117 Failures	92 (79%)	25 (21%)
Of 255 Females	169 (67%)	86 (33%)

(On probation, or placed, or in dependent institutions, or a combination of these.)

INDIVIDUALS AND NUMBER OF COMMITMENTS

Successes

	Geneva		Refuge		House of Good Shepherd	
	Ind's	Com's	Ind's	Com's	Ind's	Com's
One time	32	32	25	25	19	19
Two times	7	14	..	..	2	4
Three times	1	3	..	..	1	3
TOTALS:						
Individuals	40	..	25	..	22	..
Commitments	..	49	..	25	..	26

Failures

	Geneva		Refuge		House of Good Shepherd	
One time	30	30	24	24	31	31
Two times	9	18	2	2	8	16
Three times	1	3	1	3	2	6
Five times	2	10				
TOTALS:						
Individuals	42	..	27	..	41	..
Commitments	..	61	..	31	..	53

SUMMARY

To:

Geneva .... 82 girls. Of these 49% Successes; 51% Failures
Refuge .... 52 "   "   " 48%   "   52%   "
House of Good Sheph'd 63 "   "   " 35%   "   65%   "

Table of Total Female Juvenile Commitments

77 Successes; 100 commitments; average commitments per individual 1.3
92 Failures;   145   "   "   "   "   "   1.6

169 Females   245 commitments

TABLE 16

BOSTON 1909-1914 SERIES OF OUTCOMES

JUVENILE RECORDS—MALES

	To Juvenile Correctional Institutions	Not to Juvenile Correctional Institutions
Of the 316 Successes	84 (27%)	232 (73%)
Of the 84 Failures *	34 (40%)	50 (60%)
Of 400 Males	118 (29.5%)	282 (71%)

(* Failure in this Table being judged by adult court appearance for anything except petty infractions of law—such as do not appear in our Chicago records.)

Individuals and Commitments

	Suffolk and Parental Schools (Boys under 15; both since abolished)	Lyman School (Boys under 15)	Shirley (Boys, ages 15-17)
Successes	5	58	23
Failures	3	13	16
	8	71	39

(Concerning number of commitments for the individual it should be known that the situation is entirely different from that in Chicago, because commitment to Lyman or Shirley means that the State has authority over the individual until he is 21 years of age.)

TABLE 17

BOSTON 1918-1919 SERIES OF OUTCOMES

JUVENILE RECORDS—MALES

	To Juvenile Correctional Institutions	Not to Juvenile Correctional Institutions
Of the 297 Successes	107 (36%)	191 (64%)
Of the 103 Failures *	52 (50%)	50 (50%)
Of the 400 Males	159 (40%)	241 (60%)

(* Failure here, again, meaning adult court appearance.)

Individuals and Commitments

	Suffolk	Lyman	Shirley	Other Institutions
Successes	24	37	38	8
Failures	18	11	21	2
	42	48	59	10

(Concerning number of commitments, see note for Table 16.)

TABLE 18

CHICAGO AND BOSTON SERIES OF OUTCOMES

ADJUSTMENTS OF MALE JUVENILE REPEATED OFFENDERS

	Chicago 1909-14	Boston 1909-14	Boston 1918-19
Probation only	51	202	171
Placed only—in foster homes	19	30 *	31
To non-correctional institutions only...	8	7	6
Held to Grand Jury	..	5	..
To correctional institutions	311	118	159
Combination of treatment other than correctional institutions	31	38 *	33
	420	400	400

(* These figures are only approximately correct—being made from records not all complete.)

TABLE 19

CHICAGO AND BOSTON SERIES OF OUTCOMES

RELATION OF PROBATION TO ADULT RECORD

	Chicago 1909-14	Boston 1909-14	Boston 1918-1919
Total with probation only	51	202	171
Of the above those with adult delinquent record	15 (30%)	34 (17%)	19 (11%)

TABLE 20

SERIES OF 4000 JUVENILE DELINQUENTS

SEXES

Series		Girls	Boys	Ratio
Chicago	I.........................	306	694	1 : 2.3
"	II.........................	308	692	1 : 2.25
Boston	I.........................	242	758	1 : 3
"	II.........................	314	686	1 : 2

TABLE 21

COURT STATISTICS

RATIO OF DELINQUENTS—GIRLS TO BOYS

Chicago		Boston	
1909	1 : 3	1909	1 : 12
1910	1 : 2.5	1910	1 : 9
1911	1 : 2.7	1911	1 : 11
1912	1 : 2	1912	1 : 11
1913	1 : 2.2	1913	1 : 8
1914	1 : 3.5	1914	1 : 8.5
1915	1 : 4	1915	1 : 10
1916	1 : 3.5	1916	1 : 5.8
1921	1 : 2.6	1921	1 : 7

TABLE 22

SERIES OF 4000 JUVENILE DELINQUENTS

AGES AT THE TIME OF OUR FIRST STUDY

Years	Boys				Girls			
	Chi I	Chi II	Bost I	Bost II	Chi I	Chi II	Bost I	Bost II
5	..	..	..	1	..	..	..	1
6	5	2	2	4	3	..	2	1
7	14	3	10	7	4	..	1	4
8	22	14	21	13	6	5	5	5
9	38	18	37	39	11	3	5	6
10	41	24	56	49	12	5	12	5
11	46	45	50	48	12	12	3	9
12	78	65	79	78	23	34	10	13
13	80	76	108	88	24	30	23	30
14	114	126	139	109	33	44	39	47
15	124	164	128	127	41	50	52	54
16	132	155	111	104	73	59	64	85
17	..	..	(16)	(12)	64	56	(20)	(18)
18 + ...	..	..	(1)	(7)	..	..	(6)	(36)
Totals	694	692	758	686	306	308	242	314

The figures in parentheses are for the years over the juvenile court age.

TABLE 23

COURT STATISTICS

AGES OF FIRST AND REPEATED OFFENDERS IN CHICAGO JUVENILE COURT
YEARS 1909, 1910, 1911 TOTALLED

Years of Age	Boys		Girls	
	First time in Court	Repeated Offenders	First time in Court	Repeated Offenders
8	6	1	2	...
9	11	6	3	2
10	72	22	13	3
11	136	59	13	6
12	170	119	32	10
13	292	229	74	30
14	437	357	129	48
15	493	443	248	110
16	527	413	263	98
17	...	18	230	85
18	...	...	...	13
	2144	1667	1007	405

(The years 1909-1911 in this table and Table 24 were selected merely as fair sample years.)

TABLE 24

COURT STATISTICS AND CHICAGO SERIES OF OUTCOMES COMPARED
AGES OF FIRST COURT APPEARANCE

	Total Delinquents Chicago Court Records 1909, 1910, 1911		Our Group					
			Males			Females		
	Boys	Girls	Total	Success	Failure	Total	Success	Failure
Totals	(2144)	(1007)	(420)	(164)	(256)	(255)	(138)	(117)
Under 10 years..	1%	0.5%	11%	46%	54%	6%	53%	47%
10-14 years inclu..	52%	26 %	60%	34%	66%	38%	55%	45%
15 years	23%	24.5%	16%	38%	62%	18%	44%	56%
16 years	24%	26 %	13%	58%	42%	23%	60%	40%
17 years	....	23 %	....	....	....	15%	54%	46%

TABLE 25

CHICAGO SERIES OF OUTCOMES

NATIVITY OF PARENTS BY LANGUAGE GROUPS

	Of Boys	Of Girls
Parents born in United States	114	76
Parents born in foreign non-English speaking countries	236	142
Parents born in foreign English speaking countries	40	20
Mixed parentage	28	11
Unknown	2	6
	420	255

SUCCESS AND FAILURE ACCORDING TO NATIVITY

NATIVITY OF PARENTS

	Males		Females	
	Success	Failure	Success	Failure
United States—				
White	40 (40 %)	61 (60 %)	34 (49 %)	35 (51 %)
Colored	2 (15 %)	11 (85 %)	3 (43 %)	4 (57 %)
Slavic	30 (44 %)	38 (56 %)	6 (32 %)	13 (68 %)
Russian Jewish	24 (36 %)	43 (64 %)	20 (50 %)	16 (44 %)
Italy	9 (43 %)	12 (57 %)	5 (62.5%)	3 (37.5%)
Germanic Group ..	18 (43 %)	24 (57 %)	35 (66 %)	18 (34 %)
Ireland	14 (39 %)	22 (61 %)	4 (50 %)	4 (50 %)
Miscellaneous	27 (37.5%)	45 (62.5%)	31 (56 %)	24 (44 %)
	164	256	138	117

NATIVITY OF DELINQUENTS

	Males		Females	
	Success	Failure	Success	Failure
United States	142 (39%)	225 (61%)	104 (51%)	101 (49%)
Foreign; non-English speaking	20 (39%)	31 (61%)	23 (64%)	13 (36%)
Foreign; English speaking	2	0	9	2
Unknown			2	1
	164	256	138	117

TABLE 26

COURT STATISTICS AND CHICAGO SERIES OF OUTCOMES COMPARED

NATIVITY OF PARENTS OF REPEATED OFFENDERS IN CHICAGO JUVENILE
COURT IN 1910 AND IN OUR SERIES

	Juvenile Court 1910		Our Series	
	Boys	Girls	Boys	Girls
United States	23 %	30%	27 %	30 %
White	(18.5%)	(25%)	(24 %)	(27 %)
Colored	(4.5%)	(5%)	(3 %)	(3 %)
Slavic Group	20 %	20%	16 %	7.5%
Russian Jewish	6 %	3%	16 %	14 %
Italy	8 %	....	5 %	3.5%
Germanic Group	12 %	10%	12.5%	23 %
Ireland	14 %	7%	8.5%	3.5%
Miscellaneous	17 %	30%	15 %	18.5%
	100 %	100%	100 %	100 %
(Number of cases	517	129	420	255)

(*The year 1910 was used merely because it was a fair sample year.*)

TABLE 27

Chicago and Boston Series of Outcomes Compared—Males

NATIVITY OF PARENTS BY LANGUAGE GROUPS

	Chicago 1909-14	Boston 1909-14
United States:		
White	101 (24%)	22 (5%)
Colored	13 (3%)	11 (3%)
Foreign speaking	236 (56%)	253 (63%)
Foreign, English speaking	40 (10%)	104 (26%)
Miscellaneous (mixed parentage, unknown)	30 (7%)	10 (3%)
	420	400

NATIVITY OF PARENTS BY NATIONALITIES

	Chicago			Boston		
	Totals	Adult Record Percentage of each Nationality		Totals	Adult Record Percentage of each Nationality	
		Without court records	With court records		Without court records	With court records
United States:						
White	101 (24%)	52%	48%	22 (5%)	95%	5%
Colored	13 (3%)	46%	54%	11 (3%)	73%	27%
Slavic group	68 (16%)	56%	44%	14 (3%)	86%	14%
Russian Jewish	67 (16%)	45%	55%	91 (23%)	86%	14%
Italian	21 (5%)	43%	57%	131 (33%)	79%	21%
Irish	34 (8%)	41%	59%	95 (24%)	79%	21%
Germanic group	42 (10%)	57%	43%	4 (1%)	....	....
Miscellaneous	74 (18%)	50%	50%	32 (8%)	75%	25%
Total numbers	420 (100%)	211	209	400 (100%)	326	74

TABLE 28

Series of 4000 Juvenile Delinquents

NATIVITY AND RACIAL EXTRACTION

	Birthplace of Delinquents				Nationality of Parents			
	Chicago		Boston		Chicago		Boston	
Series	I	II	I	II	I	II	I	II
United States:								
White	783	804	759	823	251	252	245	259
Colored	27	50	45	36	42	50	29	36
Ireland	3	..	2	3	71	60	127	105
Great Britain	15	9	3	13	41	18	18	30
Canada:								
English speaking...	5	4	..	..	13	13	51	49
French speaking...	2	1	20	23	10	9	24	30
Slavic Group	33	49	9	9	133	181	32	55
Germany and Austria	29	21	3	2	123	132	19	16
Italy	22	19	61	47	60	76	217	203
Jewish—Russian, Polish, Roumanian...	38	27	71	29	76	109	155	122
Scandinavia	3	3	7	1	41	40	10	17
France and Belgium..	2	1	..	2	14	5	..	2
Holland	..	..	1	..	5	7	1	1
Bohemia	3	7	..	..	32	30	..	3
Greece	1	3	..	1	1	4	..	3
Syria and Armenia ..	..	2	1	4	..	2	13	12
Portugal and Spain...	..	..	..	3	..	..	4	8
Miscellaneous	1	..	..	3	3	4	2	3
Unknown	33	..	18	1	84	8	53	46

TABLE 29

CENSUS STATISTICS FOR NATIONALITIES
NATIONALITY—CHICAGO AND BOSTON—1910

	Chicago	Boston
Native parentage	20 %	23 %
Foreign Nationalities:		
German	20 %	4 %
Irish	8 %	26 %
Scandinavian	8 %	2 %
Italian	3 %	7.5%
British	3 %	5.5%
Polish	10.5%	1 %
Jewish	5 %	8.5%

(The last two are not enumerated as nationalities—figures are based on census of languages spoken.)

The district of Boston from which most of the cases come to the Boston Juvenile Court had, approximately, in 1910:

Irish	7%
Russian-Jewish	17%
Italian	22%

(While not of exact application to either group, these last figures restricted to a district apply more to the 400 cases of Table 27 than to the 2000 Boston cases of Table 28.)

TABLE 30

COURT STATISTICS AND CHICAGO SERIES OF OUTCOMES
RELIGIONS

	Total Delinquents in Chicago, Juvenile Court in 1910		Totals for our Series	
	Males	Females	Males	Females
Catholic	694(60%)	236(50%)	208(50%)	90(35%)
Protestant	335(29%)	197(42%)	127(30%)	116(46%)
Jewish	91 (8%)	25 (5%)	79(19%)	40(19%)
Not Stated	41 (3%)	15 (3%)	...	...
No religion	...	2	...	...
Unknown	...	...	6	0
	1161	475	420	255

Chicago 1909-1914

	Males		Females	
	Success	Failure	Success	Failure
Catholic	87(53%)	121(47%)	46(33%)	44(38%)
Protestant	49(30%)	78(31%)	62(45%)	54(46%)
Jewish	27(16%)	52(20%)	30(22%)	19(16%)
Unknown	1 (1%)	5 (2%)	0	0
	164	256	138	117

Chicago 1909-1914

	Catholic		Protestant		Jewish		Unknown	
	Males	Females	Males	Females	Males	Females	Males	Fe-males
Success	87(42%)	46(51%)	49(38%)	62(53%)	27(34%)	30(61%)	1	0
Failure	121(58%)	44(49%)	78(62%)	54(47%)	52(66%)	19(39%)	5	0
	208	90	127	116	79	49	6	0

TABLE 31

SERIES OF 4000 JUVENILE DELINQUENTS

HOME AND PARENTAL CONDITIONS

Series	Totals			
	Chicago		Boston	
	I	II	I	II
Good Home Conditions (a special study)	...	5.	10.3	...
Extreme Lack of Parental Control....	23.	46.	51.	39.5
Extreme Parental Neglect [1]	...	...	18.6	25.5
Poverty	8.	24.	19.	16.7
Excessive Quarreling in the Home [2]...	12.	8.	14.8	14.8
Alcoholism, Immorality, or Criminalism in the Home	20.	28.	19.7	15.8
Mentally Abnormal Parent in the Home	...	7.	.7	1.3
Of Illegitimate Parentage	2.6	2.8	2.	2.8
Both Parents Living at Home........	48.	55	58.	57.
Both Parents Dead	6.	2.8	2.9	3.5
One Parent Dead	26.	28.	29.	27.7
Parents Separated [3]	20.	14.	10.	12.
Step-father or Step-mother	22.7	...	10.3	16.
Mother Working away from Home...	16.5	...	22.6	20.9

[1] Boston, Series I, Males 18.0%, Females 21.0%; Series II, Males 24.0%, Females 28.0%.

[2] Boston, Series I, Males 11.7%, Females 24.4%; Series II, Males 11.8%, Females 21.0%.

[3] Parents separated includes living apart, divorced, and desertions. Desertions alone are: Chicago, I, 8.6%, II, 7.7%; Boston, I, 2.4%, II, 3.1%.

(For definition of some of the above home conditions which may not be altogether clear, the reader is referred to discussion of these conditions in the text in Chapter 12.)

TABLE 32

CHICAGO SERIES OF OUTCOMES
ECONOMIC LEVELS

	Total 675	Males		Females		Total—675	
		Success	Failure	Success	Failure	Success	Failure
Destitute	5%	8 (5%)	17 (6%)	4 (3%)	6 (5%)	4%	6%
Poverty	22%	32(19%)	65(26%)	31(22%)	23(20%)	21%	24%
Normal	35%	44(27%)	90(35%)	52(38%)	51(44%)	32%	38%
Comfortable .	34%	67(41%)	77(30%)	47(34%)	36(31%)	37%	30%
Luxury	4%	13 (8%)	7 (3%)	4 (3%)	1 (0%)	6%	2%
	100%	164	256	138	117	100%	100%

Proportion of Success and Failure at each Economic Level

	Success	Failure
Destitute	12(34%)	23(66%)
Poverty	63(42%)	88(58%)
Normal	96(40%)	141(60%)
Comfortable	114(50%)	113(50%)
Luxury	17(68%)	8(32%)
	302	373

TABLE 33

CHICAGO SERIES OF OUTCOMES
PARENTAL RELATIONSHIPS

	Boys			Girls		
	Totals	Percentage of each Parental Relationship		Totals	Percentage of each Parental Relationship	
		Success	Failure		Success	Failure
One Parent Deserted......	28 (7%)	36%	64%	13 (5%)	23%	77%
Two Parents Deserted.....	1 (0%)	0%	0%	1 (0%)	....	....
Parents Separated or Divorced	37 (9%)	40%	60%	37 (15%)	50%	50%
Both Parents Dead........	12 (3%)	33%	67%	10 (4%)	80%	20%
Father Dead	75 (18%)	30%	70%	31 (12%)	55%	45%
Mother Dead	51 (12%)	47%	53%	44 (17%)	57%	43%
Total; Broken Homes.....	204 (49%)	37%	63%	136 (53%)	54%	46%
Normally Constituted Homes	216 (51%)	41%	59%	119 (47%)	56%	44%
Total Numbers	420(100%) 164 256			255(100%) 138 117		

TABLE 34

CHICAGO SERIES OF OUTCOMES

FAMILY CONDITIONS AFTER HOMES BROKEN

	Boys		Girls	
	Success	Failure	Success	Failure
Foster Parents or Two Step-Parents	3	6	11	4
Step-father	10	22	19	12
Step-mother	15	13	15	8
In Orphanage after Death of Parents	2	6	2	0
	30	47	47	24

TABLE 35

CHICAGO AND BOSTON SERIES OF OUTCOMES

FAMILY CONDITIONS AMONG MALE OFFENDERS—1909-14

	Chicago				Boston			
	Totals		Adult Record Percentage of each Family Condition		Totals		Adult Record Percentage of each Family Condition	
			Without court records	With court records			Without court records	With court records
One Parent Deserted...	28	(7%)	36%	64%	11	(3 %)	55%	45%
Two Parents Deserted..	1	(0%)	....	....	0		0	0
Parents Separated or Divorced	37	(9%)	40%	60%	14	(3.5%)	64%	36%
Both Parents Dead.....	12	(3%)	33%	67%	9	(2.5%)	78%	22%
Father Dead	75	(18%)	30%	70%	61	(15 %)	76%	24%
Mother Dead	51	(12%)	47%	53%	26	(6.5%)	73%	27%
Total; Broken Homes..	204	(49%)	37%	63%	121	(30 %)	72%	28%
Normally Constituted Homes	216	(51%)	41%	59%	268	(67 %)	73%	27%
Unknown	..		..	....	11	(3 %)	91%	9%
Total Numbers	420	(100%)	211	209	400	(100 %)	326	74

TABLE 37

Chicago Series of Outcomes
BAD HOME CONDITIONS

In this table we have allowed no overlapping; there may have been both criminalism and alcoholism in the same home but we have placed the individual case under only one category, selecting the one which, at the time of the first study, was considered the most important.

By "alcoholic" we mean, at least occasionally intoxicated.

	Males		Females	
	Success	Failure	Success	Failure
Criminalism or sex immorality in the home	8	44	18	17
Both parents alcoholic at home.	1	3	1	2
Father alcoholic at home	4	14	6	11
Mother alcoholic at home	2	4	1	1
Father alcoholic, mother working out	6	2	0	0
Father alcoholic, mother shiftless and neglectful	4	3	1	0
Much home quarreling	3	4	1	2
Home very dirty	4	0	0	0
Father or mother takes drugs	0	2	0	0
	32	76	28	33

TABLE 38

Series of 4000 Juvenile Delinquents
ONE OR BOTH PARENTS ALCOHOLIC

Chicago		Boston	
I	II	I	II
31.0%	26.0% = Total 28.5%	51.0%	39.0% = Total 45.0%

(These figures are not identical with those for alcoholism in the home —an alcoholic parent for various reasons may have been out of the home for some time.)

TABLE 39

Chicago Series of Outcomes

52 Boys from Homes where Criminalism or Sex Immorality Existed

	Success	Failure
Probation at home or paroled home from institutions	4	38
Placed, or left home	4	6
	8	44

Of 4 Successes without leaving home, one had a vigorous mother, another worked away from home for long periods, in one case the home improved, one boy apparently withstood conditions as he became older.

Of the 6 Failures although placed, two had been in homosexual practices, one was the victim of excessively bad habits—smoking, drinking, and sex, one had a long institutional career and was soon delinquent again when placed, one, a psycho-neurotic, failed only on his return home after a short placement.

TABLE 40

CHICAGO SERIES OF OUTCOMES

35 GIRLS FROM HOMES WHERE CRIMINALISM OR SEX IMMORALITY EXISTED

SUCCESS		FAILURE	
Juvenile Adjustments	*Later Adjustments*	*Juvenile Adjustments*	*Later Adjustments*
1 Placed. Geneva.	? Later married.	19 Refuge. Geneva .	To bad home.
2 Illinois Indus.		20 Refuge	To bad home.
Sch.	Placed.	21 H. Good Shep-	
3 H. Good Shep-		herd	Home, conditions
herd	To bettered home.		unknown.
	Married.	22 Geneva	Placed. To bet-
4 Geneva	Placed. Married.		tered home.
5 Placed	Sch. for Nursing.	23 H. Good Shep-	
	Married.	herd	To bad home.
6 Refuge	To bettered home.	24 H. Good Shep-	
7 Refuge	To good rela-	herd	To house of pros-
	tives.		titution.
8 Placed	To good rela-	25 Refuge	To bad home.
	tives.	26 H. Good Shep-	
9 Placed in girls'		herd	Housework.
academy	Placed.	27 Placed	To immoral life.
10 Refuge. Geneva.		28 H. Good Shep-	
Placed	To bettered home.	herd. Geneva .	To T. B. Hos-
	Married.		pitals. Incor-
11 Chi. Indus. Sch.	To good rela-		rigible.
	tives.	29 H. Good Shep-	
12 Hosp., mental		herd	To bad home.
case	Other hospitals.	30 Placed	To bad home.
	Recovered.	31 Geneva. Lincoln	Changed institu-
	Married.		tions. Incorri-
13 Placed	Sch. for Nursing.		gible.
14 Geneva	To good rela-	32 Geneva	To bad home.
	tives. Married.	33 Placed	To bad home.
15 H. Good Shep-		34 H. Good Shep-	
herd	Housework.	herd	To bad home.
16 Geneva	Directly married.	35 Refuge	Housework.
17 H. Good Shep-			
herd	Went home which		
	became bet-		
	tered. Married.		
18 Placed. Geneva.	Placed. Married.		

SUMMARY

	Success	*Failure*
To juvenile institutions.....................	14	14
Placed as juveniles.........................	4	3
Later adjustments :		
Paroled :		
To bettered home	3	1
To home not bettered..................	1	9
To home, conditions unknown...........	0	1
Placed away from home.................	13	2
To hospitals	0	2
Directly to immoral life.................	0	2
Unknown first adjustment...............	1	0

Concerning Failures as represented in the above careers, it should be stated that for all 17 cases this means that the girls showed well-marked immoral tendencies after juvenile court age, most of them being specifically known as immoral young women.

TABLE 41

CHICAGO SERIES OF OUTCOMES

HEREDITY

Family History	Males		Females		Totals
	164 Suc-cesses	256 Fail-ures	138 Suc-cesses	117 Fail-ures	675
Normal	92	122	59	43	316(47%)
Of Abnormal Mentality.....	17	49	21	26	113(17%)
plus Delinquency	1	7	..	3	....
" Alcoholism	6	11	2	5	....
" Delinquency and Al-coholism	4	3	8	6	....
Of Delinquency	30	53	41	37	161(24%)
plus Alcoholism	14	26	16	12	....
Of Alcoholism	50	80	44	42	216(32%)
Unknown	4	3	7	2	16

In the above table there is, of course, overlapping, the same individual may be counted, for example, as both alcoholic and delinquent, and so the numbers and percentages total more than 100 per cent. The table below expresses the direct percentages of Success and Failure in each main category taken by itself.

Family History	Males		Females	
	Successes	Failures	Successes	Failures
Normal	43%	57%	58%	42%
Abnormal Mentality	26%	74%	45%	55%
Delinquency	36%	64%	52%	48%
Alcoholism	38%	62%	51%	49%

TABLE 42

CHICAGO SERIES OF OUTCOMES

MARITAL STATUS

	Males		Females	
	Success	Failure	Success	Failure
Married—Totals	23	14 [1]	83	38 [3]
Living with family.....	23	..	80	..
Divorced or separated..			3	..
Unmarried—Totals	141	242 [2]	55	79 [4]
Living with relatives...	82	..	33	..
Not with relatives—con-				
ditions good	22	..	22	..
Army or Navy	35	..	..	..
Dead after good records	2	..	..	..

Details of the Failures

MALES

[1] Married—total, 14

3 divorced or legally separated, 4 deserters or non-supporters, others loafers or in institutions

[2] Unmarried—total, 242

Most lead irregular lives; are in or out of institutions, sometimes with relatives, or vagrants, or disappeared (49 were in service, 21 of them dishonorably discharged)

FEMALES

[3] Married—total, 38

4 divorced, and probably immoral; 22 definitely reported immoral, 4 of them prostitutes; 8 deserted or badly neglected children.

[4] Unmarried—total, 79

67 reported immoral, 18 of them prostitutes; 16 had 21 illegitimate children.

TABLE 43

SERIES OF 4000 JUVENILE DELINQUENTS

PHYSICAL CONDITIONS

(Entire Table in Percentages)

	Totals				Males				Females			
	Chicago		Boston		Chicago		Boston		Chicago		Boston	
Series	I	II	I	II	I	II	I	II	I	II	I	II
Good physical condition	...	27.0	...	32.7	...	...	...	...	...	...	...	...
Marked general overdevelopment	4.5	9.0	5.7	4.7	...	5.0	4.1	4.2	...	20.0	11.0	5.7
Very poor general development	5.0	17.0	7.5	12.6	...	21.0	8.5	15.0	...	8.0	4.0	6.0
Premature puberty	7.5	14.0	8.0	9.3	...	16.0	9.0	12.6	...	9.0	4.5	2.0
Delayed puberty	1.0	5.0	3.6	3.2	...	...	4.2	4.3	...	...	0.0	0.9
Overdevelopment of sex characteristics	...	...	...	...	...	...	4.6	1.4	...	...	5.6	9.3
Sensory Defects:												
Vision	10.0	15.0	11.4	20.0	...	...	...	...	...	...	...	...
Hearing	1.5	1.6	2.2	2.5	...	...	...	...	...	...	...	...
Nose and Throat Ailments	...	18.0	25.0	23.5	...	...	...	...	...	...	...	...
Otorrhea	...	3.0	1.8	2.1	...	...	...	...	...	...	...	...
Signs of Nervous Disease	2.0	4.0	4.3	3.4	...	...	...	...	...	...	...	...
Syphilis	...	...	...	...	...	...	...	0.7	...	...	...	3.8
Gonorrhea	...	...	...	...	...	...	...	0.4	...	...	...	10.5
Stigmata of Degeneracy	13.0	3.8	5.3	3.1	...	...	...	...	...	...	...	...
Somatic Signs of Syphilis	...	5.2	5.4	3.6	...	...	...	...	...	...	...	...
Signs of Head Injury	2.0	2.7	3.7	5.8	...	...	...	...	...	...	...	...
Teeth—see below												
Goitre—see below												
Cases—Totals	1000	1000	1000	1000	694	692	758	686	306	308	242	314

TEETH

(2000 JUVENILE DELINQUENTS)

	Chicago	Boston
Good condition	39.0	79.8
Slightly carious	8.1	12.1
One or more badly carious	52.9	8.1
Cases—Totals	1000	1000

Table 42 continued on p. 270.

GOITRE

(2000 JUVENILE DELINQUENTS)

	Totals		Boys		Girls	
	Chicago	Boston	Chicago	Boston	Chicago	Boston
Just visible	4.1	0.4	3.1	0.0	6.2	1.6
Small goitre	4.9	0.1	1.1	0.0	10.4	0.4
Considerable goitre	1.7	0.0	0.4	0.0	4.6	0.0
Cases—Totals	1000	1000	694	758	306	242

TABLE 44

CHICAGO SERIES OF OUTCOMES

PHYSICAL DEVELOPMENTAL CONDITIONS

			Males		Female	
TOTALS	420 Males	255 Females	164 Success	256 Failure	138 Success	117 Failure
Normal general physical conditions; nothing pathological of marked importance	265(63%)	200(78%)	77	188	112	88
Signs of defective or poor general development	77(18%)	22 (8%)	30	47	11	11
Marked general over-development.......	13 (3%)	31(12%)	6	7	15	16
Marked sensory defect (vision or hearing)	43(10%)	33(13%)	14	29	19	14
Organic disease or defect (*diseased* tonsils, obstructive adenoids, heart disease, etc.)	54(13%)	20 (8%)	23	31	7	13
Distinct signs of congenital syphilis....	15 (3%)	10 (4%)	7	8	4	6
Suffered head injury, severe enough at least to have caused unconsciousness..	18 (4%)	1 (0%)	7	11	0	1
Marked stigmata of degeneracy........	23 (5%)	3 (1%)	6	17	2	1
Known epilepsy	15 (4%)	9 (4%)	6	9	5	4

For interpretation of the above table the following should be noted: It will be seen at a glance that data were not always gathered for all four series nor always for the sexes separately. This is mostly due to change of methods of recording data so that in the several series data were not comparable. In some matters sex differences seemed not worth separate statistics.

By *good physical condition* we mean the positive finding that no significant physical defects or ailments have been found; we have surveyed the records of only two groups for comparison of this finding.

Marked general overdevelopment does not mean nutrition in excess, but, rather, great growth of bodily structure for age.

In estimating *very poor general development* we have attempted to keep in mind standards of racial variations.

Premature puberty we have given on the basis of onset of puberty at or prior to 12 years for girls and 13 years for boys; *delayed puberty* when it begins at 16 years or later.

Overdevelopment of sex characteristics denotes structural and other secondary developmental changes.

Sensory defects.—We have counted as defective only cases where vision was less than 20/40, half normal, in either eye, uncorrected by glasses, or where there was some disabling from other ocular troubles. "Defective hearing" means, of course, more than slight defect.

Nose and throat ailments—By far the largest number listed under this category represents cases of considerably enlarged or ragged, or diseased tonsils. Slight enlargement has not been enumerated.

Otorrhea—Here means cases of active infection of the middle ear.

Signs of nervous disease—In general, this covers the distinctly neurotic types, though a diagnosis of a definite disease has sometimse been impossible. The commonest nervous disease found was chorea. (Epilepsy and head injury are omitted here.)

Syphilis and gonorrhea—We feel it unsafe to give any figures on syphilis and gonorrhea for any series earlier than Boston II, because of differences in records in these matters, and changes of methods in examination since the time of studying the Chicago series. But, we know no reason why proportions in the two cities should show much variance.

Stigmata of degeneracy—Under this heading we have placed only those who show at least two marked signs suggesting, according to the older terminology, a "degenerate" type of individual.

Somatic signs of syphilis—Here we include signs which have been formerly regarded as diagnostic of congenital syphilis. No doubt most of these do represent such defective antenatal conditions, but probably not all. On almost all of those in the Boston series a negative Wassermann has been reported; that, of course, does not prove that damage has not already been done to the organism by earlier syphilis.

Signs of head injury—Under this category we do not include scalp wounds or slight involvement of the skull. The figures given cover only cases where there have been either fracture of the skull or serious symptoms, nearly always unconsciousness following the injury.

Teeth We have taken in each city 1000 consecutive cases in which our findings are recorded in a manner to make them comparable.

Goitre—We have followed the same method, taking consecutive comparable records in 1000 cases for each city. These records show when the thyroid was palpable although not visibly enlarged. We are not at all sure that this palpability has any special significance, but we can state that such condition was found in 4.5 per cent of the Chicago cases and in 2.5 per cent of the Boston cases.

TABLE 45

Series of 4000 Juvenile Delinquents

BAD HABITS—PENCENTAGES

	Totals				Males				Females			
	Chicago		Boston		Chicago		Boston		Chicago		Boston	
Series	I	II	I	II	I	II	I	II	I	II	I	II
Tobacco in Excess.	...	...	...	...	10.8	14.4	28.2	33.8	...	...	...	...
Excessive Masturbation	10.0	11.0	12.2	7.7	...	13.0	14.0	8.3	...	7.0	6.0	6.3
Use of Alcohol....	3.0	1.7	7.5	4.5	...	...	8.5	3.5	...	...	3.7	1.2
Tea and Coffee in Excess	5.2	...	12.2	11.3	...	...	14.0	14.4	...	...	5.0	4.4

Under this heading appear facts that are known with considerable accuracy as far as stated, but there is, of course, possibility of some understatement of the total situation.

Tobacco in excess—We give figures on the use of tobacco only as somewhat, at least for the time being, of a habit. The occasional smoker is not counted.

Not being a common habit of young delinquent girls who appear in court (we have seen only one case in Chicago and one in Boston) it is fair to give percentages for boys only.

Excessive masturbation—We have enumerated masturbation only when it was a decidedly frequent habit, fairly to be termed excessive.

Use of alcohol—Even a small amount of drinking during adolescence is of great importance, and we have counted it as such.

Tea and coffee in excess—Excess in this case indicates either an undue amount of tea and coffee or the use of it at a very early age.

Use of drugs—As we stated under Offenses, the use of drugs during juvenile court age is very rare.

TABLE 46

CHICAGO SERIES OF OUTCOMES

BAD HABITS

	Males (420)		Females (255)	
	Success (164)	Failure (256)	Success (138)	Failure (117)
Excessive masturbation	18(11%)	39(15%)	17(12%)	10 (9%)
Smoking in excess................	17(10%)	28(11%)	0	1
Use of stimulants (tea and coffee) in excess	4 (2%)	15 (6%)	1	3
Frequent use of alcoholic drinks...	0	2	0	2
Use of drugs	0	2	0	0
	39	86	18	16

The percentages given above are of the total Successes and Failures—thus, 11% of the 164 male Successes were known by us to be excessively engaged in masturbation.

The figures do not represent different individuals; some engaged in more than one of the listed bad habits.

TABLE 47

SERIES OF 4000 JUVENILE DELINQUENTS

MENTAL FINDINGS

Series	Totals				Males				Females			
	Chicago		Boston		Chicago		Boston		Chicago		Boston	
	I	II	I	II	I	II	I	II	I	II	I	II
Normal Mentally..	69.5	75.0	73.8	72.0	...	77.1	75.0	71.7	...	70.0	69.9	73.2
Clearly Feeble-minded	13.5	12.5	12.0	16.2	...	10.1	11.2	15.4	...	18.1	13.5	18.0
Subnormal Mental-ity	10.1	8.2	10.6	7.7	...	9.0	10.5	8.9	...	6.4	12.0	5.0
Psychoses	6.9	4.3	1.0	1.1	5.3	3.8	1.1	1.3	10.4	5.5	0.9	1.0
Psychopathic Per-sonalities	...	...	2.6	3.0	...	...	2.2	2.7	...	...	3.7	2.8
Totals	100.0	100.0	100.0	100.0	...	100.0	100.0	100.0	...	100.0	100.0	100.0
Constitutional In-feriority	2.0	2.0	2.9	1.7	2.3	2.0	3.3	2.9	1.3	1.0	1.6	0.9
Epilepsy	7.0	4.0	2.1	1.2	...	...	...	...	...	...	...	...

(Psychopathic Personality is a term that was not used in our original classification of the Chicago series; individuals of this type were recognized but were classified among all the other groups except that of Psychoses, which were cases with frank signs of mental disease.)

Mental Classifications and Diagnoses

Normal mentally—Under this category we place those who are neither clearly defective, psychotic, nor psychopathic personalities (as judged by their intelligence quotients plus the findings on other tests and on psychiatric examination).

Clearly feebleminded—This classification represents a group diagnosed by careful interpretation of age-level and other tests. Practically all have an intelligence quotient of less than 75, and most of them of 70 or less.

Subnormal mentally—This is a group not grading low enough to be considered clearly feebleminded but yet not within the limits of certainly normal mentality. In other classifications this is called the border-line group—a term we do not use because there is no line of demarcation. The intelligence quotients of almost all of these fall between 75 and 80, but, even as in the case of the feebleminded, we use other tests and interpret them all with much care; we do not consider the I.Q. alone safely diagnostic.

Under *psychoses* we have classified cases with aberrational mental symptoms sufficient in degree to be diagnosable as mental disease.

Psychopathic personalities—We cannot readily give the figures for the large Chicago groups because earlier we were not using this terminology, which was not then greatly in use, and because in our Chicago statistics this group overlaps the others (psychopathic personalities in terms of intelligence may range from the very bright to the defective). But the group of 675 we reclassified carefully to show the outcomes of psychopathic personalities and other sub-groups.

And we frankly acknowledge that if we were similarly to review our Boston series, the percentages would be somewhat different. Indeed, we are undertaking a special study of our material better to understand and define the entire concept of psychopathic personality.

Constitutional inferiority—Under this classification are represented cases already given in the group of the mentally normal, because by mental tests they grade as normal.

Epilepsy—Our figures are only for those cases in which within recent years in the individual's life there have been active epileptic manifestations. The epileptics are distributed among the normal, defective, and psychotic in the tables of mentality; some of them are properly classified as psychopathic personalities.

TABLE 48

CHICAGO SERIES OF OUTCOMES

GENERAL FIGURES OF MENTAL STATUS

Normal intelligence	532 (79%)
Feebleminded	108 (16%)
Psychoses	35 (5%)
	675(100%)

(For a more detailed classification see Table 48)

TABLE 49

CHICAGO SERIES OF OUTCOMES

MENTALITY CLASSIFICATIONS

	Total	By Sexes		By Outcomes	
		Males	Females	Success	Failure
Mentally normal .... (Supernormal in ability 19)	426(63%)	274(65%)	152(60%)	217(51%)	209(49%)
Feebleminded	92(14%)	54(13%)	38(15%)	30(33%)	62(67%)
Psychopathic personalities ...... (Normal intelligence 79) (Feebleminded .....15)	94(14%)	57(13%)	37(15%)	31(33%)	63(67%)
Psychotic	35 (5%)	16 (4%)	19 (7%)	10(29%)	25(71%)
Psychoneurotic .... (Normal intelligence 14) (Feebleminded ..... 1)	15 (2%)	7 (2%)	8 (3%)	9(60%)	6(40%)
Constitutional inferior	13 (2%)	12 (3%)	1 (0%)	5(38%)	8(62%)
	675	420	255	302	373

In order to keep these tables simple, the border-zone group (called subnormal in tables for the larger series) has been distributed, mainly with the group of normal intelligence as found under the several headings.

TABLE 49 (*Continued*)

MENTALITY CORRELATED WITH OUTCOMES FOR SEXES SEPARATELY

	Males		Females	
	Success	Failure	Success	Failure
Mentally normal	123(45%)	151(55%)	94(62%)	58(38%)
Feebleminded	13(24%)	41(76%)	17(45%)	21(55%)
Psychopathic personalities	16(28%)	41(72%)	15(40%)	22(60%)
Psychotic	5(30%)	11(70%)	5(26%)	14(74%)
Psychoneurotic	3(13%)	4(57%)	6(75%)	2(25%)
Constitutional inferior	4(33%)	8(67%)	1	0
	164	256	138	117

SUPERNORMAL IN MENTAL ABILITY

	Success	Failure
Males	7	6
Females	6	0
Males, psychopathic personalities.......	1	1
	14	7

TABLE 50

CHICAGO SERIES OF OUTCOMES

EPILEPTICS

Males	Success	Failure
Feebleminded	3	1
Psychotic	1	0
Psychopathic	2	8

Females		
Mentally normal	0	1
Feebleminded	1	1
Psychotic	1	0
Psychopathic	3	2
	11	13

TABLE 51

CHICAGO SERIES OF OUTCOMES

TREATMENT OF MENTALLY ABNORMAL

(Among our 758 traced juvenile offenders)

5 dead (one suicide) during juvenile court age
23 remain in institutions for the feebleminded
15 remain in hospitals for mental disease
109 feebleminded either were not committed [1] as such or did not remain
     in an institution for the feebleminded
56 psychotic either were not committed as such or did not remain in
     an institution for mental disease
75 psychopathic were given no special treatment as such

___

283

(The 38 who remain in institutions have not been counted as either
Successes or Failures.)

[1] Concerning non-commitment of mentally defective juveniles, it
should be stated that when nearly all of our cases were seen, that is,
prior to 1915, juvenile courts and courts of criminal jurisdiction in
Illinois had no authority to commit. Committing to the institution for
the feebleminded depended upon consent of parents, which, on account
of general distrust of such institutions, was rarely forthcoming. But
since then many of these defectives have appeared as offenders in
adult courts, where there has been ample authority to commit under
the 1915 law, and they have not been so committed.

TABLE 52

CHICAGO SERIES OF OUTCOMES

TREATMENT OF THE MENTALLY ABNORMAL ACCORDING TO SUCCESS AND
FAILURE

221 Cases (not including 38 remaining in institutions for mentally
abnormal)

	TREATMENT AS JUVENILES					
	To Institutions for Abnormal	*To Institutions for Abnormal after Correctional Institution*	*Only to Correctional Institution*	*Placed in Country*	*Home on Probation*	*Adult Outcome*
MALES						
Successes:						
15 Feebleminded.	2	0	5	2	6	11 at home; 2 in army; 2 in foster-homes.
5 Psychotic ...	0	0	2	1	2	1 at home; 4 in army.
14 Psychopathic personality..	0	0	9	4	1	5 at home; 7 in army; 2 in foster-homes.
Failures:						
45 Feebleminded.	15	5	18	4	3	41 in court as offenders, 21 committed to correctional institution, 7 to institution for defectives (2 escaped).
11 Psychotic ...	5	1	5	0	0	11 in court as offenders, 9 committed to correctional institution, 2 to hospitals for mental diseases.
37 Psychopathic personality..	3	2	23	7	2	37 offenders, 31 in court as such, 21 committed to correctional institution; 4 to hospital for mental diseases; 3 disappeared after offenses.
FEMALES						
Successes:						
17 Feebleminded.	2	0	8	3	4	7 married; 2 at housework; 6 remain with relatives; 2 boarding and working.
5 Psychotic ...	0	0	3	1	1	3 married; 1 remains with relatives; 1 boarding and working.
15 Psychopathic personality..	0	0	9	4	2	8 married; 5 remain with relatives; 1 at housework; 1 boarding and working.
Failures:						
21 Feebleminded.	3	0	14	1	3	8 married; 21 immoral; 3 known court records; 4 known prostitutes; 6 had illegitimate children.
14 Psychotic ...	2	0	9	3	0	2 married; 10 reported immoral; 3 had illegitimate children.
22 Psychopathic personality..	0	0	20	0	2	17 reported immoral; for other offenses 2 to penitentiary, 1 to House of Correction; 2 deserted their legitimate, 3 their illegitimate children; 5 married; 7 had 10 illegitimate children.
	32	8	125	30	26	

(Of the 40 who were committed to institutions for the mentally abnormal,
some were released; many escaped.)

TABLE 53
Chicago Series of Outcomes
MENTALITY OF THE 29 INDIFFERENT SUCCESSES

19 mentally abnormal:
    11 males: 7 feebleminded (2 epileptic); 1 psychotic; 3 psychopathic personality.
    8 females: 4 feebleminded (3 epileptic); 2 psychotic; 2 psychopathic personality.
        Of these: 1 male and 5 females married; 3 other females and 9 other males remain with relatives.

10 mentally normal:
    8 males: 2 married but marital difficulty; 4 remain with relatives; 1 army; 1 disappeared.
    2 females: both married poorly.

TABLE 54
Series of 4000 Juvenile Delinquents
OFFENSES

| | BOYS | | | | GIRLS | | | |
| | Chicago | | Boston | | Chicago | | Boston | |
Series	I	II	I	II	I	II	I	II
Offenses Against Property:								
Stealing	66.	70.	72.	73.	32.	30.	40.	41.
Automobile Stealing	...	...	2.6	2.4	...	...	...	...
Major Breaking and Entering (burglary)	8.	17.	4.	3.3	...	...	...	...
Petty Breaking and Entering.	...	...	27.	34.	...	...	...	...
Picking Pockets	1.5	1.5	1.7	1.1	...	...	...	...
Forgery	1.7	2.	.8	1.6	2.	1.5	.4	.3
Arson	1.5	...	.4	1.3	1.	...	.4	0.
Offenses Against the Person:								
Robbery (hold-ups)	1.5	4.	0.	0.	...	...	...	...
Assault and Battery or.	...	...	...	...	...	...	...	...
Fighting with Weapons	6.	...	.5	0.	.7	...	...	...
Cruelty	1.5	...	.5	.7	.3	...	.4	.6
Attempted Suicide	.5	.5	...	.1	3.	3.	.5	1.
Offenses of Sex Nature:								
Immorality with Opposite Sex	4.5	4.5	4.7	7.1	60.	73.	52.	54.8
Abnormal Sex Misconduct...	4.	4.	4.3	3.7	3.	1.5	1.2	1.
Offenses Against Social Regulations:								
Carrying Concealed Weapons .	1.5	2.5	.3	1.4	...	...	...	...
Vagrancy	2.	5.	1.1	1.3	...	...	...	...
Running away from Home....	39.	48.	48.	24.	25.	37.	40.	32.
Sleeping Out Nights	12.	...	22.	21.4	10.	...	1.6	1.2
Excessive Idleness, Loafing ..	...	10.	13.	8.1	...	...	...	...
Out Late Nights	...	...	21.	16.7	...	10.	37.	37.5
Truancy	32.	43.	43.	41.	7.5	4.	3.	1.6
Excessive Lying	14.	7.	11.3	6.7	27.	14.	16.5	13.
False Accusations	1.	.2	0.	0.	5.	9.	...	2.8
Selling without License	...	...	2.	3.4	...	...	...	...
Begging	1.	...	2.2	2.9	.3	...	0.	.6
Gambling	2.	2.	3.	5.1	...	...	...	...
Alcoholic Intoxication	3.	3.	2.3	.6	3.	3.	0.	0.
Cases—Totals	694	692	758	686	306	308	242	314

(In this table where no figures are given there was no enumeration of the offense for the particular series.)

278

TABLE 55

CHICAGO SERIES OF OUTCOMES

OFFENSES KNOWN AT TIME OF FIRST STUDY OF CASE

	420 BOYS		255 GIRLS	
	Success	Failure	Success	Failure
Offenses Against Property:				
Petty Stealing	31 (49%)	32 (51%)	......	......
Larceny	51 (27%)	130 (73%)		
Stealing (including shoplifting)	......	......	49 (59%)	34 (41%)
Major Breaking and Entering (burglary)	8 (31%)	18 (69%)		
Automobile Stealing	2	3	......	......
Picking Pockets in Professional Way	1	3		
Forgery	3	2	1	1
Swindling	1	3	0	1
Arson	2	1	1	1
Offenses Against the Person:				
Violent Behavior at Home	6 (23%)	20 (77%)	1	4
Assault and Battery	5 (33%)	10 (67%)	0	2
"Hold-up"	1	2		
Cruelty to Children	1	1	......	......
Attempt to Poison	1	0	1	2
False Accusation	......	......	5	3
Offenses of Sex Nature:				
Sex (mutual masturbation with boys)	10 (37%)	17 (63%)	......	......
Abnormal Sex (homosexual affairs with men)	3 (18%)	14 (82%)		
With Opposite Sex	2	4	72 (53%)	65 (47%)*
Exhibitionism	1	2	1	0
Sex Perversions	......	......	1	2
Offenses Against Social Regulations:				
Truancy	49 (39%)	77 (61%)	9	4
Complaint of General Incorrigibility	21 (37%)	35 (63%)	16 (44%)	20 (56%)
Running away from Home	64 (37%)	110 (63%)	37 (49%)	39 (51%)
Out Late Nights or All Night	17 (49%)	18 (51%)	8 (36%)	14 (64%)
Vagrancy	2	6	......	......
Loafing (excessive)	20 (47%)	23 (53%)	5	6
Drinking (excessive)	2	2	0	1
Gambling (excessive)	4	6	......	......
Lying (excessive)	20 (44%)	25 (56%)	27 (52%)	25 (48%)

(Many individuals engaged in more than one type of offense—compare Table 55.)

* In addition to the above a special study brings out information concerning the girls as follows: 191 (75% of the total) at some time during juvenile court age had heterosexual experiences (practically always intercourse). Of these, 92 (48%) belong in our group of Successes; 99 (52%) are classed as Failures.

TABLE 56

CHICAGO SERIES BOYS OF OUTCOMES

CASES WHERE ONLY ONE TYPE OF OFFENSE WAS ENGAGED IN

	Success	Failure
Offenses Against Property		
Petty Stealing	8(67%)	4(33%)
Larceny	13(30%)	30(70%)
Breaking and Entering (Burglary)..	1	1
Automobile Stealing	1	2
Picking Pockets in Professional Way	0	1
Arson	1	0
Offenses Against the Person		
Violent Behavior at Home..........	1	2
Assault and Battery	1	0
Offenses of Sex Nature		
Definite Sex Assault on Girls........	0	2
Sex with Women or Girls...........	2	0
Touching Women on Street.........	2	0
Mutual Masturbation with Boys....	0	1
Homosexual Affairs with Boys......		
(one of each plus cruelty)	2	1
Perversions with Boys, Girls, Animals	0	1
Offenses Against Social Regulations		
Truancy	1	6
Complaint of General Incorrigibility.	1	4
Running Away from Home.........	7	9
Sleeping Away Nights..............	1	1
Vagrancy	0	1
Loafing	1	2
	43	68

TABLE 57

SOME CONDITIONS, NOT ENUMERATED ABOVE, PROBABLY DIRECTLY CAUSATIVE OF DELINQUENCY—PERCENTAGES

	TOTALS				BOYS				GIRLS			
	Chicago		Boston		Chicago		Boston		Chicago		Boston	
Series	I	II	I	II	I	II	I	II	I	II	I	II
Mental Conflict	7.		5.7	6.2								
Adolescent Instability and Impulses	21.		18.4	15.5	18.		16.5	11.		27.	24.	24.8
Extreme Social Suggestibility	3.		7.6	3.8								
Extremely Early Improper Sex Experiences	15.		10.4	11.8	13.		8.4	10.4		23.	16.	15.
Bad Companions	55.		64.	67.			65.	68.			59.	64.
Motion Pictures	1.1		1.7	.9			2.1	1.			.4	.6
Love of Adventure	1.2		2.1	3.9			2.6	4.8			.4	1.9
Other Probable Direct Causations												
School Dissatisfaction			9.8	8.6			10.	12.5			3.	1.2
Vocational Dissatisfaction			1.5	3.8			1.4	4.8			3.	1.5
Sudden Impulse				7.2				8.3				4.7
Recurrent or Obsessive Ideation			.8	5.9				4.5				8.9
Recurrent or Obsessive Imagery				.9			1.	1.2			0.	.4
Street Life in Excess			11.6	11.5			14.	16.4			3.	.9
Poor Types of Recreations			21.4	20.4			19.	18.8			26.	23.8
Formation of Habit of Delinquency			3.5	8.6			4.	10.3			1.2	4.7
Premature Puberty (as direct causation, distinguished from mere physical finding)			2.9	3.3			2.	4			4	1.5
Physical Conditions (of all sorts, and as direct causations only, distinguished from physical findings)			3.7	7.5			3.	6.2			2.	10.

(The lower part of the above table contains no figures for the Chicago series because our terminology for data has changed with the years.)

TABLE 58

CHICAGO SERIES OF OUTCOMES

SOME MENTAL FACTORS RELATED TO SUCCESS AND FAILURE AMONG 500
CASES ANALYZED FOR CAUSATIVE FACTORS—NUMBER OF CASES

	313 Males		187 Females	
	Success	Failure	Success	Failure
Mental Conflict, clear cases....	20	10	17	12
Early Bad Sex Experiences or Sex Teaching, known to create unfortunate mental results	18	16	22	12
Definite Criminalistic Impulsions	2	2	1	0
Social Suggestibility in Excess..	3	5	1	0
Excessive Love of Adventure...	4	4	0	0
Obsessive Ideation and Imagery	4	2	4	1
Marked Adolescent Instability.	21	14	18	9
Masturbatory Mental Concomitants, subversive of morale.	12	17	9	5

(It is to be noted that this table does not cover the entire series of
675 Success and Failure outcomes; not all of these were originally
analyzed for causative factors.)

APPENDIX II

APPENDIX II

CHARTS OF INDIVIDUAL CAREERS

Showing Separate Steps of Official Treatment

The details of individual careers are vastly instructive and worth careful representation. If the number and sequence of adjustments can be vividly pictured, a very definite estimate can be made of the effectiveness or the lack of effectiveness of special forms of social treatment. To this end we have attempted a semi-diagrammatic scheme of reproduction of the measures undertaken for the treatment of delinquency in our Chicago series.

Such graphic representations have been attempted by Gruhle and Glueck. The method of the former involves a diagram that is too minutely complex to be of practical value in depicting the facts for a large group. Glueck's form requires nearly a page for each individual and hence is suitable for illustrating only a few cases. We wish to show for our series the separate steps of official treatment for each individual, but as compared with that given others and especially according to Success and Failure of treatment by different methods. For this purpose we group those who have been committed to each institution. We have used a two dimensional scheme: the height of a column shows the number of individuals who have had the treatment which is the central theme of the given graph; the horizontal line specifies the items of treatment which each individual has received and the length of this line suggests at once the extent to which different measures of treatment have been undertaken. The pyramidal distribution is to facilitate comparisons of the careers of individuals as showing the proportion of Success and Failure following any one type of treatment—on each line there is given, on either side of the central item of treatment, the main facts of the antecedent and the subsequent career.

It will be readily seen that these graphs offer material for conclusions on points of varied interest.

KEY TO ABBREVIATIONS

PRO probation, as enumerated always meaning for a new offense
PLA placing in foster home
DEP commitment to institution for dependents
PTL   "   " Chicago Parental School
JWS   "   " John Worthy School
SC   "   " St. Charles State School for Boys
CCS   "   " Chicago and Cook County School for Boys
GEN   "   " Geneva School for Girls
HGS   "   " House of the Good Shepherd
RFG   "   " "The Refuge," Chicago Home for Girls
FM   "   " Institution for the Feebleminded

284

INS commitment to Hospital for the Insane
REF   "   " State Reformatory
HC   "   " House of Correction
JL   "   " County Jail
PEN   "   " Penitentiary
CT Adult Court appearance
SER Army or Navy Service
  fm a feebleminded individual
  ps an individual showing signs of mental disease (psychosis)
  pp an individual of psychopathic personality

The adult career is distinguished by heavy type and is separated from the juvenile career by a long and heavy dash.

Parentheses are used to indicate treatment that involves confinement in an institution. The central theme of each diagram is one particular form of treatment which is represented by the pivotal column of the page. Naturally, the same individual sometimes appears on a number of charts.

Individuals abnormal mentally are designated by the symbols in small type indicating their special class of abnormality. Occasional cases show more than one abnormality.

Illustration:

(PTL)–(PTL)–(JWS)–(SC)—**CT–(REF)** indicates that a boy, mentally normal, was committed first to the Parental School, then recommitted, then sent to the John Worthy School, and next to St. Charles. As a young adult he appeared in court, and then on some new charge he was sentenced to the State Reformatory.

(Those records among the Failures which show no adult careers represent the individuals who were chronic vagrants, loafers, etc., although never in court; particularly the females show adult careers only blank, their immorality did not lead to court record.)

The criterion of Success and Failure of the treatment of these juvenile offenders, we may reiterate, is for us in this study the adult career, in nearly all cases whether or not there was adult court record.

BOYS IN DEPENDENT INSTITUTIONS—SUCCESS

```
                              [DEP]
                              [DEP]
                              [DEP]
                              [DEP]
           ps-fmPLA–PLA–[DEP]
                              [DEP]–[DEP]
                              [DEP]–[DEP]
                    PRO–[DEP]–[DEP]
                              [DEP]–PRO
                              [DEP]–PRO
                              [DEP]–PRO
                    PRO–[DEP]–PRO
                        pp[DEP]–PLA
                              [DEP]–PLA
                              [DEP]–PLA
                    PRO-[DEP]–PLA
                              [DEP]–[SC]
                              [DEP]–[SC]
                              [DEP]–[JWS]
                              [DEP]–[JWS]–PRO
                   PLA–[DEP]–[SC]–PLA
         [PTL]–PLA–[DEP]–[PTL]–[SC]
            [PTL]–[DEP]–[SC]–PRO–PRO
                              [DEP]–[DEP]–PRO–[JWS]
                              [DEP]–[PTL]–[PTL]–PLA
                              [DEP]–[DEP]–[PTL]–PRO–PLA
                    fm[DEP]–[JWS]–[JWS]–[JWS]–[SC]
                              [DEP]–[DEP]–[DEP]–[JWS]–[JWS]–PLA
                              [DEP]–[DEP]–[PTL]–[DEP]–[JWS]–PLA
                              [DEP]–PLA–PLA–[JWS]–[INS]–[SC]–PLA
                              [DEP]–[DEP]–[PTL]–[SC]–[SC]–[JWS]–[JWS]–[JWS]–PLA
         [PTL]–[DEP]–[JWS]–[JWS]–PRO–PRO–PRO–PRO–PRO–[SC]–[JWS]
```

An astonishing number of delinquent boys in our group, Successes and Failures, are shown to have been in dependent institutions, 87 out of 420, over 20 per cent. If we think of the series of 420 boys, as we naturally would, as coming from the general population, the proportion who have been in dependent institutions seems enormous.

It would be interesting to know how large a proportion of the total repeated offenders in court over a period of years have been in dependent institutions; and, conversely, how many of the total number of boys in dependent institutions have become delinquent.

Other points arise: How many of those committed to dependent institutions already had delinquent tendencies? And how fair or how effectual is it to send delinquent children to an institution for dependents? We are raising questions certainly worthy of practical research.

BOYS IN DEPENDENT INSTITUTIONS—FAILURE

```
            [DEP]—
            [DEP]-[DEP]—
            [DEP]—CT
            [DEP]-PRO—SER
            [DEP]-PLA—[INS]
            [DEP]-[SC]—[REF]
            [DEP]-[SC]—[PEN]
      pp[JWS]-[DEP]-[JWS]-[SC]—
    m[PTL]-[SC]-[DEP]-PLA—CT
            [DEP]-PRO-PRO-[JWS]—
            [DEP]-PRO-[SC]—[REF]
            [DEP]-[PTL]-[DEP]-[JWS]—
        fm[DEP]-[SC]-PLA—CT
        fm[DEP]-[SC]-[FM]—[FM]
        fm[DEP]-[SC]-[FM]-[FM]
            [DEP]-[SC]-PLA-[SC]—CT
            [DEP]-[PTL]-[SC]-SER—CT
            [DEP]-[PTL]-[JWS]—SER-CT
            [DEP]-PLA-[DEP]-PLA-[SC]—
        fm[DEP]-[DEP]-[JWS]-PLA—CT
            [DEP]-PRO-[SC]-[SC]—[REF]
        ps[DEP]-[PTL]-[SC]-[SC]—SER
            [DEP]-[JWS]—[HC]-[PEN]-CT
      [PTL]-[DEP]-[JWS]-[SC]-PRO-CT—
    pp[PTL]-[DEP] [DEP]-[SC]-[JWS]—[REF]
            [DEP]-[SC]- PLA—CT-CT-CT
            [DEP]-[SC]-[PTL]-[SC]-[SC]—CT
            [DEP]-[JWS]-PRO-[JWS]-CT—[PEN]
            [DEP]-[JWS]-[JWS]-PLA-[SC]—[JL]
            [DEP]-[SC]—[HC]-[HC]-[HC]-[REF]
            [DEP]-[JWS]-[JWS]-[SC]—[HC]-[REF]
        PRO-[DEP]-PRO—CT-[REF]-[JL]-CT
    [PTL]-[DEP]-PRO-[JWS]-[JWS]-PLA—[HC]
            [DEP]-PLA—CT-CT-CT-CT-CT
      pp-fm[DEP]-PRO-[FM]—CT-CT-CT-CT
            [DEP]-PLA-PRO-CT—SER-[HC]-[REF]
        pp[DEP]-[DEP]-[JWS]-[SC]—[HC]-[HC] [JL]
            [DEP]-PRO-PRO-[SC]-[JWS]—[SC] PLA
        pp[DEP]-[JWS]-[PTL]-[JWS]—CT-[HC]-[HC]
        pp[DEP] [JWS]-[JWS]-[JWS]-[JWS]-PLA-[HC]—
            [DEP]-[SC]-[SC]-[JWS]-[SC]-[JWS]—[REF]
      [JWS]-[DEP]-[DEP]-PRO-[SC]-[DEP]—CT-[HC]
        pp[DEP]-[JWS]-PLA-PLA-[JWS]-PLA—[HC]-[JL]
        pp[DEP]-[PTL]-[PTL]-[DEP]-PLA-[SC]-PRO—[HC]
            [DEP]-PLA-[JWS]-[JWS]-[JWS]-[JWS]—[HC]-[HC]
        fm[DEP]-[DEP]-[JWS]-PLA-[SC]—[HC]-[JL]-SER
            [DEP]-[PTL]-[JWS]-[DEP]-PLA—[HC]-[PEN]-[PEN]
            [DEP]-[PTL]—CT-CT-CT-CT-CT-[HC]-CT
            [DEP]-[PTL]-[JWS]-[SC]—CT-CT-CT-CT-CT
            [DEP]-PLA-[DEP]-[JWS]-PLA-[SC]-[SC]-[SC]-[SC]—
        pp[DEP]-[PTL]-[JWS]-PLA-[SC]-[SC]—SER-[HC]-[PEN]-[REF]
        pp[DEP]-[PTL]-[PTL]-[PTL]-[PTL]-[PTL]-[DEP]-[SC]—[HC]-[REF]
            [DEP]-[DEP]-PLA-PLA-PLA-PLA-PLA-[SC]-[SC]—CT-[HC]
        pp[DEP]-[DEP]-[PTL]-PLA—CT-CT-CT-CT-CT-[HC]-CT
            [DEP]-[DEP]-[PTL]-[PTL]-[JWS]-[JWS]—[JL]-[REF]-[REF]-[JL]-[REF]-[JL]-[HC]-[PEN]
```

PROBATION—BOYS

We offer no graph of the cases which were placed on probation, merely because of the necessity for saving space and the fact that such a large number received probation who appear (almost all of the Failures) on the graphs of other types of treatment. We need only to give totals and figures for those who as juveniles received probation as the only form of official treatment.

Of the 164 male Successes, 96 were specifically placed on probation as juveniles. Of these 31 were once placed on probation only—they had no other treatment; 5 were twice put on probation and then were Successes.

Of the 256 male Failures, 124 were sometime placed on probation as juveniles. Of these 13 had only probation once as juvenile offenders; 2 were twice placed on probation. What happened to these 15 as adults may be seen under the charts which deal with adult treatment.

We have not undertaken to publish our charts of cases placed, mainly because of the difficulty of ascertaining reliably the facts about the placing of those who went out for a time to foster homes from the various institutions. It seems, however, that we can make a satisfactory general statement about the cases placed from the court,—and the fact of such placing appears on other graphs in nearly all cases, the main exception being the 19 for whom it was the single adjustment.

Of the 164 male Successes 50 had placement as one part of their treatment; of these:

  11 placement only
   6 " following probation
   3 "   " dependent institution
  15 "   " correctional institution
   3 probation following placement
  12 correctional institution following placement

Of the 256 male Failures, 68 had placement as one part of their treatment, with juvenile correctional institution following in 30 cases. Of the total 68:

  8 only placement as juveniles
  5 probation prior to placement
  7 only dependent institution prior to placement
 44 correctional institution prior to placement

BOYS IN PARENTAL SCHOOL—SUCCESS

```
                              fm[PTL]
                              DD[PTL]
                              DD[PTL]
                                [PTL]
                                [PTL]
                           PRO-[PTL]
                           PLA-[PTL]
                  [SC]-[SC]-[PTL]
                              fm[PTL]-PRO
                                [PTL]-PRO
                                [PTL]-PRO
                                [PTL]-[SC]
                                [PTL]-[SC]
                                [PTL]-[JWS]
                           PRO-[PTL]-[PTL]
                        fmPRO-[PTL]-[SC]
                                [PTL]-PRO-PRO
                              fm[PTL]-PRO-[FM]
                                [PTL]-[JWS]-PRO
                                [PTL]-[JWS]-PRO
                                [PTL]-[JWS]-PLA
                                [PTL]-[PTL]-[SC]
                        fmPRO-[PTL]-[PTL]-[SC]
                           [DEP]-[PTL]-[PTL]-PLA
                  [DEP]-[DEP]-[PTL]-PRO-PLA
                                [PTL]-[PTL]-PLA-[JWS]
                                [PTL]-PRO-[CCS]-[CCS]
                           PRO-[PTL]-[PTL]-PLA-[CCS]
                  [DEP]-[DEP]-[PTL]-[DEP]-[JWS]-PLA
                                [PTL]-[DEP]-[SC]-PRO-PRO
                                [PTL]-PLA-[DEP]-[PTL]-[SC]
                                [PTL]-[PTL]-[PTL]-[JWS]-[SC]
                              DD[PTL]-[PTL]-[PTL]-[CCS]-[SC]
                           PRO-[PTL]-[PTL]-PRO-[CCS]-[JWS]
                      PRO-[PTL]-[PTL]-[PTL]-[PTL]-[PTL]-PRO-PLA
             [DEP]-[DEP]-[PTL]-[SC]-[SC]-[JWS]-[JWS]-[JWS]-[CCS]-PLA
                      [PTL]-[DEP]-[JWS]-[JWS]-PRO-PRO-PRO-PRO-PRO-[SC]-[JWS]
```

Perhaps the most striking fact represented by these graphs concerning Parental School commitments is that only 9 out of these 118 boys who were committed made a Success following treatment by the Parental School only. And the reader may see for himself that almost none of the cases had any prior correctional institution experience, so the Parental School received them early as comparatively mild delinquents and had the most favorable time for influencing them.

BOYS IN PARENTAL SCHOOL—FAILURE

```
                              fm[PTL]—CT
                  PRO-PRO-PRO-[PTL]—[REF]
                                [PTL]-PLA-PRO—
                              fm[PTL]-[PTL]-[JWS]—
                              fm[PTL]-[PTL]-[SC]—
                                [PTL]-[JWS]—CT
                                [PTL]-[JWS]—[REF]
                                [PTL]-[SC]—[REF]
                           [DEP]-[PTL]-[DEP]-[JWS]—
                  PRO-PRO-PRO-PRO-[PTL]-[SC]-[SC]—
                                [PTL]-PRO—CT-SER
                              ps[PTL]-PRO-[INS]—[HC]
                                [PTL]-PLA—CT-SER
```

BOYS IN PARENTAL SCHOOL—FAILURE (Continued)

```
              pp[PTL]–[PTL]–PRO—SER
              fm[PTL]–[PTL]–[JWS]—[HC]
                 [PTL]–[SC]—CT–[REF]
              fm[PTL]–[FM]—CT–[REF]
              fm[PTL]–[FM]–[JWS]—[INS]
          [DEP]–[PTL]–[SC]–SER—CT
          [DEP]–[PTL]–[JWS]—SER–CT
            ps[DEP]–[PTL]–[SC]–[SC]—SER
      [DEP]–[SC]–[PTL]–[SC]–[SC]—CT
              pp[PTL]–PRO–PLA—SER–CT
                 [PTL]–PLA–[SC]—[JL]–[REF]
                 [PTL]–[PTL]–PRO–PRO—[REF]
                 [PTL]–[PTL]–[JWS]—CT–[HC]
                 [PTL]–[PTL]–[SC]–[SC]–SER
              pp[PTL]–[JWS]–[HC]–[JWS]—[REF]
                 [PTL]–[JWS]–[SC]—[JL]–SER
              fm[PTL]–[JWS]–[FM]—CT–[FM]
                 [PTL]–[SC]—CT–CT–SER
                 [PTL]–[SC]—CT–CT–[REF]
              fm[PTL]–[SC]–[DEP]–PLA—CT
             PRO–[PTL]–[JWS]–[SC]–[SC]—CT
             psPLA–[PTL]–[INS]—CT–CT–[INS]
      pp[DEP]–[JWS]–[PTL]–[JWS]—CT–[HC]–[HC]
                 [PTL]–[DEP]–[JWS]–[SC]–PRO—CT
              pp[PTL]–[PTL]–PLA–CT—SER–CT
              fm[PTL]–[PTL]–[SC]—[HC]–[HC]–[JL]
                 [PTL]–[PTL]–PRO–[SC]—CT–[JL]
                 [PTL]–[PTL]–[JWS]–[HC]–[JL]–[JWS]—
              pp[PTL]–[DEP]–[DEP]–[SC]–[JWS]—[REF]
                 [PTL]–[PTL]–[SC]–[SC]—CT–[JL]
          pp-fm[PTL]–[JWS]—[HC]–[HC]–[HC]–[INS]
                 [PTL]–[JWS]–[JWS]–PLA–[SC]—[HC]
                 [PTL]–[JWS]–[JWS]—[HC]–[HC]–[REF]
             PRO–[PTL]–[SC]–[JWS]–[JWS]–[SC]—[PEN]
                 [PTL]–[DEP]–PRO–[JWS]–[JWS]–PLA—[HC]
                 [PTL]–[SC]–[SC]—CT–CT–[JL]–[REF]
                 [PTL]–[PTL]–[SC]—CT–CT–CT–CT
                 [PTL]–[PTL]–[JWS]–[SC]—CT–[REF]–CT
                 [PTL]–PLA–[JWS]—[HC]–[HC]–[HC]–[HC]
                 [PTL]–[PTL]–[PTL]–[SC]—[REF]–[JL]–[REF]
              ps[PTL]–[PTL]–[JWS]–PRO–PLA–[SC]—[PEN]
                 [PTL]–[PTL]–[JWS]–PLA–[JWS]–PLA—[REF]
             PRO–[PTL]–[PTL]–[CCS]–[CCS]–[CCS]–SER—[CCS]
              pp[DEP]–[PTL]–[PTL]–[DEP]–PLA–[SC]–PRO—[HC]
                 [DEP]–[PTL]–[JWS]–[DEP]–PLA—[HC]–[PEN]–[PEN]
              fm[JWS]–[PTL]–[FM]—CT–[FM]–CT–[REF]–[HC]
             PRO–[JWS]–[JWS]–[PTL]–[SC]–[JWS]–[SC]—[HC]–[HC]–[HC]
                 [PTL]–PRO–PRO–PRO–PRO–PRO—[JL]–[JL]
                 [PTL]–[PTL]–[PTL]—CT–[JL]–CT–CT–CT–CT
              fm[PTL]–[PTL]–[SC]–[FM]—CT–[HC]–[FM]–CT
                 [PTL]–[PTL]–PRO–PLA—[REF]–[PEN]–[REF]–[PEN]
             PRO–[PTL]–[JWS]–[SC]–[SC]–[SC]–[SC]–[SC]—[REF]
             PRO–[PTL]–[PTL]–[PTL]–[PTL]–[SC]–[SC]–[CCS]—[JL]
          [DEP]–[PTL]–[JWS]–[SC]—CT–CT–CT–CT–CT
          [DEP]–[PTL]—CT–CT–CT–CT–CT–[HC]–CT
PRO–PRO–PRO–PRO–PRO–[PTL]–[JWS]–[SC]–[SC]–[SC]–[SC]–[SC]—[REF]
                 [PTL]–[PTL]–PRO–PRO–PRO–PRO–PRO—SER–[INS]
                 [PTL]–[JWS]–PRO–[SC]—CT–CT–CT–CT–CT
              pp[DEP]–[PTL]–[PTL]–[PTL]–[PTL]–[PTL]–[DEP]–[SC]—[HC]–[REF]
              pp[DEP]–[PTL]–[JWS]–PLA–[SC]–[SC]—SER–[HC]–[PEN]–[REF]
      pp[DEP]–[DEP]–[PTL]–PLA—CT–CT–CT–CT–CT–[HC]–CT
                 [PTL]–PRO–[PTL]–[PTL]—[JL]–CT–CT–CT–CT–CT
              pp[PTL]–[PTL]–[PTL]–PLA–PRO–PRO–[SC]—[HC]–PLA–[REF]–SER
                 [PTL]–[JWS]–PRO—[HC]–[HC]–[JL]–[JL]–[JL]–[JL]–[JL]–SER
                 [PTL]–[PTL]–[PTL]–[JWS]–[JWS]–[JWS]—[HC]–[HC]–[HC]–[HC]–[HC]
                 [PTL]–[PTL]–[PTL]–PRO–PRO–PRO–PRO–CT–[SC]—CT
      [DEP]–[DEP]–[PTL]–[PTL]–[JWS]–[JWS]—[JL]–[REF]–[REF]–[JL]–[REF]–[JL]–[HC]–[PEN]
              pp[PTL]–[JWS]–[SC]–[JWS]–[SC]–PLA–[JWS]—[HC]–[HC]–[HC]–[HC]–[HC]–[JL]
```

BOYS IN ST. CHARLES—SUCCESS

```
                                      pp[SC]
                                        [SC]
                                        [SC]
                                        [SC]
                                      fm[SC]
                                  ppPLA–[SC]
                                    PLA–[SC]
                                    PLA–[SC]
                                    PRO–[SC]
                                  ppPRO–[SC]
                                    PRO–[SC]
                                    PRO–[SC]
                                   [DEP]–[SC]
                                   [DEP]–[SC]
                                   [PTL]–[SC]
                                   [PTL]–[SC]
                            fmPRO–[PTL]–[SC]
                          ppPRO–[JWS]–[SC]
                             [PTL]–[PTL]–[SC]
                             PLA–[DEP]–[SC]
                       PRO–[JWS]–PLA–[SC]
                   fmPRO–[PTL]–[PTL]–[SC]
                [PTL]–PLA–[DEP]–[PTL]–[SC]
               [PTL]–[PTL]–[PTL]–[JWS]–[SC]
            pp[PTL]–[PTL]–[PTL]–[CCS]–[SC]
          fm[DEP]–[JWS]–[JWS]–[JWS]–[SC]
                                      pp[SC]–PLA
                                        [SC]–PLA
                                        [SC]–PLA
                                        [SC]–[SC]
                                 PRO–[SC]–[JWS]
                                 PLA–[SC]–[SC]
                                 PLA–[SC]–[JWS]
                           PRO–[JWS]–[SC]–PLA
                        fmPRO–[JWS]–[SC]–PLA
              [DEP]–PLA–PLA–[JWS]–[CCS]–[SC]–PLA
[PTL]–[DEP]–[JWS]–[JWS]–PRO–PRO–PRO–PRO–PRO–[SC]–[JWS]
                                      [SC]–[SC]–[SC]
                                      [SC]–[SC]–[PTL]
                               ppPRO–[SC]–PRO–SER
                          [PTL]–[DEP]–[SC]–PRO–PRO
                          [JWS]–[JWS]–[SC]–[JWS]–PRO
   [DEP]–[DEP]–[PTL]–[SC]–[SC]–[JWS]–[JWS]–[JWS]–[CCS]–PLA
```

One of the greatest surprises to us has been the outcome of cases sent
to St. Charles, an institution which in some ways had and has an
unusually fine equipment for what is supposed to be effective in the
reformation of boys.

BOYS IN ST. CHARLES—FAILURE

PRO–[SC]—
ppPRO–[SC]—
ppPLA–[SC]—
fm[PTL]–[PTL]–[SC]—
[JWS]–[JWS]–[SC]—
pp[JWS]–[DEP]–[JWS]–[SC]—
[DEP]–PLA–[DEP]–PLA–[SC]—
pp[SC]—**[REF]**
[SC]—**[REF]**
pp-fmPRO–[SC]–[SC]—
ppPRO–[SC]–**PRO**—
PRO–[SC]—**[REF]**
[DEP]–[SC]—**[PEN]**
[DEP]–[SC]—**[REF]**
[JWS]–[SC]—**[JL]**
[JWS]–[SC]—**[REF]**
[JWS]–[SC]—**CT**
[PTL]–[SC]—**[REF**
PRO–PLA–[SC]—**CT**
PRO–[JWS]–[SC]—**[HC]**
PRO–[JWS]–[SC]—**[HC]**
[DEP]–PRO–[SC]—**[REF**
[JWS]–PRO–[SC]–SER—
[DEP]–[JWS]–[JWS]–PLA–[SC]—**[JL]**
[PTL]–[JWS]–[JWS]–PLA–[SC]—**[HC]**
ps[PTL]–[PTL]–[JWS]–PRO–PLA–[SC]—**[PEN]**
PRO–[JWS]–[JWS]–[JWS]–PRO–PLA–[SC]—**[REF]**
PRO–PRO–PRO–PRO–PRO–[PTL]–[SC]–[SC]—
[SC]—**[HC]**–**[HC]**
ps[SC]–[JWS]—**[PEN]**
ps[SC]–[INS]—**[INS**
PRO–[SC]–[SC]—**[REF]]**
PRO–[SC]–[SC]—**SER**
PRO–[SC]–[SC]—**[SC]**
PRO–[SC]—**CT**–**[REF]**
PRO–[SC]—**CT–SER**
ppPRO–[SC]–[INS]—**[INS**
PRO–[SC]—**[JL]**–**[JL]**
ppPRO–[SC]—**[HC]**–**[HC]**
fm[DEP]–[SC]–PLA—**CT**
fm[DEP]–[SC]–**[FM]**–**[FM]**
fm[DEP]–[SC]–[FM]–[FM]—
ppPLA–[SC]—**CT–CT**
[PTL]–[SC]—**CT**–**[REF]**
pp-fmJWS]–[SC]—**[REF]–SER**
PRO–[CCS]–[SC]–[SC]—**SER**
PRO–[JWS]–[SC]—**[HC]**–**[REF**
[DEP]–PRO–[SC]–[SC]—**[REF]**
[DEP]–[PTL]–[SC]–SER—**CT**
ps[DEP]–[PTL]–[SC]–[SC]—**SER**
[PTL]–[PTL]–[SC]–[SC]—**SER**
[PTL]–[JWS]–[SC]—**[JL]–SER**
[PTL]–PLA–[SC]—**[JL]**–**[REF]**
PRO–[PTL]–[JWS]–[SC]–[SC]—**CT**
[DEP]–[JWS]–[JWS]–[SC]—**[HC]**–**[REF]**
[PTL]–[DEP]–[JWS]–[SC]–PRO—**CT**
pp[PTL]–[DEP]–[DEP]–[SC]–[JWS]—**[REF]**
[PTL]–[PTL]–PRO–[SC]—**CT**–**[JL]**
pp[DEP]–[PTL]–[PTL]–[DEP]–PLA–[SC]–PRO—**[HC]**
pp[DEP]–[PTL]–[PTL]–[PTL]–[PTL]–[PTL]–[DEP]–[SC]—**[HC]**–**[REF]**
fm[SC]–[FM]—**CT**–**[FM]**
pp[SC]–PRO–[FM]—**[JL]**
[SC]–PLA–[PEN]—**[PEN]**

BOYS IN ST. CHARLES—FAILURE (Continued)

```
              PRO-[SC]-[SC]—[JL]-[REF]
              PRO-[SC]-[JWS]—[REF]-CT
           fmPRO-[SC]-PLA—CT-[FM]
          psPRO-[SC]—[REF]-[INS]-[REF]
            [DEP]-[SC]-PLA-[SC]—CT
            [JWS]-[SC]—[REF]-[REF]-SER
          fm[JWS]-[SC]-PRO-[SC]—[REF]
            [PTL]-[SC]—CT-CT-SER
            [PTL]-[SC]—CT-CT-[REF]
          fm[PTL]-[SC]-[DEP]-PLA—CT
        fmPRO-[JWS]-[SC]-PLA—[HC]-[REF]
            [PTL]-[PTL]-[SC]-[SC]—CT-[JL]
          fm[PTL]-[PTL]-[SC]—[HC]-[HC]-[JL]
        [DEP]-PRO-PRO-[SC]-[JWS]—[SC]-PLA
        DD[DEP]-[DEP]-[JWS]-[SC]—[HC]-[HC]-[JL]
          [PTL]-[PTL]-[JWS]-[SC]—CT-[REF]-CT
          [PTL]-[PTL]-[PTL]-[SC]—[REF]-[JL]-[REF
        fm[DEP]-[DEP]-[JWS]-PLA-[SC]—[HC]-[JL]-SER
          [JWS]-[DEP]-[DEP]-PRO-[SC]-[DEP]—CT-[REF]
          [JWS]-[DEP]-[DEP]-PRO-[SC]-[DEP]—CT-[HC]
      PRO-[PTL]-[PTL]-[PTL]-[PTL]-[SC]-[SC]-[CCS]—[JL]
    [DEP]-[DEP]-PLA-PLA-PLA-PLA-PLA-[SC]-[SC]—CT-[HC]
PTL]-[PTL]-[PTL]-PRO-PRO-PRO-PRO-PRO-[SC]-CT-[SC]—CT
                  [SC]-PLA—[HC]-[HC]-[JL]
              DDPRO-[SC]-[SC]—[REF]-[JL]-[REF]
              PRO-[SC]-PRO [JWS] [SC]—[REF]
              PRO-[SC]—CT-[HC]-CT-[PEN]
            fmPRO-[SC]—[REF]-CT-CT-CT
            [DEP]-[SC]-PLA—CT-CT-CT
            [DEP]-[SC]-[PTL]-[SC]-[SC]—CT
            [DEP]-[SC]—[HC]-[HC]-[HC]-[REF]
            PRO-[PTL]-[SC]-[JWS]-[JWS]-[SC]—[PEN]
            [PTL]-[PTL]-[SC]—CT-CT-CT-CT
            PRO-[JWS]-PRO-[SC]—[JL]-[REF]-[REF]-SER
        [DEP]-PLA-[DEP]-[JWS]-PLA-[SC]-[SC]-[SC]-[SC]-
        DD[PTL]-[PTL]-[PTL]-PLA-PRO-PRO-[SC]—[HC]-PLA-[REF]-SER
            [DEP]-[SC]-[SC]-[JWS]-[SC]-[JWS]—[REF]
            PLA-[SC]—PLA-PLA PLA-PLA-PLA
            [PTL]-[SC]-[SC]—OT-CT [JL] [REF]
          fm[PTL]-[PTL] [SC]-[FM]—CT-[HC]-[FM]-CT
          [PTL]-[JWS]-PRO-[SC]—CT-CT-CT-CT-CT
          [DEP]-[PTL]-[JWS]-[SC]—CT-CT-CT-CT-CT
        PRO-[JWS]-[JWS]-[PTL]-[SC]-[JWS]-[SC]—[HC]-[HC]-[HC]
        DD[DEP]-[PTL]-[JWS]-PLA-[SC]-[SC]—SER-[HC]-[PEN]-[REF]
        PRO-[PTL]-[JWS]-[SC]-[SC]-[SC]-[SC]-[SC]-[SC]—[REF]
            [SC]-[JWS]-[SC]-[SC]-[SC]-[SC]-[SC]-[SC]—
        [JWS]-[JWS]-[SC]-PRO-[SC]-[JWS]—[HC]-[HC]-[REF]
              fm[SC]-[SC]—[JL]-[REF]-[HC]-CT-[REF]-SER
        PRO-PRO-[SC]-PLA-[SC]-[SC]—SER-SER-CT-[HC]
            fm[SC]-[SC]—CT-CT-CT-[HC]-[HC]-[HC]-[JL]-SER-[REF]
      DD[PTL]-[JWS]-[SC]-[JWS]-[SC]-PLA-[JWS]—[HC]-[HC]-[HC]-[HC]-[HC]-[JL]
        PRO-[SC]-PRO-[SC]-[JWS]-PLA-PRO-PRO-PRO-PRO-PRO-[JWS]—
                                              [REF]-[PEN]
```

The John Worthy School no longer being in existence, as earlier stated in describing the correctional institutions, we deem it unnecessary to reproduce the long graphs which would be necessary for representation of the many Failures and few Successes which followed incarceration there.

There were 36 cases with ultimate Success among the 145 who at some time in their career were at the John Worthy School. Among the 36 there were 5 who had as treatment commitment to the John Worthy School only once; 5 others had probation earlier; 8 more had no other subsequent treatment, though they had various prior adjustments; 4 succeeded after two or three terms at this institution.

Concerning the extraordinary records of a large number of the Failures (101 out of the total 256 Failures of our whole group) who had been at the John Worthy School we may say that these are apparent in the graphs for the adult institutions.

MALES IN COUNTY JAIL

```
                    ppPRO—[JL]-SER
                   ps[INS]-[JL]-[REF]-SER
                fm[FM]—CT-[JL]
                [JWS]-[SC]—[JL]
                PRO-[SC]—[JL]-[JL]
                PRO—SER-[JL]-[JL]-[REF]
                 fm[SC]-[SC]—[JL]-[REF]-[HC]-CT-[REF]-SER
                 pp[JWS]-[JWS]-[JL]-[REF]—[HC]
                PRO—[HC]-CT [JL]
                pp[SC]-PRO-[FM]—[JL]
                PRO-[JWS]-[JWS]—[JL]
                 PRO-[SC]-[SC]—[JL]-[REF]
                [PTL]-PLA-[SC]—[JL]-[REF]
                [PTL]-[JWS]-[SC]—[JL]-SER
                 [SC]-PLA—[HC]-[HC]-[JL]
               ppPRO-[SC]-[SC]—[REF]-[JL]-[REF]
              [PTL]-[PTL]-[JWS]-[HC]-[JL]-[JWS]—
               [PTL]-[PTL]-[PTL]—CT-[JL]-CT-CT-CT-CT
                PRO-[JWS]-PRO-[SC]—[JL]-[REF]-[REF]-SER
              [PTL]-PRO-[PTL]-[PTL]—[JL]-CT-CT-CT-CT-CT
               [PTL] [PTL]-PRO-[SC]—CT-[JL]
               [PTL]-[PTL]-[SC]-[SC]—CT-[JL]
              [PTL] [JWS] PRO—[HC] [HC] [JL] [JL]-[JL]-[JL]-SER
              fm[PTL]-[PTL]-[SC]—[HC]-[HC]-[JL]
             pp[FM]-[JWS]-PRO-[JWS]—[HC]-[JL]
              [DEP]-[JWS]-[JWS]-PLA-[SC]—[JL]
              PRO-[DEP]-PRO—CT-[REF]-[JL]-CT
               [PTL]-[SC]-[SC]—CT-CT-[JL]-[REF]
              [PTL]-[PTL]-[PTL]-[SC]—[REF]-[JL]-[REF]
             PRO-[JWS]—[HC]-[HC]-[HC]-[HC]-[JL]
            pp[DEP]-[DEP]-[JWS]-[SC]—[HC]-[HC]-[JL]
             [PTL]-PRO-PRO-PRO-PRO-PRO—[JL]-[JL]
             PRO-PRO-PRO-PRO-PRO-[JWS]—[JL]-[HC]
           fm[DEP]-[DEP]-[JWS]-PLA-[SC]—[HC]-[JL]-SER
            [DEP]-[DEP]-[PTL]-[PTL]-[JWS]-[JWS]—[JL]-[REF]-[REF]-[JL]-[REF]-[JL]-[REF]-[PEN]
          pp[DEP] [JWS] PLA-PLA [JWS]-PLA—[HC] [JI]
            [SC]-[SC]—CT-CT-CT-[HC]-[HC]-[HC]-[JL]-SER-[REF]
         PRO-[PTL]-[PTL]-[PTL] [PTL]-[SC]-[SC]-[CCS]—[JL]
   l]-[JWS]-[SC]-[JWS]-[SC]-PLA-[JWS]—[HC]-[HC]-[HC]-[HC]-[HC]-[JL]
```

The above represent commitments to a county jail over and beyond those in connection with offenses for which sentence was given to a reformatory or penitentiary.

We have omitted from this graph six individuals whose commitment to the County Jail was out of the ordinary, such as those who were held as adults and later found to be juveniles.

ᴅᴅ[SC]—[REF]
[SC]—[REF]
PRO—[REF]–[HC]
PRO—[HC]–[REF]
PRO–[SC]—[REF]
[DEP]–[SC]—[REF]
[DEP]–PRO–[REF]
[PTL]–[SC]—[REF]
[PTL]–JWS]—[REF]
[JWS]–[SC]—[REF]
[JWS]–PRO–[REF]
ꜰᵐPRO–PRO—[REF]–SER
ᴅᴅ-ꜰᵐ[JWS]–[SC]—[REF]–SER
ᴅᴅPLA–[JWS]—[REF]–SER
ᴅˢ[INS]—[JL]—[REF]–SER
PRO–[SC]—[REF]–[INS]–SER
ᴅˢPRO–[SC]—[REF]–CT–CT–CT
[JWS]–[SC]—[REF]–[REF]–SER
PRO–[SC]–[SC]—[REF]
PRO—CT–CT–[REF]
PRO–[SC]—CT–[REF]
PRO–[JWS]–PRO–[REF]
ꜰᵐPRO–[FM]—[HC]–[REF]
[DEP]–PRO–[SC]—[REF]
[DEP]–[DEP]–PRO–[REF]
ꜰᵐ[PTL]–[FM]—CT–[REF]
[PTL]–[SC]—CT–[REF]
PRO–[JWS]–CT–[REF]–[REF]
PRO–[JWS]–JWS]—[REF]–[REF]
PRO–[SC]–[JWS]—[REF]–CT
ᴅᴅ[JWS]–[JWS]–[JL]–[REF]–[HC]
ᴅᴅPRO–[SC]–[SC]—[REF]–[JL]–[REF]
ꜰᵐ[SC]–[SC]—[JL]—[REF]–[HC]–CT–[REF]–SER
PLA—CT–CT–CT–[REF]
ᴅᴅPLA–PLA—SER–CT–[REF]
PTL–[SC]—CT–CT–[REF]
ꜰᵐ[JWS]–[SC]–PRO–[SC]—[REF]
PRO–PRO–PRO–[PTL]—[REF]
PRO—SER–[JL]–[JL]—[REF]
[PTL]–PLA–[SC]—[JL]–[REF]
[PTL]–[PTL]–PRO–PRO—[REF]
PRO–[SC]–[SC]—[JL]–[REF]
[DEP]–PRO–[SC]–[SC]—[REF]
PRO–[JWS]–[SC]—[HC]–[REF]
ᴅᴅ[PTL]–[JWS]–[HC]–[JWS]—[REF]
PRO–[JWS]–PRO–[JWS]—[REF]–[REF]
PRO–[DEP]–PRO—CT–[REF]–[JL]–CT
[PTL]–[PTL]–[PTL]–[SC]—[REF]–[JL]–[REF]
[PTL]–[PTL]–PRO–PLA—[REF]–[PEN]–[REF]–[PEN]
ꜰᵐPRO–[JWS]–[SC]–PLA—[HC]–[REF]
PRO–[SC]–PRO–[JWS]–[SC]—[REF]
[DEP]–[SC]—[HC]–[HC]–[HC]—[REF]
[DEP]–[JWS]–[JWS]–[SC]—[HC]–[REF]
[PTL]–[JWS]–[JWS]—[HC]–[HC]—[REF]
ᴅᴅ[PTL]–[DEP]–[DEP]–[SC]–[JWS]—[REF]
[PTL]–[PTL]–[JWS]–[SC]—CT–[REF]–CT
PRO–[JWS]–PRO–[SC]—[JL]—[REF]–[REF]–SER
[DEP]–PLA–PRO–CT—SER–[HC]–[REF]
[PTL]–[SC]–[SC]—CT–CT–[JL]–[REF]
[PTL]–[PTL]–[JWS]–PLA–[JWS]–PLA—[REF]
[DEP]–[SC]–[SC]–[JWS]–[SC]–[JWS]—[REF]
ꜰᵐ[JWS]–[PTL]–[FM]—CT–[FM]–CT–[REF]–[HC]
PRO–[JWS]–[JWS]–JWS]–PRO–PLA–[SC]—[REF]
PRO–PRO–PRO–PRO–PRO–[JWS]–[JWS]—[REF]–[PEN]
[JWS]–[DEP]–[DEP]–PRO–[SC]–[DEP]—CT–[REF]
PRO–[PTL]–[JWS]–[SC]–[SC]–[SC]–[SC]–[SC]—[REF]
[JWS]–[JWS]–[SC]–PRO–[SC]–[JWS]—[HC]–[HC]–[REF]
ꜰᵐ[SC]–[SC]—CT–CT–CT–[HC]–[HC]–[HC]–[JL]–SER–[REF]
ᴅᴅ[DEP]–[PTL]–[JWS]–PLA–[SC]–[SC]—SER–[HC]–[PEN]–[REF]
[DEP]–[PTL]–[PTL]–[PTL]–[PTL]–[DEP]–[SC]—[HC]–[REF]
ᴅᴅ[PTL]–[PTL]–[PTL]–PLA–PRO–PRO–[SC]—[HC]–PLA–[REF]–SER
PRO–[SC]–PRO–[SC]–[JWS]–PLA–PRO–PRO–PRO–PRO–[JWS]—[REF]–[PEN]
PRO–PRO–PRO–PRO–PRO–[PTL]–[JWS]–[SC]–[SC]–[SC]–[SC]–[SC]–[SC]—[REF]

PRO—[HC]
fmPLA—[HC]
fm[JWS]—[HC]
fm[FM]—[HC]
[SC]—[HC]-[HC]
PRO—[HC]-[REF]
PRO—[HC]-CT-[JL]
PRO—[REF]-[HC]
fmPRO-[JWS]—[HC]
psPRO-[JWS]—[HC]
PRO-[JWS]—[HC]-[PEN]
ppPRO-[SC]—[HC]-[HC]
fmPRO-[FM]—[HC]-[REF]
[SC]-PLA—[HC]-[HC]-[JL]
PRO-PRO—[HC]-CT-[PEN]
[DEP]-[JWS]—[HC]-[PEN]-CT
pp[PTL]-[JWS]-[HC]-[JWS]—[REF]
pp-fm[PTL]-[JWS]—[HC]-[HC]-[HC]-[INS]
[DEP]-[SC]—[HC]-[HC]-[HC]-[REF]
ppPRO-[JWS]—[HC]-[HC]-[HC]-[HC]-[HC]
PRO-[JWS]—[HC]-[HC]-[HC]-[HC]-[JL]
PRO-[JWS]-[SC]—[HC]
PRO-[JWS]-[SC]—[HC]
fm[PTL]-[PTL]-[JWS]—[HC]
ps[PTL]-PRO-[INS]—[HC]
PRO-[JWS]-[SC]—[HC]-[REF]
PRO-[SC]-CT—[HC]-CT-[PEN]
fm[PTL]-[PTL]-[SC]—[HC]-[HC]-[JL]
[PTL]-[JWS]-[JWS]—[HC]-[HC]-[REF]
[PTL]-[PTL]-[JWS]—[HC]-[JL]-[JWS]
[PTL]-PLA-[JWS]—[HC]-[HC]-[HC]-[HC]
[PTL]-[JWS]-PRO—[HC]-[HC]-[JL]-[JL]-[JL]-[JL]-[JL]-[SER]
PRO-[JWS]-[JWS]—CT-[HC]
[JWS]-PLA-[JWS]—CT-[HC]
pp[JWS]-[JWS]-[JL]-[REF]—[HC]
[PTL]-[PTL]-[JWS]—CT-[HC]
PRO-PRO-[JWS]-[JWS]—[HC]-SER
ppPRO-PLA—CT-CT-[HC]-[HC]
fmPRO-[JWS]-[SC]-PLA—[HC]-[REF]
[DEP]-[JWS]-[JWS]-[SC]—[HC]-[REF]
pp[FM]-[JWS]-PRO-[JWS]—[HC]-[JL]
pp[DEP]-[DEP]-[JWS]-[SC]—[HC]-[HC]-[JL]
fm[SC]-[SC]—[JL]-[REF]-[HC]-CT-[REF]-SER
[PTL]-[JWS]-[JWS]-PLA-[SC]—[HC]
[DEP]-PLA-PRO-CT—SER-[HC]-[REF]
pp[DEP]-[JWS]-[PTL]-[JWS]—CT-[HC]-[HC]
[JWS]-[JWS]-[JWS]-[JWS]-PRO—[HC]-[HC]
fm[DEP]-[DEP]-[JWS]-PLA-[SC]—[HC]-[JL]-SER
[DEP]-[PTL]-[JWS]-[DEP]-PLA—[HC]-[PEN]-[PEN]
fm[PTL]-[PTL]-[SC]-[FM]—CT-[HC]-[FM]-CT
fm[SC]-[SC]—CT-CT-CT—[HC]-[HC]-[HC]-[JL]-SER-[REF]
pp[DEP]-[JWS]-[JWS]-[JWS]-[JWS]-PLA-[HC]—
[PTL]-[DEP]-PRO-[JWS]-[JWS]-PLA—[HC]
pp[DEP]-[JWS]-PLA-PLA-[JWS]-PLA—[HC]-[JL]
[DEP]-PLA-[JWS]-[JWS]-[JWS]-[JWS]—[HC]-[HC]
[DEP]-[JWS]-[JWS]-PLA-[JWS]-[JWS]—[HC]-[HC]
[JWS]-[JWS]-[SC]-PRO-[SC]-[JWS]—[HC]-[HC]-[REF]
[PTL]-[PTL]-[PTL]-[JWS]-[JWS]-[JWS]—[HC]-[HC]-[HC]-[HC]-[HC]
PRO-PRO-PRO-PRO-PRO-[JWS]—[JL]-[HC]
pp[DEP]-[PTL]-[PTL]-[DEP]-PLA-[SC]-PRO—[HC]
fm[JWS]-[PTL]-[FM]—CT-[FM]-CT-[REF]-[HC]
[JWS]-[DEP]-[DEP]-PRO-[SC]-[DEP]—CT-[HC]
[DEP]-[PTL]—CT-CT-CT-CT-CT—[HC]-CT
pp[DEP]-[PTL]-[JWS]-PLA-[SC]-[SC]—SER-[HC]-[PEN]-[REF]
PRO-[JWS]-[JWS]-[PTL]-[SC]-[JWS]-[SC]—[HC]-[HC]-[HC]
pp[PTL]-[PTL]-[PTL]-PLA-PRO-PRO-[SC]—[HC]-PLA-[REF]-SER
pp[PTL]-[JWS]-[SC]-[JWS]-[SC]-PLA-[JWS]—[HC]-[HC]-[HC]-[HC]-[HC]-[JL]
pp[DEP]-[PTL]-[PTL]-[PTL]-[PTL]-[PTL]-[DEP]-[SC]—[HC]-[REF]
PRO-PRO-PLA-[SC]-[SC]—SER-SER-CT-[HC]
pp[DEP]-[DEP]-[PTL]-PLA—CT-CT-CT-CT-CT-[HC]-CT
[DEP]-[DEP]-PLA-PLA-PLA-PLA-PLA-[SC]-[SC]—CT-[HC]
-[DEP]-[PTL]-[PTL]-[JWS]-[JWS]—[JL]-[REF]-[REF]-[JL]-[REF]-[JL]-[HC]-[PEN]

MALES IN PENITENTIARY

```
                              PRO—[PEN]
                          PRO-PLA—[PEN]
                        PRO-[JWS]—[PEN]
                      [DEP]-[SC]—[PEN]
                    ps[SC]-[JWS]—[PEN]
                      [SC]-PLA-[PEN]—[PEN]
                 PRO—CT-SER-[PEN]
                 PRO-[JWS]—[HC]-[PEN]
                 [DEP]-[JWS]—[HC]·[PEN]-CT
             PRO-PRO-[JWS]-PLA—[PEN]
             PRO-PRO—[HC]-CT-[PEN]
             PRO-[SC]—CT-[HC]-CT-[PEN]
          fmPRO-[FM]- [FM]-[FM]—CT-[PEN]
          [DEP]-[JWS]-PRO-[JWS]-CT—[PEN]
          [PTL]-[PTL]-PRO-PLA—[REF]-[PEN]-[REF]-[PEN]
       PRO-[PTL]-[SC]- [JWS]-[JWS]-[SC]—[PEN]
       [DEP]-[PTL]-[JWS]-[DEP]-PLA—[HC]-[PEN]-[PEN]
         ps[PTL]-[PTL]-[JWS]-PRO-PLA-[SC]—[PEN]
    pp[DEP]- [PTL]-[JWS]-PLA- [SC]-[SC]—SER-[HC]-[PEN]-[REF]
       PRO-PRO-PRO-PRO-PRO-[JWS]-[JWS]—[REF]-[PEN]
 PRO-[SC]-PRO- [SC]- [JWS]-PLA-PRO-PRO-PRO-PRO-[JWS]—[REF]-[PEN]
[DEP]-[DEP]-[PTL]-[PTL]-[JWS]-[JWS]—[JL]-[REF]-[REF]- [JL]-[REF]-[JL]-[HC]-[PEN]
```

Since the above chart was made we know that there has been at least one more penitentiary commitment, this one a life sentence.

MALE ADULT COURT APPEARANCES OF THOSE NOT IN ADULT INSTITUTIONS

```
                          PRO—CT
                          PRO—CT
                          PRO—CT-CT
                       fmPRO—CT-SER
                          PRO—CT-SER-CT
                       fmPRO—CT-CT-CT-CT-CT
                       fmPLA—CT
                       fmPLA—CT-CT
                          PLA—CT-SER
                       fm[FM]—CT-[FM]
                      DD[DEP]—CT
                       fm[PTL]—CT
                      PRO-PLA—CT-CT
                      PRO-[SC]—CT-SER
                      PRO-[JWS]—CT-SER
                     [DEP]-PLA—CT-CT-CT-CT-CT
                      PLA-PRO—CT
                    DDPLA-[SC]—CT-CT
                     [PTL]-PRO—CT-SER
                     [PTL]-PLA—CT-SER
                     [PTL]-[JWS]—CT
                     [PTL]-[SC]—CT-CT-SER
                     [JWS]-[SC]—CT
                     fm[SC]-[FM]—CT-[FM]
                     fm[FM]-PRO—CT-CT
                    PRO-PLA-PLA—CT
                    PRO-PLA-[SC]—CT
                 fm[FM]-[FM]-[FM]—CT-SER
                 fmPRO-[SC]-PLA—CT-[FM]
               DD-fm[DEP]-PRO-[FM]—CT-CT-CT-CT
               fm[DEP]-[SC]-PLA—CT
                [DEP]-[SC]-PLA—CT-CT-CT
                DapPLA-[PTL]-[INS]—CT-CT-[INS]
               DD[PTL]-[PTL]-PLA-CT—SER-CT
                [PTL]-[PTL]-[SC]—CT-CT-CT-CT
               fm[PTL]-[JWS]-[FM]—CT-[FM]
               PRO-PRO-[JWS]-PLA—CT
            fm[DEP]-[DEP]-[JWS]-PLA—CT
             [DEP]-[PTL]-[JWS]—SER-CT
             [DEP]-[PTL]-[JWS]-[SC]—CT-CT-CT-CT-CT
             [DEP]-[PTL]-[SC]-SER—CT
             [DEP]-[SC]-PLA-[SC]—CT
            DD[PTL]-PRO-PLA—SER-CT
             [PTL]-[JWS]-PRO-[SC]—CT-CT-CT-CT-CT
            fm[PTL]-[SC]-[DEP]-PLA—CT
            DD[JWS]-[INS]-[JWS]—SER-CT-CT-SER
          [PTL]-[DEP]-[JWS]-[SC]-PRO—CT
          PRO-[PTL]-[JWS]-[SC]-[SC]—CT
          [DEP]-[SC]-[PTL]-[SC]-[SC]—CT
[PTL]-[PTL]-[PTL]-PRO-PRO-PRO-PRO-PRO-[SC]-CT-[SC]—CT
```

The above does not represent the total number of court appearances. Of course all sentenced had court appearance; nowhere have we enumerated appearance which had this outcome. Then some had court appearance who for another offense were sentenced; these are represented on graphs for the adult institutions. Above are given only those who never were sentenced.

GIRLS ON PROBATION——SUCCESS

fmPRO
fmPRO
fmPRO
fmPRO
psPRO
ppPRO
ppPRO
ppPRO
PRO
PRO
PRO
PRO
PRO
PRO
PRO
PRO
PRO
PRO
PRO
PRO
PRO
fmPRO–PLA
PRO–PLA
PRO–PLA
PRO–[DEP]
PRO–[DEP]
PRO–[HGS]
PRO–[HGS]
fmPRO–[HGS]
PRO–[HGS]
fmPRO–[GEN]
PRO–[GEN]
PRO–[GEN]
PRO–[GEN]
PRO–[GEN]
PRO–[GEN]
PRO–[GEN]
PRO–[GEN]
PRO–[GEN]
fmPRO–[RFG]
PRO–[RFG]
PRO–[RFG]
PRO–[RFG]
PRO–[RFG]
ppPRO-[HGS]-[GEN]
PRO-[GEN]-[GEN]
PRO-[GEN]-[REF]
PRO-[REF]-[GEN]
fmPRO-[HGS]-[HGS]
PRO–[HGS]-[HGS]-[HGS]
PRO–[HGS]-[GEN]-PLA
PRO–PLA–PLA–PLA–PLA–PLA
pp[DEP]–[DEP]–[GEN]–[REF]–PRO–PLA–PLA–PLA–PLA–PLA–[GEN]

GIRLS ON PROBATION—FAILURE

```
                fmPRO—
                fmPRO—
                fmPRO—
                ppPRO—CT–[HC]
                ppPRO—
                ppPRO—
                ppPRO—
                  PRO—
                  PRO—
                  PRO—
                  PRO—
                  PRO—
                  PRO—
                  PRO—
             [DEP]–PLA–PRO—
             PLA–[RFG]–PRO—
       psPLA–PLA–PLA–PLA–PLA–PRO—
    [GEN]–[DEP]–[GEN]–PLA–[GEN]–PRO—
                  psPRO–PLA—CT
                  PRO–PLA—
                fmPRO–[HGS]—
                  PRO–[HGS]—
                  PRO–[HGS]—
                  PRO–[HGS]—
                  PRO–[HGS]—
                  psPRO–[GEN]—
                  ppPRO–[GEN]—
                  PRO–[GEN]—CT–CT–CT–[HC]
                  psPRO–[RFG]—CT
                  psPRO–[RFG]—[HC]–[HC]
                  PRO–[RFG]—CT
                  PRO–[RFG]—
                  PRO–[RFG]—
             PLA–PRO–[RFG]—
               ppPRO–PRO–[GEN]—CT–[HC]
               PRO–PLA [RFG]—
             ppPRO–[HGS]–[HGS]—
               PRO–[GEN]–[GEN]—
               PRO–[GEN]–[GEN]—
               PRO–[GEN]–[GEN]—
          [RFG]–PRO–PRO–[RFG]—
          ps[RFG]–PRO–[RFG]–[RFG]—
          [HGS]–PRO–[GEN]–[GEN]—
     fm[RFG]–[RFG]–PRO–[HGS]–PLA—
  [DEP]–[RFG]–[GEN]–PRO–PRO–[GEN]—CT–CT
          fmPRO–PLA–[RFG]–PLA—
  [DEP]–PRO–PLA–PLA–[HGS]–[HGS]—
     PRO–[GEN]–[GEN]–[GEN]–[GEN]–[GEN]—
     PRO–PRO–PRO–PRO–PRO–PLA–[RFG]—
```

The most significant feature of these graphs for girls on probation is that such a small proportion of the total number of the delinquent girls find representation here; only 102 out of 255 girls were placed on probation at any time. In most of the remaining cases the immediate recourse was to institutional commitment.

GIRLS PLACED IN FOSTER HOMES—SUCCESS

```
                              ᴅᴅPLA
                               PLA
                               PLA
                               PLA
                               PLA
                               PLA
                               PLA
                            ғᴍPRO–PLA
                              PRO–PLA
                              PRO–PLA
                            ғᴍ[DEP]–PLA
                             [[DEP]–PLA
                              [DEP]–PLA
                            ᴅᴅHGS]–PLA
                              [HGS]–PLA
                              [GEN]–PLA
                              [GEN]–PLA
                              [GEN]–PLA
                    ᴅᴅ[DEP]–[DEP]–PLA
                    PRO–[HGS]–[GEN]–PLA
                                PLA–PRO
                                PLA–PLA
                                PLA–PLA
                                PLA–PLA
                                PLA–[DEP]
                                PLA–[DEP]
                                PLA–[HGS]
                                PLA–[HGS]
                            ғᴍPLA–[GEN]
                                PLA–[GEN]
                                PLA–[GEN]
                                PLA–[GEN]
                        ғᴍ[GEN]–PLA–[GEN]
                        ᴅˢ[RFG]–PLA–[GEN]
                         [DEP]–PLA–[RFG]
                            PLA–PLA–PLA
                            PLA–[DEP]–PLA
                            PLA–[RFG]–PLA
                            PLA–[RFG]–PLA
                            PLA–[GEN]–[GEN]
                    ᴅᴅ[HGS]–PLA–[GEN]–PLA
                        PLA–[GEN]–[GEN]–[GEN]–PLA
                    PRO–PLA–PLA–PLA–PLA–PLA
    ᴅᴅ[DEP]–[DEP]–[GEN]–[RFG]–PRO–PLA–PLA–PLA-PLA–PLA–[GEN]
```

    The graphs for the girls show very different in form from those representing the boys' careers. This is mainly due to the fact that the girls who are Failures so infrequently appear in adult courts or have adult commitments. The Failures have such similarity in nature of offense (see Chapter 3) that we have thought adult offenses hardly worth showing.

    We have given a chart representing the placement in foster homes of the girls because of the relative greater frequency, compared to the boys, with which this form of treatment was used and the interesting results which followed. When PLA follows institution, such as [GEN] or [RFG], it means placing on parole; otherwise it stands for placing on probation. And probation is a term used to mean direct action by the court.

GIRLS PLACED IN FOSTER HOMES—FAILURE

```
                   PLA—
                   PLA—
                   PLA—
             psPRO-PLA—CT
                PRO-PLA—
       [DEP]-[GEN]-PLA—[HC]-[HC]
       [DEP]-[RFG]-PLA—
         ps[GEN]-[GEN]-PLA—[INS]
fm[RFG]-[RFG]-PRO-[HGS]-PLA—
                PRO-PLA-[RFG]—
            fm[DEP]-PLA-PLA—
          [DEP]-PLA-PRO—
       [HGS]-[RFG]-PLA-[GEN]—CT
PRO-PRO-PRO-PRO-PRO-PLA-[RFG]—
                PLA-PRO-[RFG]—
                PLA-[RFG]-PRO—
          fmPRO-PLA-[RFG]-PLA—
        [DEP]-PLA-[GEN]-PLA—
     [DEP]-[HGS]-PLA-PLA-[GEN]—
[GEN]-[DEP]-[GEN]-PLA-[GEN]-PRO—
   [DEP]-PRO-PLA-PLA-[HGS]-[HGS]—
          psPLA-PLA-PLA-PLA-PLA-PRO—
```

GIRLS IN "THE REFUGE"—SUCCESS

pp-fm[RFG]
ps[RFG]
pp[RFG]
[RFG]
[RFG]
[RFG]
[RFG]
[RFG]
[RFG]
[RFG]
fmPRO-[RFG]
PRO-[RFG]
PRO-[RFG]
PRO-[RFG]
PRO-[RFG]
PRO-[RFG]
[DEP]-PLA-[RFG]
PRO-[GEN]-[RFG]
[RFG]-[GEN]
PLA-[RFG]-PLA
PLA-[RFG]-PLA
PRO-[RFG]-[GEN]
ps[RFG]-PLA-[GEN]
pp[RFG]-[GEN]-[GEN]
pp[DEP]-[DEP]-[GEN]-[RFG]-PRO-PLA-PLA-PLA-PLA-PLA-[GEN]

GIRLS IN "THE REFUGE"—FAILURE

```
                        fm[RFG]—
                        fm[RFG]—
                        pp[RFG]—
                          [RFG]—CT
                          [RFG]—CT
                     ps PRO–[RFG]—CT
                     ps PRO–[RFG]—[HC]-[HC]
                       PRO–[RFG]—CT
                       PRO–[RFG]—
                       PRO–[RFG]—
                    pp[HGS]-[RFG]—[PEN]-[INS]
                    PRO–PLA–[RFG]—
                    PLA–PRO–[RFG]—
                 pp[GEN]-[HGS]-[RFG]—CT-[HC]-CT-CT-[PEN]
    PRO–PRO–PRO–PRO–PRO–PLA–[RFG]—
                       ps[RFG]-[INS]—
                         [RFG]-[GEN]—
                     PLA–[RFG]-PRO—
                     [DEP]-[RFG]-PLA—
                     [DEP]-[RFG]-[GEN]—
                 fm PRO–PLA–[RFG]-PLA—
                         [RFG]-[HGS]-[HGS]—
                 [HGS]-[RFG]-PLA–[GEN]—CT
                         [RFG]-PRO–PRO–[RFG]—
                     ps[RFG]-PRO–[RFG]-[RFG]—
                 fm[RFG]-[RFG]–PRO–[HGS]-PLA—
             DEP]-[RFG]-[GEN]-PRO–PRO–[GEN]—CT-CT
```

GIRLS IN HOUSE OF GOOD SHEPHERD—SUCCESS

```
             fm[HGS]
               [HGS]
               [HGS]
               [HGS]
               [HGS]
         fmPRO-[HGS]
           PRO-[HGS]
           PRO-[HGS]
           PRO-[HGS]
           PLA-[HGS]
           PLA-[HGS]
         [DEP]-[HGS]
         [DEP]-[HGS]
               pp[HGS]-PLA
                 [HGS]-PLA
           ppPRO-[HGS]-[GEN]
           fmPRO-[HGS]-[HGS]
                 [HGS]-[HGS]-[GEN]
                 [HGS]-[GEN]-[GEN]
             PRO-[HGS]-[GEN]-PLA
             PRO-[HGS]-[HGS]-[HGS]
                 pp[HGS]-PLA-[GEN]-PLA
```

GIRLS IN HOUSE OF GOOD SHEPHERD—FAILURE

```
                    fm[HGS]—CT
                    fm[HGS]—CT
                    fm[HGS]—
                    fm[HGS]—
                    fm[HGS]—
                    fm[HGS]—
                    ps[HGS]—
                    ps[HGS]—
                    pp[HGS]—CT
                    pp[HGS]—
                    pp[HGS]—
                       [HGS]—[HC]
                       [HGS]—CT-CT
                       [HGS]—
                       [HGS]—
                fmPRO-[HGS]—
                ppPRO-[HGS]—
                   PRO-[HGS]—
                   PRO-[HGS]—
                   PRO-[HGS]—
             ps[INS]-[HGS]—[INS]
     [GEN]-[DEP]-[HGS]—
                    fm[HGS]-[HGS]—CT
                    pp[HGS]-[HGS]—
                       [HGS]-[HGS]—
                       [HGS]-[HGS]—
                       [HGS]-[GEN]—
                    pp[HGS]-[RFG]—[PEN]-[INS]
               ppPRO-[HGS]-[HGS]—
                  [RFG]-[HGS]-[HGS]—
                pp[GEN]-[HGS]-[RFG]—CT-[HC]-CT-CT-[PEN]
       fm[RFG]-[RFG] PRO [HGS]-PLA—
 [DEP]-PRO-PLA-PLA-[HGS]-[HGS]—
                    fm[HGS] [DEP]-[GEN]—
                    fm[HGS]-[HGS]-[GEN]—
                    pp[HGS]-[GEN]-[GEN]—
               ps[DEP] [HGS]-[HGS]-[HGS]—
                       [HGS]-PRO-[GEN]-[GEN]—
                       [HGS] [RFG] PLA [GEN]—OT
                       [HGS]-[HGS]-[HGS]-[GEN]—
                pp[DEP]-[HGS]-PLA-PLA-[GEN]—
```

GIRLS IN GENEVA—SUCCESS

ₚₛ[GEN]
ₚₚ[GEN]
ₚₚ[GEN]
[GEN]
[GEN]
[GEN]
[GEN]
[GEN]
fmPRO–[GEN]
PRO–[GEN]
PRO–[GEN]
PRO–[GEN]
PRO–[GEN]
PRO–[GEN]
PRO–[GEN]
PRO–[GEN]
PRO–[GEN]
fmPLA–[GEN]
PLA–[GEN]
PLA–[GEN]
ₚₚ[DEP]–[GEN]
[RFG]–[GEN]
fm[FM]–[GEN]
ₚₚPRO–[HGS]–[GEN]
ₚₚPRO–[RFG]–[GEN]
ₚₛ[RFG]–PLA–[GEN]
[HGS]–[HGS]–[GEN]
[GEN]–PLA
[GEN]–PLA
[GEN]–PLA
[GEN]–[GEN]
PLA–[GEN]–[GEN]
ₚₚ[RFG]–[GEN]–[GEN]
[HGS]–[GEN]–[GEN]
[DEP]–[GEN]–[GEN]
ₚₚ[HGS]–PLA–[GEN]–PLA
PRO–[HGS]–[GEN]–PLA
fm[GEN]–PLA–[GEN]
PLA–[GEN]–[GEN]–[GEN]–PLA
ₚₚ[DEP]–[DEP]–[GEN]–[RFG]–PRO–PLA–PLA–PLA–PLA–PLA–[GEN]

GIRLS IN GENEVA—FAILURE

```
            pp[GEN]—
              [GEN]—CT
              [GEN]—
              [GEN]—
              [GEN]—
              [GEN]—
              [GEN]—
          psPRO-[GEN]—
          ppPRO-[GEN]—
            PRO-[GEN]—CT-CT-CT-[HC]]
            PLA-[GEN]—
            PLA-[GEN]—
          pp[DEP]-[GEN]—
          pp[DEP]-[GEN]—
            [HGS]-[GEN]—
            [RFG]-[GEN]—
        ppPRO-PRO-[GEN]—CT-[HC]
         [HGS]-PRO-[GEN]—
       fm[HGS]-[HGS]-[GEN]—
       fm[HGS]-[DEP]-[GEN]—
         [DEP]-[RFG]-[GEN]—
       [HGS]-[RFG]-PLA-[GEN]—CT
      [HGS]-[HGS]-[HGS]-[GEN]—
   pp[DEP]-[HGS]-PLA-PLA-[GEN]—
              [GEN]-[GEN]—CT
              [GEN]-[GEN]—
              [GEN]-[GEN]—
              [GEN]-[FM]—[FM]
           fm[GEN]-[FM]—
            PRO-[GEN]-[GEN]—
            PRO-[GEN]-[GEN]—
            PRO-[GEN]-[GEN]—
             [DEP]-[GEN] PLA [HC] [HC]
          pp[HGS]-[GEN]-[GEN]—
          [DEP] PLA-[GEN]-PLA—
              ps[GEN]-[GEN]-PLA—[INS]
              pp[GEN]-[HGS]-[RFG]—CT-[HC]-CT-CT-[PEN]
                [GEN]-[DEP] [HGS]
      [DEP]-[RFG]-[GEN]-PRO-PRO-[GEN]—CT-CT
              pp[GEN]-[GEN] [GEN]-[GEN]-[GEN]—
            PRO-[GEN] [GEN] [GEN] [GEN]-[GEN]—
              [GEN]-[DEP]-[GEN]-PLA-[GEN]-PRO—
```

INDEX

A

Abnormal mentality, 149, 156, 205, 208, 210.
Abnormal mentality, table, 274.
Adenoids, 141.
Adolescent instability, 179.
Adult commitments, 62, 64 ff., 67, 202.
Adult court appearances, 202, 301.
Adult criminality, 201.
Adult record and juvenile commitment, 77.
Adventure, love of, 181.
Age at first delinquency, 95.
Age correlations with delinquency, 207.
Age of murderers, 32.
Age statistics, 90.
Ages, tables, 255 ff.
Alcohol, use of, 147, 173, 175.
Alcoholism, 98, 126; tables, 265, 267.
Army findings for intelligence, 153.
Army or navy service, 23.
Arson, 167, 175.
Assault and battery, 169.
Automobile stealing, 167.

B

Bad companions, 179.
Begging, 173, 175.
Biological findings, 136 ff.
Boston and Chicago, comparison of, 183, 203.
Boston, conditions in, 194.
Boston outcomes, data for first series, 18; data for second series, 19.
Breaking and entering, 166.
Broken homes, 121, 123, 208; tables, 262 ff, 264.
Burglary, 166.

C

Carrying concealed weapons, 172.
Cases in courts, number of, table, 250.
Cases of murderers, 40 ff.
Cases with follow-up, 16.
Case records, 15.
Cases, types illustrated, 39.
Causations, 179, 181.
Causations, direct, table, 281.
Causative mental factors, table, 282.
Chicago and Boston, comparison of, 182, 203.
Chicago and Cook County School, 20.
Chicago, conditions in, 192.
Chicago Home for Girls, 21.
Child placing, 193, 196.
Child-placing agencies, 85, 189, 194.
Church activities, 114 ff.
Civic life, 183.
Commitment, 204, 218; juvenile, 69.
Commitments, adult, table, 248.
Commitments or court appearances, table, 247.
Commitment without probation, 84.
Community differences, 183, 190.
Community spirit, 152, 183, 190, 211.
Comparison of series, 37.
Comparison, series utilized for, 59.
Comparison, value of, 12.
Conclusions, negative, 209.
Constitutional inferiority, 153, 156.
Correctional institutions, efficacy of, 79.
Correctional methods, failure of, 201.
Court appearances, 62, 65; Boston, table, 249.

313

V 10
3